OUR MAN IN VIENNA

THE SPYMASTERS' WAR
AT THE HEART OF EUROPE

PANAGIOTIS DIMITRAKIS

NEW HAVEN PUBLISHING

First Edition 2021
NEW HAVEN PUBLISHING LTD
www.newhavenpublishingltd.com
newhavenpublishing@gmail.com

Cover design © Panagiotis Dimitrakis

Panagiotis Dimitrakis holds a doctorate from the Department of War Studies, King's College London, and is an expert on intelligence and military history.

By the same author

Greece and the English: British Diplomacy and the Kings of Greece

Military Intelligence in Cyprus: From the Great War to Middle East Crises

Greek Military Intelligence and the Crescent: Estimating the Turkish Threat – Crises, Leadership and Strategic Analyses, 1974-1996

Failed Alliances of the Cold War: Britain's Strategy and Ambitions in Asiaand the Middle East

The Secret War in Afghanistan: The Soviet Union, China and Anglo-American Intelligence in the Afghan War

The Hidden Wars in China and Greece: The CIA, MI6 and the Civil Wars

Secrets and Lies in Vietnam: Spies, Intelligence and Covert Operations in the Vietnam Wars

The Secret War for China: Espionage, Revolution and the Rise of Mao

The Hidden War in Argentina: British and American Espionage in World War II

Content

ACKNOWLEDGEMENTS

Professor Joe Maiolo of the Department of War Studies, King's College London, helped me considerably with sources, and I thank him for this. Special thanks to Rosalie Spire for her prompt aid and advice with reference to the UK National Archives and Carol Trow for editing. I owe a great debt to my family for their support and encouragement.

ABBREVIATIONS AND GLOSSARY

Abwehr	Military intelligence service (Nazi Germany)
AVH	State Protection Authority (Hungary)
CIA	Central Intelligence Agency (US)
CIC	Counter Intelligence Corps (US Army)
CIG	Central Intelligence Group (US)
Evidenzbureau	Bureau for military intelligence (Austria)
FRUS	Foreign Relations of the United States series
GC&CS	Government Communications and Cipher School (UK)
Gestapo	Geheimstaatspolizei (Nazi Secret Police)
Hauptsturmführer	Nazi Party paramilitary officer rank
JIC	Joint Intelligence Committee (UK)
KGB	Committee for State Security (Soviet Union)
Kriminalpolizei	Criminal Police (Austria)
MI5	Security Service (UK)
MI6/SIS	Secret Intelligence Service (UK)
MGB	Ministry of State Security (Soviet Union)
MoI	Ministry of Information (UK)
MIS	Military Intelligence Service (US Army)
NKVD	People's Commissariat for Internal Affairs (Soviet Union)
OB	Order of Battle
Obstf	Obersturmführer Nazi Party paramilitary rank
OGPU	All-Union State Political Administration and Unified State Political Directorate (Soviet Union)
OKH	OberKommando des Heeres (Nazi Germany)
OKW	OberKommando der Wehrmacht (Nazi Germany)
OSS	Office of Strategic Services (USA)
RSHA	Reichssicherheitshauptamt, Reich Main Security Office (Nazi Germany)
SD	Sicherheitsdienst (Nazi Security Service)
SIPO	Sicherheitspolizei, Security Police (Nazi Germany)
SOE	Special Operations Executive (UK)
SSU	Strategic Services Unit (US)
Staatspolizei	State Police (Austria)
TNA	The National Archives (UK)
UNRRA	United Nations Relief and Rehabilitation Administration
w/t	wireless transmitter

Prologue

The Third Man (1949) is a film noir, voted 'the greatest British film of all time.' In post war Vienna, smuggler Harry Lime (Orson Welles) fakes his own death to evade his pursuers, the British military police. The film is based on the novella of the same name by Graham Greene, originally not meant for separate publication but merely as a preparation for the screenplay. Greene afterwards admitted that the film was far better than the book; an unusual admission for a writer to make. Harry Lime is not, as people often suppose, a hero: he had been selling adulterated penicillin, and was thus responsible for children's deaths. This is based on an actual case which Greene was told about by a spy working for Soviet Intelligence. The Allied occupation authorities in Vienna, where the population suffered from all sorts of privations, tolerate and occasionally use Lime - just as happened in post-war Vienna.

Looking into the secret history of Vienna and the spymasters who operated there, we realise that Greene wrote something beyond a simple story of criminal activities. All the protagonists and their families have a dark past. Even elegant Anna Schmidt (Alida Valli), the devoted girlfriend of Lime, had a father who collaborated with the Nazis. Nothing could be kept secret in such a city; geographically the centre of Europe, with spies - with their secret populations, always on the move, supported by evolving bureaucracies, the modern secret services - on missions to reach other cities of Europe. Acclaimed film director Carol Reed says in the voice-over introduction of *The Third Man*: 'I never knew the old Vienna before the war with its Strauss music, its glamour and easy charm. Constantinople suited me better.' Reed did not know that SOE spies and couriers for Austria were recruited in Constantinople (Istanbul).

The Third Man touched on the layers of intrigue and deception in Vienna, the place of spies indeed, from the interwar period, the Second World War and the Cold War. In the film, Lime's loyal friend, author Holly Martins (Joseph Cotten), says that he is writing a story 'based on facts.' Truth is stranger than fiction; 'Life is a great screenwriter,' film director Francis Ford Coppola remarked in a recent interview. This most certainly applies in the history of espionage, the never-ending spy game of wartime and peacetime.

The real Third Men, the intelligence gatherers and the deceivers, are the noted British, American, German and Soviet spymasters as well as

American diplomats assigned to political intelligence. Some cautious professionals, some overzealous and reckless amateurs, they were forged in the violent and ideologically divergent labyrinth of the otherwise musical and culture-rich Vienna, a city forever haunted by its past, lost glory. The capital of the Hapsburgs remained the epicentre of Central European politics and trade despite the collapse of the Austro-Hungarian Empire in 1918. The spies based in the city were interested in politics in Austria and in other Central European countries, namely Czechoslovakia and Hungary, as well as Germany and Italy. They were desperate to collect military information for the near-constant upcoming crises, be it with Nazi Germany, fascist Italy or the Soviet Union; they also did not hesitate to enjoy life with waltzing and champagne - 'the easy charm' of Carol Reed.

Vienna's geographical location compelled all spymasters to take account of the city as a centre for regional operations, from the time of the Bolshevik Cheka to the CIA in the 1950s and beyond. The post Great War and post Second World War decayed Vienna was the hub of espionage, a place for spies as well as somewhere from which to communicate with an opponent and reach an agreement. Vienna would retain this distinction; in 2010, the CIA and the SVR (Soviet Foreign Intelligence Service) arranged to swap, in broad daylight, arrested spies at the city airport. The CIA Director at the time, Leon Panetta, wrote in his memoirs, 'The Cold War was over, but the scene [at the airport] in Vienna was proof that the old games were alive and well. All that was missing was the sound of the zither playing the theme of the movie *The Third Man*.'[1] Authors were always thrilled with this city. Frederick Forsyth in *The Day of the Jackal* had the members of the French terrorist organisation OAS to meet with a British hitman in Vienna and plot the murder of President de Gaulle.

Graham Greene, a former SIS officer working under Kim Philby, had an eye for detail, and he used this in his films and books. Philby, the infamous Soviet spy within British Intelligence, began his career in Vienna as a secret communist courier back in 1934 during the riots, but he did not reveal this to Greene for a long time. It was in Vienna where Philby took his first personal risk on a mission, when fear and commitment tested his character. In 1950, as *The Third Man* was screened in cinemas, disclosing the real Vienna of violence and crime, Philby was in the United States as SIS liaison officer with the CIA and the FBI. Ironically, Philby would be called 'the third man' by the speculating

---

[1] Panetta, Leon, *Worthy Fights: A Memoir of Leadership in War and Peace* (New York: Penguin, 2014), p.284; see also West, Nigel, *Spy Swap: The Humiliation of Putin's Intelligence Services* (Barnsley: Frontline, 2021).

press, suspected of espionage after the defection of his friends and spies, Guy Burgess and Donald Maclean, in 1951.

The Austrian historian Thomas Riegler assumed that Greene was portraying Harold Adrian Philby in Harry Lime. The *Harold* turned to *Harry*. Most significantly, Philby and Lime had a certain 'dark charm.' The sewer system chase reminded everyone in the know of Philby's 1934 experience in Vienna. At the time of writing *The Third Man* Greene did not know that his former superior at the SIS was a Russian spy. Nonetheless, he had worked for Philby in 1941-44 and they remained friends. Greene had a true author's sense when it came to bringing the people he had been working and drinking with to the page or silver screen.[2]

The Third Man is an excellent introduction to the real world of espionage in Vienna, and, as this book will show, truth can indeed be stranger than fiction.

---

[2] Riegler, Thomas, 'The Spy Story Behind the Third Man' *Journal of Austrian-American History*, Vol.4 (2020). p.27; Beer, Siegfried, ' "The Third Man" and British Intelligence', *History Today* Vol. 51 Issue 5 (2001), pp.45-51.

Introduction

The Secret Legacy of a City

'I'm basically a romantic. I believe in human agency. I love the fact that individuals can make a difference,' Alex Younger the SIS chief admitted in an interview.[3] One can tell that all spymasters, especially British ones, in history thought the same. Spymasters are forged by their experiences. Every spymaster was once a humble, inexperienced, over-eager, untrained rookie operative working in a labyrinth of rumour, deception and fear without, usually, any background knowledge (beyond a hasty briefing) of the area or country in which he or she had to operate. Richard Moore, Younger's successor, remarked of his experience of espionage: 'I had a brilliant time. There is something about trying to work out who might be prepared to help us — a bit of the thrill of the chase, as you try to find a way in which you can get alongside them, and then the fascinating business of working with people, having to do some pretty wild things, you know after dark on the streets of Islamabad, when the adrenaline is rushing.'[4] Perhaps the song 'Philby' (1979) by Rory Gallagher best describes the adrenaline and darkness of a spy's life.

In the interwar period, the starting point of our espionage narrative, the Secret Intelligence Service (SIS/MI6) training focused on ciphers, codes and book-keeping accounts. Nicholas Elliot, an SIS station chief in Vienna between 1953 and 1956, a loyal and eventually disappointed and betrayed friend of Kim Philby, noted:

> 'The successful Field Officers will be generally found to have three important characteristics. They will be personalities in their own right. They will have humanity and a capacity for friendship and they will have a sense of humour which will enable them to avoid the ridiculous mumbo-jumbo of over-secrecy.'[5]

---

[3] 'Alex Younger: "The Russians did not create the things that divide us — we did that" Interview to Roula Khalaf, *Financial Times*, 30 September 2020.

[4] 'MI6's 'C': We warned Putin what would happen if he invaded Ukraine' *The Sunday Times*, 23 April 2021.

[5] Quoted from Nicholas Elliot's *With My Little Eye* (1994) in Hastings, Stephen, 'Obituary: Nicholas Elliot' The Independent, 18 April 1994, available at:

Admiral Sir Hugh Sinclair, the head of the SIS, advised the newly-recruited Frederick Winterbotham (a former Royal Flying Corps pilot who fought in the Great War and was captured by the Germans) in January 1930:

> 'If you can listen to someone important telling somebody else equally important about some event of importance and, knowing the story to be quite inaccurate, you can keep your mouth shut, you may in due course make a good Intelligence officer.'[6]

Winterbotham understood that an instinct develops:

> 'It is recognised in intelligence circles that after a while one develops a "nose", whether it be the ability to spot the real thing from the fake, or a feeling that such and such a person knows more than he is telling and is likely to be useful to one. I also possessed the ability to tuck away bits of information in the back of my mind, ready to bring out when they fitted some new part of the puzzle.'[7]

A contemporary of Winterbotham was SIS officer Leslie Nicholson. Briefly, he was posted in the Vienna SIS station under Thomas Kendrick, a seasoned military intelligence officer. The young officer was eager to learn the second oldest profession and asked Kendrick:

> '"Could you give me any idea of how to begin?...Are there any standard rules?...or could you give me some practical advice?" He [Kendrick] thought for a bit. "I don't think there are, really; you'll just have to work it out for yourself. I think everyone has his own methods and I can't think of anything I can tell you.'[8]

<https://www.independent.co.uk/news/people/obituary-nicholas-elliott-1370833.html? accessed 29 October 2020.

[6]Quoted in Winterbotham, Frederick, W. *The Nazi Connection* (New York: Dell Books, 1978), pp.28-29.

[7]Ibid., p.49.

[8] Quoted in Leslie Nicholson (writing as John Whitwell), *British Agent* (New York, William Kimber & Co, 1967), p.26.

Setting priorities in intelligence gathering was another formidable issue for rookie spies; thus 'information [was wanted] on every subject under the sun, political, military, industrial, economic, social scandal in high places'.[9] Nicholson met with Kendrick. Now a seasoned intelligence officer, Nicholson remembered his questions to Kendrick and remarked in his memoirs:

> 'I remembered only too vividly my abortive interview with him so many years before in 1930...now looking back, I can see that he was right. If I had to advise a budding agent today on how to start as a spy, I could think of nothing very practical to impart him. There are no rules of thumb in my profession - if there were, they would be obsolete as soon as they were laid down.'[10]

A sinister episode, betrayal of trust or a violent encounter of the past would always be remembered. In their quest for intelligence, spymasters assess people, their targets, and try to foresee their possible actions. Graham Greene had served with the SIS in the Second World War under the supervision of Kim Philby. In 1949 he wrote *The Third Man*, where Major Calloway of the British Military Police in Vienna elaborated: '...for it is my profession to balance possibilities, human possibilities, and the drive of destiny can never find a place in my files.'[11]

John Bruce Lockhart, another SIS officer with decades-old experience admitted:

> 'The suspicion or actual evidence that your own intelligence service has a traitor within the house is the most miserable event that can happen to a service. All secret intelligence services have been through this trauma. It destroys morale, upsets judgments, destroys personal relationships, and gravely threatens inter-allied confidence.'[12]

James 'Jesus' Angleton, the ever-suspicious of deception, infamous future CIA counter-espionage head, had a close associate in the 1940s:

[9]Ibid., p.20.

[10]Ibid., p.220.

[11] Greene, Graham, *The Third Man &The Fallen Idol* (London: Heinemann, 1950), p.56.

[12] Lockhart quoted in West Nigel ed. *The Faber Book of Espionage* sited in Lathrop, Charles, E. ed..*The Literary Spy* (New Haven: Yale University Press, 2004), p.396.

Kim Philby, who defected in January 1963 showing the world, and Angleton, that he had been a spy for Moscow for decades.

Following people for years, spymasters – and readers of books like this one – do know that mistakes with names rarely occur; a name *leads* to a name. Sooner or later a spy ring unravels when a member is detected, watched and arrested. Turning enemy spies is the next step for the spymaster.

This book explores the secret war for Austria. US and British Intelligence confronted the Soviet Intelligence, the OGPU and its successor the NKVD, the forerunner of the KGB. Brute force, kidnappings, beatings, terror and murder were a daily routine of the spy games in the Austrian capital. Intelligence operatives would have to learn fast to survive the Vienna streets. Daphne Park, the legendary SIS female spymaster who had worked in Vienna in 1946, in her first years in intelligence, admitted: 'I had seen them [Soviet Intelligence] on the streets of Vienna and how they behaved and I felt anger.'[13] Kidnapping was a practice of both the Americans and the Russians, but it seemed that the Soviet Intelligence had a widespread kidnapping policy. Indeed, in Vienna, 'many of the scientists were being kidnapped by the Russians. It was this that made me want to learn Russian and serve in the Soviet Union, and see what it was really like there...I watched them [Soviet Intelligence] swallow up Czechs, Poles – people I had known. I wanted to meet and understand the people who lived under such a regime,' Park said.[14]

Graham Greene was laconic, writing the script of *The Third War* in Vienna during the actual days of kidnapping and intrigue:

'She was scared the Russians would pick her up.'

'Why should they want to?'

'We can't always figure out why they do these things. Perhaps just to show that it's not healthy being friends with an Englishman.'[15]

Reviewing the history of Anglo-American counter-espionage in the Cold War and all its controversies, failures and witch-hunts, one could argue that perhaps the overwhelming, intense experiences of the past deprived British and American operatives, the future spymasters, of key lessons in successful clandestine warfare and the related mentality; spying meant being secret, ingenious, not to draw attention, not to brawl or threaten.

---

[13] Daphne Park quoted in Corera, Gordon, *The Art of Betrayal: Life and Death in the British Intelligence* (London: Weidenfeld& Nicolson 2011), p.36.

[14] Ibid.

[15] Greene, *The Third Man*...p.59.

Soviet Intelligence escalated the violence in the spying game, drawing the attention of US and British Intelligence, whose veterans in Vienna perhaps later on did not suspect that *the other face* of Soviet espionage was sophisticated – culminating in the game played by Kim Philby and his colleagues and the legendary illegals from the 1930s to the 1960s.

Kim Philby belongs to the secret history of Vienna; he was forged there. In June 1933 the over-eager Cambridge University graduate confided, 'My life must be devoted to Communism.' He supported the activities of the International Workers Relief Organisation (MOPR), a Soviet Intelligence front organisation. He turned into a risk-taking secret courier of the Austrian Communist Party. The young British communist went into Czechoslovakia six times and twice into Hungary to transfer messages and packages.

The regime of Engelbert Dollfuss crushed the socialist rebellion in February 1934. Dollfuss went against the Revolutionary Socialists (an alliance of communists and socialists) arresting a total of 1,500 members and executing their leaders.[16] The children of the executed communists were adopted by the Soviet Union and lived there until the war. Once war broke out, the Comintern recruited them as spies with a mission to penetrate Austria; in the majority of cases they were arrested and executed after a deception game of the Gestapo, to be explored in a following chapter.

Death and violence against communists cemented Philby's beliefs. A future political figure was also influenced by these events. In 1934 Hugh Gaitskell, the future Labour leader, was on a Rockefeller scholarship at the University of Vienna. He witnessed the harsh government crackdown. Eventually he realised that socialism, not Marxism, offered solutions to social problems. During the war, Gaitskell served as Principal Private Secretary to Hugh Dalton, the head of the Ministry of Economic Warfare, overviewing the Special Operations Executive (SOE) activities.[17]

In Vienna, Philby met and married Litzi Friedman, a committed communist. By 1934 she was wanted by the authorities. His new wife had a friend: photographer Edith Tudor-Hart, born Suschitzky, an Austrian who ran a bookshop as a secret communication centre. Philby, as a secret messenger, was introduced to konspiratsiya and duplicity. He learned how to use sewers; through them communists could escape the police.[18]

---

[16] Macintyre, Ben, *A Spy Among Friends: Kim Philby and the Great Betrayal* (London: Broadway Books, 2014), p. 39.

[17] Knightley, Philip, *Philby: KGB Masterspy* (London: Andre Deutsch, 1988), p.83.

[18] West, W.L. *The Quest for Graham Greene* (London: Weidenfeld& Nicolson, 1997), p.128.

Edith Tudor-Hart was recruited by the OPGU in 1929 after the recommendation of Arnold Deutsch, who had known Edith since 1926 and abetted in her recruitment. The Austrian police found out about Tudor-Hart and she fled the bookshop. She and her husband reached London and she was the one who insisted that Philby be recruited for Soviet Intelligence. In Vienna she had evaluated Philby for future secret work.

In May 1934, Philby and his wife moved to London. A month earlier, the British Passport Control Officer in Vienna granted Litzi her visa to enter Britain. She was a known communist in a relatively small city. The British Passport Control Officer was SIS station chief Thomas Kendrick. Philby's marriage to a communist would not have been pinpointed by MI5 and SIS until it was too late. With the benefit of hindsight this was 'the Vienna mistake' of SIS and a lesson learned; a spy might be hidden not necessarily in the dark, but his trail could be found in applications for his wife's visa.

Philby himself commented about mistakes:

'We tend to look for a solid logical line in the various cleaner decisions of the intelligence services. But every such decision involved the human factor. And that means that you can never exclude the possibility of a mistake, simple stupidity, as in chess. By the way, that is the great lack in spy novels, where the authors write their plots, even complicated ones, very logically. The most complicated logical construction is predictable and expected. These writers exclude the human factor, that is, error, in their work. There is only one writer who writes about intelligence with the human factor always present. That, of course, is Graham Greene. There is always some completely illogical, unexpected thing in his books. That's why they are all so truthful and human.'[19]

In July 1934, Philby met his recruiter, Arnold Deutsch. In the history of interwar espionage, Deutsch is one of the most charismatic spymasters. Born in 1904, he obtained a PhD from the University of Vienna at the age of twenty-four. He was fluent in English, German and French and operated under the codename *Otto*. By the mid-1930s, he had recruited

---

[19]Philby's interview quoted in Borovik, Genrikh, *ThePhilby Files: The Secret Life of Master Spy Kim Philby* (Boston: Little brown 1994), p.323.

and handled sixteen secret agents in Britain, including the Cambridge spy ring. In 1938 he was recalled to Moscow and miraculously survived the Great Terror. He stayed until 1942, when he was ordered to go to the United States to spy as an illegal rezidentura (station) head. A German U-Boat torpedoed the ship. Deutsch drowned alongside other passengers. It was reported that he showed heroism in his last hours.[20]

In London, during a walk in the park, Deutsch opened up, telling Philby: 'We need people who could penetrate into the bourgeois institutions. Penetrate them for us!' Philby assumed that he was entering the secret organisation of Comintern to fight international fascism, and agreed to avoid any contact with overt communist organisations. [21] Deutsch focused on lecturing the fascinated Philby about tradecraft. In 1963, Philby revealed how Deutsch trained him:

> 'Our meetings always took place in outlying districts of London, such as Ealing, Acton, Park Royal, etc. and almost always in the open air. The regular drill consisted of synchronising watches with a neighbouring clock, appearing at the rendezvous on the dot, taking at least three taxis both to and from the rendezvous to ensure that nobody followed. At each meeting, a time and place was fixed for the next one...'[22]
>
> 'For the first year or so, I contributed very little, and Otto (Deutsch) devoted most of his time to lessons on tradecraft, emphasising securing above all things. He was always setting little traps for me, in order to determine whether I had really broken off all connection with Communist friends, was following the taxi drill etc.'

Deutsch reported to Moscow:

> 'It's amazing that such a young man is so widely and deeply knowledgeable. In conversation with him, you always sense the patrician in him. He is very modest, even too modest. In discussing plans of work, he never raises any doubts about his personal life. The question simply does not

[20] Pringle, Robert, W., *Historical Dictionary of Russian & Soviet intelligence* (Lanham, Maryland: Scarecrow Press, 2006), p.68.
[21] Andrew, Christopher &Mitrokhin, Vasili, *The Sword and the Shield: The Mitrokhin Archive and the Secret History of the KGB* (London: Basic Books, 1999), pp.58-9.
[22] Extract from notes handed by Philby, 12 June 1964, KV 2/4428 TNA.

exist for him. He is so serious that he forgets that he is only 25. He has only one flaw: he stutters severely..."Sonny" [Philby] is very shy, indecisive, and physically clumsy. His stutter makes him even more insecure..."Sonny" has studied Marxist teaching quite deeply. In general, he studies everything thoroughly, but always says that he knows a little. By nature he is gentle and kind...Sonny's moods fluctuate significantly sometimes...'[23]

Deutsch departed like a ghost, as Philby remembered:

'One evening (in June 1936), our telephone rang, and Otto asked if we were alone at home. I replied that we were, and he told me that he would be round in a half-an-hour. I was much astonished at this, since it was completely at variance with his normal security-mindedness. He arrived in a state of great agitation with a suitcase. He used my telephone to book an air passage to Paris, and left the following morning. I never saw him again...from then on, Theo [the new OGPU handler] took over direct contact with me.'[24]

An Austrian refugee recalled his admiration and suspicion of Philby in his Vienna days:

'Here was a young Englishman, determined to risk much to help the underground freedom movement in a small country which must have been of very limited interest to him. But doubts began to dawn on me when Philby appeared as a communist go-between and when he declared that he could provide all money we needed for our work. The money which Philby offered could only have come from the Russians.'[25]

The refugee was wrong in this respect. Philby paid out of his own pocket. In fact, his father, St John 'Jack' Philby, had given him a

---

[23] Deutsch report on Philby quoted in Borovik, Genrikh, *The Philby Files: The Secret Life of Master Spy Kim Philby* (Boston: Little, Brown & Co, 1994), p.55.
[24] Extract from notes handed by Philby, 12 June 1964, KV 2/4428 TNA.
[25] Quoted in Smith, Michal, *New Cloak, Old Dagger: How Britain's Spies Came In From the Cold* (London: Victor Gollancz, 1996), p.127.

considerable amount of money to live in Vienna for a year.[26]

Tim Milne, a long-time co-student, friend and SIS colleague of Philby wrote:

> 'I myself had a hazy but erroneous impression that he was doing a postgraduate year at Vienna University. (His German was already good; if he had been thinking only of the Foreign Service it would have made much more sense to go to France for a year. Good French was more or less obligatory.) Perhaps his chief reason for going to Austria was to get into the thick of European politics. If so, he chose well: the winter of 1933-34 saw Viennese socialism crushed by Chancellor Dollfuss, and the huge socialist-built blocks of workers' flats blasted by government artillery. Kim, as he is now known, threw himself into the task of aiding left-wingers in danger from the police, including refugees from Nazi Germany, and helping to organise assistance and escape.'[27]

Yuri Modin, Philby's handler in the late 1940s, remembered:

> 'In later years, Kim often told me that the Soviet intelligence services had shown considerable interest in him during his time in Vienna. This seems to me unlikely, although he must have had his reasons for saying so. What I can say with some certainty is that the decisive influence in persuading him to become a Soviet agent came not from his friends but from Litzi. Neither Theodor Maly, an NKVD agent, nor anyone else recruited him. He was won over by his wife – not directly, of course, and not on behalf of the NKVD (she was not a member) – but in the name of the Comintern, the international Soviet Communist organisation (also called the Third International), whose purpose was to promote world revolution, for which she was an agent.'[28]

Modin insisted about the recruitment of Philby:

---

[26] Borovik, *The Philby Files*, p.14.

[27] Milne, Tim, *Kim Philby: A story of Friendship and Betrayal* (London: Biteback,2014), pp.37-8.

[28] Modin, Yuri, *My Five Cambridge Friends: Burgess, Maclean, Philby, Blunt, and Cairncross by Their KGB Controller* (New York: Farrar and Giroux, 1994), p. 51.

'Kim Philby, deeply moved and outraged by the atrocities he had witnessed in Vienna, simply went along with Litzi. Neither their political convictions nor their engagement with Communism was the prime mover; they were just a young couple in love, who shared a bitter loathing of Fascism.'[29]

Teddy Kollek, a British Zionist and former SIS agent, met James Angleton in Rome after the war; Angleton was a friend of Philby and soon to become head of counterintelligence at the CIA. In the autumn of 1950, Kollek met again Angleton at the CIA headquarters. He later wrote: 'I was walking towards Angleton's office...when suddenly I spotted a familiar face at the other end of the hallway...I burst into Angleton's office and said "Jim, you'll never guess who I saw in the hallway. It was Kim Philby!"' Kollek was in Vienna during the 1934 crisis and knew that Philby helped communists to escape. He told Angleton that Philby may have been recruited to Soviet Intelligence. Angleton did not pay much attention and Kollek never raised the issue again.

It was in Vienna that Philby listened attentively to Theodor Maly, the seasoned NKVD agent who did not approach him at that time. Maly (a former priest and artilleryman in the Austro-Hungarian army) was speaking against fascism.

Ironically, Arnold Deutsch, the seasoned intelligence officer of OGPU and chief recruiter of Philby and the Cambridge spy ring, was arrested by German police in 1933 and later in 1934 by Austrian police on charges of being a communist as well as of being involved in indecent publications (he was accused of promoting Wilhelm's Reich sexologist theories).

The internal newsletter *Befehlsblatt des Chefs der Sicherheitspolizei under des SD*, in its 29 January 1943 issue, published the obituary of decorated Hauptsturmführer Willi Lehmann of the Gestapo, who gave his life 'for the Führer and Fatherland'. Born in 1884, Lehmann had joined the Kriminalpolizei of Berlin in 1911 and by 1920 he had risen to deputy chief of counter-espionage. In 1933 he joined the Gestapo and was active in the Night of the Long Knives (June 30 to July 2, 1934) when at least eighty-five Nazi officials were executed. He admitted that he felt 'sick' of the experience, hinting that he had himself had killed someone.

Back in September 1929, Lehmann needed money to support his

---

[29] Ibid., p.52.

gambling, his wife and his mistress. The Soviet Legation officials in Berlin were initially perplexed by the appearance of Ernst Kuhr, a demoted policeman. He wanted to take revenge on the Polizei and was willing to give the Soviets secret documents in return for money. Soviet agents followed Kuhr and soon established that behind him was the offer of Lehmanm, a high-ranking police officer. Colonel Pawel Kornel of the NKVD recruited Lehmann the same year as agent A-201 to be paid a handsome 580 DM per month.

In 1933, Arnold Deutsch was arrested in Berlin. Notified by his NKVD handlers, Lehmann arranged for Deutsch to walk free and go to Austria. Lehmann was the right man in the right place at the right time and was the key person (some would say) who enabled the charismatic Deutsch to meet Philby and persuade the already committed communist to spy on behalf of Moscow.

Lehmann continued supplying Moscow with intelligence on rocket projects and submarine construction and warned on 19 June 1941 of the impending invasion of Russia. In late 1942, Lehmann, now 59 years old, was discovered by the Gestapo. In his interrogation by British Military Intelligence after the war, Horst Kopkow (a senior Gestapo officer who investigated the July 1944 attempt against Hitler) revealed the role of Lehmann as a spy of Moscow, remarking 'as an old official Lehmann had a considerable insight into the activities of Abwehrabteilung III, especially as regards to espionage in the East.'[30] Kriminal-Inspektor Lehmann 'was shot on written instruction from Himmler, who had forbidden any court proceedings since he did not wish it to become known, to Nazi judges, that an official of the Gestapo (*Gegeim Staats Amnt*) had been working for the Russian IS (Intelligence Service) for years. The whole matter was hushed up and a statement issued that Lehmann had been murdered by partisans on a journey to Bialystok; a fictitious grave was photographed and shown to Lehmann's wife, who was promised a pension.'[31]

Vienna was a hub for revolutionaries prior to 1917. In 1921, Soviet Intelligence built a station – a rezidentura – of the Foreign Department of the GPU and the Registration Directorate of the General Staff of the Red Army. Initially it was a joint organisation (the KGB and GRU working together in Cold War terms). Joseph J. Krasny, a seasoned revolutionary (and co-worker of Felix Dzerzhinsky, the chief of the Cheka) was head of the rezidentura in the early 1920s before he was assigned to the London rezidentura. The Vienna rezidentura reported to the Berlin rezidentura and

---

[30]Field interrogation Report of Horst Kopkow, 11 September 1945, p.24, KV 2/1500 TNA.
[31]Third interim report on Stubaf Horst Kopkow, p.7, KV 2/1501 TNA.

it was the base for operations in the Balkans.

Moscow was informed of the efforts of the rezidentura and its sub-stations. Krasny boasted to a letter to Mikhail Trilisser (27 March 1922):

> 'My organisation for the Balkans is fairly large and has the potential for expansion, as the need may arise. Certain contacts are extremely valuable. I have, for instance, somebody who frequents [General] Wrangel's house and another individual is a good acquaintance of General Klimovick, the Chief of Wrangel's intelligence department.'

In October 1922, he wrote from Vienna that he had wound up his affairs and was about to move to London and had applied for a visa. General Pyotr Nikolayevich Wrangel had led the anti-Bolshevik White Army in Southern Russia in the Civil War. After the defeat he fled to Constantinople and then to Serbia in 1922. Two years later, he established in Sremski Karlovci the Russian All-Military Union to unite anti-Bolshevik émigrés. In 1927 he moved to Brussels. He died on 25 April 1928, some fearing that he was poisoned by a Russian agent, his brother's butler.

In the 1920s, a notable coup by Soviet Intelligence in Vienna was the recruitment of clerks in the Ministry of Foreign Affairs, who leaked classified documents. Eventually, in May 1927, the Austrian police arrested the spy network in the ministry.

From the interwar period to the Second World War and the Cold War, Vienna was an eco-system of spies fighting interconnected secret wars: SIS against Comintern spies; Nazi espionage against Austrian Intelligence and later the OSS and SOE; American secret agents against NKVD spymasters. Vienna was also the gateway for spies going from Nazi Germany or Russia into Europe, to Britain or the Balkans.

What kind of spies does Vienna produce? An historian cannot put together a documented and coherent answer. But a former intelligence officer who served in the 1950s in Austria turned author, John le Carré (David Cornwell), can perhaps give us some leads into the psyche of the Vienna spy. He writes of the fictional Toby Esterhase in *Tinker, Taylor, Soldier, Spy* and in a couple of other novels. Esterhase is a top operative and Hungarian by birth. He entered the world of espionage out of desperation: George Smiley recruited him in Vienna during the Allied occupation, when he was a 'starving' student living in the 'ruins of a museum' where his late uncle was a curator. Esterhase was a man who never smiled and was fearless in operations; he was a polyglot ('Toby spoke no known language perfectly, but he spoke them all.') His odd syntax in English was always noted as well as his frantic effort to be accepted by SIS rank and file as an English gentleman. He dressed impeccably; 'dressing like a male model' was the joke. Esterhase had the ability to manage and lead a motley crew of characters, the section called the 'Lamplighters', a group of wiretapping operatives, petty thieves, and housewives; effectively the people who carried out secret operations. Esterhase had a taste for fine arts, and was selling, occasionally, forgeries. He was loyal to himself only, but he would never defect to Moscow; he believed in the West and what it represented. He proved himself an efficient spymaster.[32]

This book concentrates on espionage narrative, distinguishable from war-time military, diplomatic and strategic intelligence history or biography. The attention to detail helps us understand the world of the spy; after all, the very survival of the spy depends on the detail. For example, a genuine-looking Soviet identity card has to have rusty staples colouring the photograph of the holder - otherwise he/she will be executed almost on the spot. And the spymaster is interested in the detail: MGB Major Pyotr Deryabin, based in Vienna in the early 1950s, who defected to US Intelligence, was nonetheless proud in stating the Americans 'cannot really appreciate the diligence with which the Soviets pursued tiny tidbits of information...'[33]

Spymasters may seem like ghosts in this book; they appear and disappear in a haunted Vienna, a city that forged their past. The narratives focus on the activities of each spymaster, and each 'ghost's' story covers a specific time period of the secret war. 'We may have to concede that while truth is indeed stranger than fiction, fiction is substantially better arranged.'[34] Any spymaster ought to take note of a remark by Klemens von Metternich, the nineteenth century Austrian Chancellor, infamous for his oppressive policies: 'Any plan conceived in moderation must fail when the circumstances are set in extremes.' Indeed, this book narrates the extreme circumstances of the spy game.

---

[32]Le Carré, John, *Tinker, Tailor, Soldier, Spy* (London: Hodder & Stoughton, 1989), pp.91-92, 150, 179, 323; Le Carré, *Smiley's People* (London: Hodder & Stoughton, 1992), p.314; Le Carré, *The Secret Pilgrim* (London: Hodder & Stoughton, 1991), pp.144-45.

[33] Debriefing of Peter Deryabin concerning operation Zeppelin, 6 February 1964, available at:<https://www.cia.gov/library/readingroom/docs/KURRECK%2C%20WALTER_0025.pdf > accessed 28 August 2019.

[34] Finch, Charles, 'Murderous Husbands, Flapper-Era Gun Molls and Korean Assassins: The Best Winter Thrillers' *New York Times*, 28 January 2019, available at: <https://www.nytimes.com/2019/01/28/books/review/new-winter-thrillers.html> accessed 4 February 2019.

1

Our Man in Vienna

On 31 October 1918, in the last days of the Great War, the Hungarian parliament voted to terminate the union with Austria. Emperor Charles I of Austria relinquished any authority over government on 11 November, the day of the Armistice. The peace Treaty of Versailles was concluded on 28 June 1919. Austria and Hungary were not among the signatories.

The Republic of German Austria signed the Treaty of Saint-Germain-en-Laye with the victorious Allies. Social Democrat Chancellor Karl Renner reached Saint-Germain in May 1919 to attend the negotiations. French Prime Minister Georges Clemenceau had taken the lead and effectively issued an ultimatum to Renner, and the Chancellor had no other choice but to concede. Years later, in May 1945, Renner headed the first post-war Austrian government, eventually keeping Soviet influence at arm's length, despite the fact that it was Stalin who sent for him as the Third Reich was collapsing. The Republic was compelled to eliminate any reference to ethnic Germans and 'German' (as an adjective in the official name), and not to unite with Germany.

Winston Churchill called the breakup of the Austro-Hungarian Empire 'a cardinal tragedy'.[35] The Treaty of St. Germain-en-Laye was signed on 10 September 1919 at the Chateau Neuf. The British delegation was led by Arthur James Balfour, the Foreign Secretary. All 381 articles, written in French, English and Italian, made sure that Austria, the country at the centre of Europe, would be weak and at the mercy of politico-military pressures from neighbouring states. A weak Austria could be put under strong pressure by Nazi Germany and Soviet Russia - and therefore also their hundreds of spies and propagandists. Under the provisions of the treaty, Austria recognised the independence of Czechoslovakia, Poland, Hungary, and the Kingdom of the Serbs, Croats, and Slovenes (Yugoslavia). The humiliated former Austro-Hungarian Empire also lost eastern Galicia, Trento, southern Tirol, Trieste, and Istria. Plebiscites determined that Carinthia would remain in Austria, and Sopron in Hungary; ethnic German Austrians were included in the territories of Czechoslovakia and Italy. Austria was compelled to

---

[35] Churchill, Winston S. *The Second World War: The Gathering Storm* (Boston: Houghton Mifflin, 1948), p.10.

renounce trading rights in treaties with Morocco, Egypt, Siam and China. The new Republic of Austria retained a maximum of 30,000 troops; the import and export of arms was prohibited; and only one, state-owned factory could produce arms. The surviving warships and submarines of the former empire would be surrendered to the Allies. Renner accepted article 177, with Austria taking responsibility for 'the war imposed upon them [the Entente] by the aggression of Austria-Hungary and her allies'.[36]

Colonel Lambert Ward, a Tory Member of Parliament, was asked by Austen Chamberlain (then the Chancellor of the Exchequer) to go to Vienna. Chamberlain was a proponent of secret intelligence and was aware of the post-1918 limitations of SIS in human resources and funding.[37] The Chancellor would have liked further information on economic matters. Major H. Visher, the SIS station head in Bern after the end of the war, was directed to establish SIS stations in Vienna, Prague and Budapest. Captain Ernan Forbes-Dennis was named head of the Vienna station, serving overtly as a Passport Control Officer until October 1922. Chamberlain circulated Colonel Ward's report to the Cabinet. Ward, a spy of everyday economy, kept a low profile in the city and mingled with the crowds. He wrote to Chamberlain of his impressions 'apart from statistics' of the Austrian government as he put it:

'...conditions at the present moment were not nearly as bad there as people [Austrian officials] are endeavouring to make out. There is an absolute orgy of gaiety and extravagance going on amongst the richer people. Theatres, restaurants, and music-halls are packed...Every hotel is full...There is apparently no coal to bring the necessities of life to the city, but there is any amount to run electric light...To give you one example only - on Shrove Tuesday a Ball was given at the Concert House, which you probably know, is as large as the Albert Hall. Certainly 10,000 people were there, each of whom had paid the pre-war equivalent of £4 per ticket. The only drink being served was Champagne...There is no doubt a large amount of real suffering amongst the middle and professional classes whose incomes have not been raised in proportion to the increased cost of living...I must say I

---

[36] See FO 93/11/74 TNA; FO 608/23/1 TNA; see Suppan, Arnold, *The Imperialist Peace Order in Central Europe: Saint-Germain and Trianon, 1919-1920* (Vienna: Austrian Academy of Sciences Press, 2019).

[37] Quoted in Andrew, Christopher, 'intelligence, international relations and 'under-theorisation' *Intelligence and National Security*, Vol.19, No 2 summer 2004, p.171.

looked for signs of misery in the crowded streets and did not find them. The people were well-dressed and looked well-fed, and were certainly not in the pitiable condition of the French and Belgian refugees in the early days of the War...Children between the ages of 1 and 5 no doubt, suffer from the lack of milk, and will doubtless feel the effects for the rest of their lives...Personally, I can see no reason for the heart-breaking accounts of the sufferings in Vienna which have appeared in the papers, and I cannot account for them. I am inclined to suspect some subsidised scheme of newspaper propaganda designed to discredit the Treaty of Peace and to soften the hearts and loosen the purse strings of the Allies.' [38]

Ward put emphasis on the fact that Vienna was *the* city for 'amusement and luxury for the whole of Austro-Hungary.' Now, the capital of Austria 'no longer has any raison d'être in the life of Central Europe.' Nonetheless, he was wrong: Vienna would be ideal for foreign spymasters, namely British and Russian, to establish their regional headquarters as Austrian politics radicalised to the far left and far right and the Austrian government tolerated the presence of foreign spies – as long as they did not steal Austrian secrets.

The colonel insisted that the population of 2½ million could not be supported because so many major industries were now in Czechoslovakian territories. The Austrians sought international aid credit to purchase coal and raw materials. [39] The diplomats at the British Legation in Vienna never hid their suspicion towards him and he later blamed them for being 'still very much of the old school who cultivated the members of the old aristocratic families.' The Legation were experts in elite-centred intelligence. Forbes-Dennis attempted to create 'a firm relationship' with Dr Johannes Schober, who served as Chancellor from June 1921 to May 1922. Earlier, in his police career, at a time of anarchist terrorist attacks against royals and politicians, Schober was assigned security duties for King Edward IV and the Austrian royal family. He was the founder of the International Criminal Police Association, the predecessor of Interpol. There was an exchange of intelligence about subversive organisations and individuals. But Forbes-Dennis did not establish a network of secret agents. Besides, his budget was meagre and Austria had a low priority in London's intelligence-tasking in the 1920s.[40]

---

[38] Situation in Vienna, 3 March 1920, CAB 24/99/84 TNA.
[39] Ibid.
[40] Jeffery, *MI6*, pp.201-2.

After Forbes-Dennis' resignation, the acting head of station was named his deputy. Forbes-Dennis assumed that he had 'decidedly leftish views' and served for three years until 1925 when Captain Thomas J. Kendrick took over in December.

London received streams of reports on the organisation of the Soviet espionage machinery in central Europe. An agent of SIS in Czechoslovakia reported that until 1922 the Bolshevik military intelligence was alarmist and inaccurate. A major re-organisation was put in place only after the Soviet defeat in Poland. Commissars took over as spymasters with military officers as assistants. In Vienna their headquarters were at Gumpendorferstrasse no 87. This agent insisted:

'The work of the agents is very carefully regulated; they are given in the first place economic missions, observation of industrial centres; later they are entrusted with military espionage. The missions have instructions to compromise the agents with the police of the country in which they work, so to have them completely in their hands; they are then sent to work in other countries. Each agent who proves his worth is allowed to engage other agents, and to become the head of a sub-organisation called Rezidentur; this Rezidentur is in touch with the Vienna centre through intermediaries or under cover addresses. A Rezident who is successful is promoted to the rank of a Red officer; as a special favour they get the Order of the Red Flag.'[41]

The secret agent was anti-Semitic: 'In Poland it is more difficult because of the genuine patriotism; there however they can make use of the Jews who as a rule can be bought.'[42]

Every six months, Moscow dispatched a very detailed list of intelligence requirements to their centre in Berlin. The Vienna centre was informed by Berlin; many secret rezidents received the same intelligence requirements.

'decipher invisible ink and prepare two groups of reports, one of which is purely military. Documents are photographed in Vienna itself...Vienna makes three types...one of which they file, and the other two are sent to

---

[41] The Bolshevik SS (Secret Service) in Central Europe, 10 July 1923, KV 3/230 TNA.
[42] Ibid.

Berlin. The information obtained from these sources is chiefly collated by the Russian general staff, who every few months issue a highly confidential volume, containing their summaries.'[43]

The secret courier service between the Vienna and Berlin centres ran every week; and Vienna reported also on every month of their activities while 'special and urgent communications with Berlin are always made by telephone.'[44]

In July 1924, the SIS station in Vienna reported that the Soviet rezidentura was 'enlarged'. One Lettish Lieutenant under the pseudonym Franz headed the organisation; his assistants were called Fedorovitch, Ruszko and Baum. Their main interest was military intelligence on Romania and Poland. The agent reporting put emphasis that 'the military espionage is very extensive and exact, and the agents have also been ordered to organise a guerrilla war in case of a Russo-Romanian war.'[45]

Captain Thomas Kendrick was 44 years old when he took charge of the SIS Vienna station in January 1925. He was a seasoned military intelligence officer (mainly in the field of intelligence security – counterintelligence) who had served in the Great War and with MI 1(c) in Cologne after the Armistice. Kendrick worked with a staff of three secretaries at the Passport Control Office, which was not covered by diplomatic immunity. The office was located at 6 Metternichstrasse in central Vienna.

Kendrick had secret agents and access to the correspondence of the OGPU rezidentura with their headquarters in Moscow, soon to be renamed to NKVD. A close reading of the reports shows his many secret coups.

In April 1925, the SIS station informed London that the head of the Soviet delegation in Vienna, called Yoffe, was a member of the executive committee of Comintern in Vienna. Levitski, the counsellor of the Soviet Legation, was also a member of the committee. Moscow was dispatching specialists to Vienna as advisers. Two advisers of military affairs were noted by the British. One was K.G. Pavlov, a former officer of the general staff of the Russian Imperial Army, considered 'a highly trusted agent and friend of Grigory Zinoviev' (chairman of the Comintern until November 1926). Pavlov was in Bulgaria and Romania in late 1924, inspecting the activities of the Bulgarian and Romanian Communist Parties.

---

[43] Ibid.
[44] Ibid.
[45] MI1c to MI5, Extract of a report 10 July 1924, KV 3/230 TNA.

The other adviser was Neiz Schultz, 'an ex-officer of the German army in which he served with distinction during the Great War where he came under the influence of the Comintern.' He was a member of the German Social-Democratic Party. Kendrick reported that the Comintern did not trust the Balkan communist parties and 'for this reason prefers to maintain its own network of agents in the Balkans to whom all important work is entrusted.' A plan was drafted for the penetration of the Macedonian Revolutionary Organisation with Comintern agents; the Balkan communist parties would not get involved in this endeavour.

In Yugoslavia, ninety-eight Comintern agents had been active; 'This large number is considered necessary owing to the weakness of communism', it was claimed in a report. In addition to the Comintern agents, the OGPU maintained a separate presence in Vienna. [46] Kendrick reported on the head of this organisation:

'Anderson recently succeeded Zavadski as chief of the Soviet intelligence in the Balkans. Although nominally working direct with Moscow, Anderson is to a greater extent under the control of Yoffe and the latter obtains copies of all intelligence reports. Anderson is known to employ an intelligence officer in Bulgaria and another in Romania...The duties of these two officers are to report to Anderson all information affecting communism from a military point of view and to render periodical reports on the military forces of the countries to which they are appointed...The relations between the Soviet diplomatic and commercial missions in Vienna and the branch of the Comintern in Vienna are conducted in complete secrecy and their meetings and conference are usually held in private houses. Yoffe seldom attends these meetings but Levitski is always present. The money furnished by Moscow for revolutionary work in the Balkans is paid by the Vienna centre to delegates of the Balkan communist parties working in Vienna and is transmitted by them to the various Balkan communist parties.'[47]

Key secret couriers known to British Intelligence included Gabriel Eugene Kunzitine, 'a well educated man, speaking many languages, 30-32

---

[46] Ibid., p.2.
[47] Ibid., p.4.

years old. A former student of a commercial high school and attached to the Vienna Soviet diplomatic mission.' Another secret courier named Vrublevski 'travels continuously between Vienna and Salonika through Bulgaria and Constantinople on a Polish passport. Is highly trusted courier...'[48]

Kendrick's coups continued to amaze London. In April 1926, he managed to intercept a summary of a report 'by a highly placed communist official who visited Vienna on duty...and who came into personal contact with the various sections of the Centre of the Comintern.' They directed activities in Yugoslavia, Bulgaria, Italy, Greece, Hungary, Czechoslovakia, Rumania and Switzerland. The Comintern did not conduct operations in Austria out of fear of provoking the government and bringing a police crackdown. The report also stated that in summer 1925 the reorganisation of the Comintern led to the Greek Communist Party being directed by Moscow only. A year later, control of the Greek Communist Party was transferred to the Vienna centre. Klimov, the Soviet diplomatic representative in Greece, moved to Vienna as special delegate of the Comintern for the Balkans. In Greece the dictatorship under General Theodoros Pangalos compelled the Comintern to abolish the centres in Athens and Salonica; thus Vienna would direct all Comintern activities for Greece.[49]

A military intelligence section operated in Vienna manned with five intelligence officers for Greece, Bulgaria, Czechoslovakia, Yugoslavia and Hungary; 'The military operations section aimed to direct the military activity of the Balkans and southeast Europe communist parties; to supply arms and to arrange the transport and safe storage of arms and ammunition.'[50]

Kendrick found out the mission of two Soviet secret agents. 'Nadia Zachariova a contre-espionage agent of Moscow Comintern headquarters sent for (sic) anti-British intelligence. She poses as a Russian refugee.' The second agent named Swagens was an 'agent of the contre-espionage of the Comintern in Moscow.' His mission in Vienna was to shadow the SIS station.[51]

In September 1927, a spy story hit the press. The correspondent of the *Daily Mail* in Vienna wrote of the arrest of a very beautiful woman in Budapest on charges of being a communist spy:

---

[48] Ibid., p.5.
[49] The Vienna center of the communist international, 17 May 1926, KV 3/230 TNA.
[50] Ibid., p.2.
[51] Ibid.

'A woman calling herself Alexandra Romanova and claiming to be a Russian duchess who was arrested at Budapest has been proved by the Hungarian police to be the widow of a Russian doctor named Kleitschovitsch. The widow who is beautiful was convicted in 1915 of espionage against Austria and sentenced to six months imprisonment. Afterwards she came to Vienna where she was imprisoned for theft. After her release she served the communist government which was then in power in Budapest, doing duty as a hospital nurse and collecting war prisoners' confidences. She was able to do this as she speaks nine languages fluently. Since then she had organised an espionage service at Vienna for the Bolsheviks and it is believed that her reports caused the Soviet minister's recall recently. She has made several journeys to Moscow with a Soviet secret service agent, Balmovski.'[52]

Kendrick became aware of Soviet suspicions of Italian espionage. He intercepted a letter dated 22 September 1927 from the OGPU in Vienna to Moscow. A certain Sonia Alberovaya was reported as working against Soviet interests on behalf of Italian Intelligence – she was already known to Moscow. There was a Comrade M. Schmidt undertaking the mission 'of watching and reporting upon the activities' of Sonia Alberovaya.[53]

Kendrick set up networks of spies in Czechoslovakia while reporting on Italy, Hungary and Yugoslavia. In Czechoslovakia his key sources were an ethnic German former officer of the Austrian army, now working in the Czechoslovak Ministry of Defence, an electrical engineer doing his national service (and securing call signs and codes for Kendrick); another spy, on the general staff, had access to mobilisation maps; another one worked in the Skoda aircraft factory. There was a secret source too in the office of the President of Czechoslovakia. He reported until the early 1930s when SIS in London started fearing that his reports might have been fake.[54]

Gradually, Kendrick and his wife immersed themselves in the Viennese circles and British expatriate community, holding parties at their apartment at 25 Wattmanngasse.[55] Vienna was a small city; people talked,

[52] 'Beautiful Red Spy' 21 September 1927, *Daily Mail*, KV 3/230 TNA.
[53] Bolshevik activity abroad SIS to MI5, 21 October 1927, KV 3/230 TNA.
[54] Jeffery, *MI6*, pp.202- 203.
[55] Fry, Helen, *Spymaster: the Secret Life of Kendrick* (London: Marranos Press, 2018), pp.39-40.

and Kendrick, the spymaster, stayed there too long.

His secretaries (Clara Holmes, Evelyn Stamper and Betty Hogson) were handpicked by him and were committed in their administrative tasks. While keeping the Passport Control Office running, they wrote messages with secret ink, decrypted incoming secret correspondence and wrote secret messages in innocent letters to recipients in Czechoslovakia, Hungary, Italy and Sicily. In Italy the new strongman, Benito Mussolini, had drawn the attention of British Intelligence with his fascist ideology and policies, especially in Sicily where he unleashed Cesare Mori, the prefect who crippled the mafia.

Kendrick's intelligence officers were Rex Pearson and Charles Howard Ellis, the latter having served with SIS in Berlin until posted to Vienna. They both acted as journalists. George Eric Rove Gedye, a First World War veteran, was a left-wing journalist who was connected to Kendrick's organisation and during the Second World War he would become an SOE recruiter in Constantinople. (See chapter 6.)

In Vienna, Kendrick's spies and informers shadowed the Soviet Legation and kept track of key communist spies seeking to go to Britain; the cases of Béla Kun (discussed later) and Schueller are representative of the warning MI5 received from Kendrick. In January 1926, one agent attended a secret communist session in Czechoslovakia. The spymaster was aware of the Russian espionage effort against the Czech military. The Comintern correspondence was dispatched with the Soviet diplomatic bag. The Russians in Vienna coordinated their intelligence and Comintern propaganda for Yugoslavia, Italy, Greece, Bulgaria, Romania, Czechoslovakia, Hungary and Switzerland. The Comintern activities in Syria, Palestine and North Africa were directed by rezidentura in Constantinople.[56]

Kendrick and his agents witnessed the crisis of July 1927. Austrian politics became radicalised when the Social Democrats confronted right-wing parties and the Catholic Church. On 15 July 1927, Vienna was shaken by violent demonstrations. The police fired at the crowd, killing 89 protesters. Five policemen were also killed and the more than 1,200 were wounded on both sides. The involvement of left-wing and right-wing paramilitary organisations was another aspect of the violence. The nationalist Frontkämpfervereinigung Deutsch-Österreichs under Colonel Hermann Hiltl and the Social Democratic Republikanischer Schutzbund clashed. On 30 January 1927, three Frontkämpfer had been accused of shooting a veteran and an 8-year-old boy, and they were brought to trial in

---

[56] Ibid., p.50.

July. The jury acquitted them. Demonstrations followed. The government, under Christian Social Party Chancellor Ignaz Seipel, was put in a difficult position. On 15 July, protesters made an attempt against the Vienna University building in the Ringstrasse. Afterwards a police station was raided, together with newspaper offices. Soon, the large crowd turned against Parliament. The police pushed back and the new centre of conflict became the square outside the Palace of Justice. The protesters invaded the courthouse and set it on fire, while preventing the fire brigade from putting it out. Johann Schober, the chief of police, after failing to persuade Social Democrat mayor Karl Seitz to bring in the army, distributed rifles to the police, who were ordered to open fire.

Gedye was an eyewitness to the demonstrations and knew that Socialists had many arms caches at their disposal. He wrote of false information and rumour leading to the escalation of the crisis:

> '...the police had been inflamed during the day, deliberately or accidentally, by all kinds of atrocity stories. The cap and uniform jacket of a policeman were hung derisively on a lamp-post outside a small police station from which the police were driven out. In an hour all the police believed a dozen policemen had been hanged there. The police took a terrible toll of the civilian population that afternoon. They started firing indiscriminately, not only in the neighbourhood of the Ringstrasse but in many other parts of the city...'[57]

Meanwhile, the SIS station in Vienna continued collecting intelligence on 'every subject under the sun, political, military, industrial, economic, social scandal in high places' as SIS officer Leslie Nicholson put it.

In 1928, the station penetrated the rezidentura in Vienna, securing at least two letters from Stanislas Kalina of the special section of the Soviet Legation in Vienna to the NKVD in Moscow. Kalina had in his possession military intelligence on Yugoslavia. An agent in Bulgaria had received money and instructions to urge a Bulgarian garrison to revolt against the government there. Kendrick also reported to London about the detailed Soviet reporting on Czech military organisation.

The British spymaster followed the case of Hungarian prominent communist leader Béla Kun, who was arrested by Austrian police in

---

[57] Ibid., p.25.

Vienna for not having a passport or any identification papers. The Austrian police assured the press that they were aware 'for some time' that Béla Kun was in the country. On 26 April 1928, he was arrested in a drug store he had rented under a false name. Béla Kun was no ordinary communist. In 1914 he was recruited to the Austro-Hungarian army and was captured by the Russians in 1916. At a prison camp in the Urals, he was converted to communism. By 1919 he was considered the leader of Hungarian communists, establishing the Hungarian Soviet Republic. Serving as Commissar for Foreign Affairs, he boasted to Lenin: 'My personal influence in the Revolutionary Governing Council is such that the dictatorship of the proletariat is firmly established, since the masses are backing me.' The Soviet government lasted for 133 days. After the invasion of the Romanian army and the taking over of Budapest, the communist regime collapsed. Béla Kun fled to Austria. In 1920, he was arrested by the police but soon was exchanged for Austrian prisoners of war helped by the Soviets. After moving to Moscow, he started working for the Comintern. In 1920-21, he was named head of the Crimean Revolutionary Committee and was directly implicated in a terror campaign there. In March 1921 Béla Kun reached Berlin to advise the German Communist Party. Eventually their coup attempt failed. In a secret speech, Lenin accused Kun of this failure, but the Hungarian communist continued to work for the Comintern.

Kendrick read carefully what Kalina wrote about the arrest of Kun. The Soviet spymaster was critical in his 28 April 1928 message to Moscow:

> 'I consider it necessary to make a few observations in connection with the arrest of Comrade B.K. [Béla Kun], although the whole question, as the O.O. is aware, is outside the sphere of my jurisdiction and full explanations have already been given by Comrade Segal both to the INO of the OGPU and to the Presidium of the IKKI. It is my deep conviction that the Presidium of the IKKI committed an unpardonable error with regard to Comrade B.K., to which, at my instigation, Comrade Segal has already drawn attention. I refer to the long stay of Comrade B.K. in Vienna, and the fact that he occupied private rooms, whereas he might have had certain security with the Diplomatic Representation or Trade Delegation.'[58]

---

[58] Arrest of Béla Kun and his Associates', 4 June 1928, KV 2/578 TNA.

34

Kalina added: 'I do not wish to contest the principle, that in order to preserve outward appearance, Comintern workers should not be sheltered by our diplomatic representatives. Nevertheless, every rule has exceptions, and such an exception is certainly Comrade Bela Kun.'[59]

For the time being, Kalina could not assess the damage of Kun's arrest on Soviet espionage in Austria. He had information that Kun was threatened with imprisonment by the Austrian authorities for one year and three months. Indeed, 'it is absolutely certain that Béla Kun will not be surrendered to Hungary.' Meanwhile Kalina and his staff were urging the Social-Democrat and the 'Left-bourgeois' press in Austria to support Kun:

> '...with regard to influencing public opinion, I can assure you that I have literally set every spring in motion and, as far as the press is concerned, have obtained entirely favourable results. I trusted this part of the business to Comrade Almasov, to whom I have transferred 20,000 Austrian schillings and have given "carte blanche" in the disposal of the sum.'[60]

> 'We are in possession of a written assurance from the Social-Democrats with regards to cooperation in the matter of the liberation of Comrade B.K., as well as concerning his unhindered and safe dispatch to the USSR...In case of unfavourable issues of the affairs, I am also taking measures for the forcible liberation of BK which I would endeavour to realise if the worst happened. Naturally no employee of the Political Representation or Trade Delegation has any immediate part in the matter - nor will have so that the Soviet Government will not be compromised in any way. The technical part of the plan is dependent upon circumstances, and the people will be supplied by the Austrian Communist Party and the Hungarian Group 'K', in whom I have the greatest confidence. [emphasis of the author] I hope, however, that the affair will be settled without resorting to these measures.'[61]

In addition, Kalina reassured Moscow:

---

[59] Ibid.
[60] CX/ 737, Memo 'the Arrest of Bela Kun ', 15 May 1928, KV 2/578 TNA.
[61] Ibid.

'...in any case the arrest of Comrade B.K. has had no effect on the communication lines and on the activity of my section, as, in accordance with the instructions of the O.O., I have always carried on my work parallel to, but independently of, the activities of the Comintern.'[62]

Kendrick intercepted another letter of Kalina to Moscow dated 4 June 1928. Kalina remarked:

'In connection with the approaching settlement of the question relating to Béla Kun's fate, I am of opinion that in the interests of his personal safety every possible effort should be made to treat as strictly secret the decision of the Austrian Government to deport him to Russia and also the granting of a transit visa by the German Government. According to my information, the whole question will only be definitely settled after the result of the trial of the German engineers who were implicated in the Shakhtin (Donetz Basin) affair becomes known. Further, I am personally convinced that the arrest of Bela Kun was in a great measure the result of the arrest of the German engineers in Russia and I request that my view in this connection be submitted to the proper authorities.'[63]

In 1928, the OGPU accused a group of engineers in the North Caucasus town of Shakhty of conspiring and sabotaging the Soviet industrial effort. The show trial of fifty Russians and three Germans led to fifty-three death sentences; another forty-four who were arrested languished in prison. In the Politburo, Josef Stalin declared that the international capitalists would 'weaken our economic power by means of invisible economic intervention, not always obvious but fairly serious, organising sabotage, planning all kinds of "crises" in one branch of industry or another, and thus facilitating the possibility of future military intervention...We have internal enemies. We have external enemies. We cannot forget this for a moment.'[64] Stanislas Kalina played safe with the escalating paranoia, by claiming that German espionage was threatening Russian economy and industry.

Kendrick read with interest a letter dated 11 June 1928 from Kalina to

---

[62] Memo 'Arrest of Béla Kun and his Associates', 4 June 1928, KV 2/578 TNA.
[63] Memo 'Arrest of Béla Kun', 20 June 1928 KV 2/578 TNA.
[64] Kotkin, *Stalin*, pp.702-5.

Moscow:

> 'With regard to the activity of our information section, Comrade Dikman has proved himself particularly useful, having succeeded within the past two weeks in collecting exhaustive material dealing, on the one hand, with the status, organisation, concentration and orders of the [Czech] Cs,S1.Army (Material N-X11-3233) and, on the other, with the Vienna centre of the Eurasians which he had failed to obtain in spite of our endeavours and considerable expenditure.'[65]

The SIS station in Vienna intercepted another letter dated 29 June 1928 from the Special Section of the Soviet Legation in Vienna to the Special Section of NKVD in Moscow. Kalina was playing up the case of German espionage in the Soviet Union. Kendrick followed the writing of his opponent, who boasted in a letter to Moscow dated 14 July 1929:

> 'I am in possession of indisputable evidence from two agents, (A-XVI and O.34), entirely separate from each other, which shows that, as a result of the Shakhtin affair, both German and Austrian industrial circles are filled with the utmost distrust for anything emanating from the Soviet Government or from any of the organs thereof...'

Kalina warned Moscow: 'as I am of the opinion that the continued activity of the German spy apparatus is capable of completely destroying our plans with regard to Germany, and partly also with regard to Austria, I beg to call the attention of the OO [Special Section] to these facts and to request that they may be brought to the notice of the INO/Foreign Department of the OGPU'.[66]

Kendrick assured London that he had a 'first-hand source' reporting the 'Special Section'. The British spymaster had read Kalina's brief to Moscow:

> 'In reply to your strictly confidential question concerning Comrade Yurenev [the Soviet Minister in Vienna], I can inform you that on the question of the struggle

---

[65] 'Soviet SS (Secret Service) activities in Vienna, SIS to MI5, 22 June 1928, KV 3/230 TNA.
[66] German Espionage in the USSR, SIS to MI5, 25 July 1928, KV 3/230 TNA.

of the Party majority with the Opposition (both with the Left and with the Right) Comrade Yurenev adopts an extremely cautious and somewhat temporising attitude…Nevertheless I have every reason to assume (for the present I cannot "affirm") that Comrade Yurenev is not only in sympathy with the Right opposition, but is not also in permanent connection therewith, as for instance with Comrade Uglanov up to the present, that is to say, ever since the resolutions of the Central Committee of the Austrian Communist Party with regard to the Moscow Party organisation.'[67]

Another letter, dated 25 February 1929, was intercepted by British Intelligence. Kalina wrote of a secret plan in the making by a certain Kuschnir-Kushnarev who lived in Graz. He was 'an experienced provocateur-adventurer and is entirely in my hands.' Kalina sought to create a false organisation. 'I think that with his assistance we shall be able to organise a "Russian émigrés' Committee" in Austria (of a monarchist nature formed by adherents of the Antoniyevski movement) through which we shall, without difficulty, take upon ourselves the protection of Russian émigrés' interests in Austria.'[68]

Meanwhile, the SIS representative in Czechoslovakia had 'a completely separate and absolutely unconnected source [to Kalina's residentura]', to the effect that a Czechoslovak agent in Vienna had gathered from a conversation with an Austrian official that 'Bela Kun would be neither kept by the Austrians nor surrendered to Hungary, because he was wanted by Germany for exchange against the German engineers not under arrest and trial in Russia for sabotage in Donetz Basin.'[69]

Eventually, Béla Kun was freed, and returned to Moscow. In 1937 he was arrested by NKVD and accused of Trotskyism. He was tried and executed in 1938. The Béla Kun affair showed the capabilities and plans of Soviet espionage in Austria during times of social upheaval. The fact that SIS had access to the secret correspondence of Kalina proves a coup of British Intelligence in shadowing Soviet spymasters. We do not know if Kendrick or the British Embassy informed the Austrian authorities about the intelligence of Soviet plans. Probably they did not, out of fear that this would prompt the Austrians to fear more and thus tolerate the Russians.

In the summer 1930, a young SIS officer, Leslie Nicholson, was

---

[67] Surveillance over Soviet Representatives Abroad, 26 November 1928, KV 3/230 TNA..
[68] SIS to MI5, 13 March 1929, KV 3/230 TNA.
[69] Ibid.

dispatched to the Vienna station before he moved to Czechoslovakia. He remarked of life in Vienna, 'From what I observed during my all too brief stay, the Viennese were still incorrigibly romantic; café and night life flourished in all its variations in spite of the general shortage of money.'[70] He had dinner with station chief Kendrick, which 'was a formal affair and the talk was mostly about the political set-up in Vienna and - which was closely connected - the state of the Austrian Exchequer.'[71]

Nicholson had concluded that out of the three countries born from the defunct Hapsburg empire, Czechoslovakia was prosperous with 'first class industries' and thus economic potential. Hungary was an agricultural country whose leaders blamed the 1920 Treaty of Trianon for costing them territories ceded. Hungary was now landlocked with only 28 per cent of the territories of the kingdom of Hungary and an army of only 35,000 men. Romania, Czechoslovakia and Yugoslavia benefited from the Trianon Treaty dividing Hungarian territories where non-Hungarians had been living. Hungarians also paid war reparations. The Hungarian dictator, Admiral Miklós Horthy, had turned against Jews and communists. Austria was about to face severe economic problems after the bankruptcy of the bank Credit-Anstalt (to happen in May 1931) causing additional financial problems even to Britain, eventually compelling London to abandon the gold standard.

Nicholson recalled of Kendrick:

'[Kendrick] was a man of great charm, a keen sense of humour and wit, an air of middle-aged respectability which I found reassuring in view of his stories. He gave me the run of all his files [of the SIS station in Vienna], but I could not make nothing of them (sic). The operational files contained little more than a series of question and answer exchanges with London. They revealed nothing of how it was done and to the uninitiated reader, it was almost impossible to see what they were all about... at the end of a wearisome day I told him that I was getting nowhere with the files and he agreed that perhaps they were not much help.'[72]

Later, Nicholson, Kendrick and some other intelligence officers went out for a dinner:

---

[70] Whitwell (Nicholson), *British Agent*, p.28.

[71] Ibid., p.22.

[72] Ibid.,p.26.

'We went on to a well-known restaurant and here my colleague pointed out to me a swarthy-looking Austrian dining with a big party who was the chief of the political police. This man had once demonstrated local methods of interrogation by striking a prisoner he happened to be questioning across the face with a rubber truncheon, much to the discomfort of my colleague [of the SIS] who at that moment was ushered into the office.'[73]

The only comment one could make was that in Vienna, the nest of spies, spymasters bumped into to each other in restaurants.

---

[73] Ibid.,p.27.

2

The Americans

George Earle, the US Chargé d'Affaires in Vienna, was a seasoned businessman, war veteran and Republican politician. Back in 1916 he was commissioned to fight on the Mexican border in the Pancho Villa Expedition and, in 1918, he was awarded the Navy Cross for 'averting an explosion' aboard the ship he was commanding. Earle was surprised by what Nazi diplomat Kurt Rieth, the head of the German Legation in Vienna, had been telling him. He rushed to inform Washington:

> 'Have just had long interview with German Minister Rieth. He states that he has agents throughout Austria in every class and occupation; that he knows Nazi secret organization in Austria grows daily in strength; that it already includes 50 percent of the people; that it may seize control at any time and that Dollfuss government cannot possibly last more than 6 months; and that with Nazi control will come great anti-Semitic action in Vienna. I think Rieth believes all this.'[74]

Chancellor Engelbert Dollfuss, who in early 1933 had sidelined parliament, boosting his authoritarian style, had banned the Austrian National Socialist Party, fearing its potential. The Staatspolizei and the Evidenzbureau of the general staff were the key intelligence services keeping check on the Nazis. The Viennese police was a professional force. In 1930, Norman Kendal of Scotland Yard visited the police of Berlin, Dresden, and Vienna and reported:

> 'In all three places, and particularly at Berlin, it is obvious that the amount of money spent on wireless installations could not possibly be justified, except for the fact that at the back of their mind all the time is the fear of political trouble. They believe it necessary to have a complete reserve method of communication in case the

---

[74] Earle to the Secretary of State, 14 November 1933, Foreign Relations of the United States (FRUS) *1934. Europe, Near East and Africa*, (1934), p.3.

telegraph and telephone should be tampered with. In the meantime they are making use of their systems for purposes of original investigation and urging other countries to adopt wireless for police work.'[75]

In the 1920s and early 1930s, there was no military intelligence service similar to the wartime Evidenzbureau. Spymaster Maximilen Ronge was advisor to the Dollfuss regime. Major General Erwin von Lahousen wrote:

'Vienna in the years after the First World War was an internation[al] [sic] center for espionage. This condition was favored by the fact that by the law at that time, espionage in Austria was not punishable at all, and espionage against Austria would be punished in the most extreme and aggravated case only by a maximum imprisonment of ten years. In practice, sentences of over two years hardly occurred. Especially Balkan espionage and the Soviet Union liked to do business in Vienna.'

Lahousen descended from an Austrian noble family and had served in the Austro-Hungarian army during the Great War. He witnessed the Nazi threat to Austrian in the late 1920s and early 1930s as a member of counterintelligence. From 1932 the activity of Nazis was noted by the authorities. Ronge was aware of the activities of the 2ieme Bureau of the Czechoslovak general staff employing spies against Austria. Once the Dollfuss regime started to discharge pro-Nazi officers the Czech espionage approached them via their military attaché in Berlin to spy for them. Ronge proved himself a master of spy hunt; in 1913 he was the one who trapped the infamous Colonel Alfred Redl, the spy from the Russian general staff. Now, in 1932, he laid a trap for Czech Intelligence officer Major Bartik, who received the incriminating evidence just before his arrest. The whole operation of Ronge was organised and 'carried out quite "privately" and on his own by Ronge' as Lahousen remarked. President Benes of Czechoslovakia intervened with Dollfuss for Bratik to be released. Dollfuss was persuaded that his regime needed a modernised intelligence machinery and put in Ronge as head of the state police Special Bureau in his Chancellery (Staatspolizeiliches Sonderbüro). It was Ronge who, in 1933, insisted on an intelligence section to be established

[75] 'Visit to the Police at Vienna, Dresden and Berlin' MEPO 3/2036 TNA.

at the Ministry of Defence; Major General Franz Bohme took over the helm. Soon the counter-espionage department at the Ministry of Defence worked closely with the Staatspolizei and Ronge. Dr Bermann, the head of Staatspolizei, remained in his post until the coming of the Nazis in 1938. Soon he was saved by Lahousen and sent to the Abwehr station (Ausenstelle, Ast) in Vienna.

In this period, Austrian Military Intelligence focused on Czechoslovakia and Yugoslavia. There was a strict prohibition against espionage in the South Tyrol in order not to provoke Mussolini. In 1936-38 the Military Intelligence and the Staatspolizei focused more on Nazi subversion and terrorism, mainly bomb attacks. The Austrian military exchanged information on Czechoslovakia with Germany and Italy. Until 1934 and the assassination of Dollfuss, there was a system of exchange of information with the Abwehr station in Munich. The new phase of Austro-German intelligence sharing came in 1937 after an agreement of General Alfred Jansa, the chief of the Austrian General Staff, and Admiral Wilhelm Canaris, the chief of the Abwehr; the target was Czechoslovakia.

Nonetheless, the resourceful Ronge did not uncover the Nazi spy in time. Otto Steinhäusl was the head of the Vienna police, but had secretly joined the Nazi party. In July 1933, he was involved in the kidnap attempt of Otto Strasser, a left-wing Nazi aiming to split the Nazi party under Hitler. Strasser and his faction wanted the Nazi party to nationalise banks and industries and cultivate good relations with the Soviet Union. Investigations of the Staatspolizei revealed his Nazi identity, effectively his espionage and subversion role.

Dollfuss trusted the Heimwehr (Home Guard), a paramilitary nationalist group backed by their political party, the Heimatblock. In October 1933, Rudolf Dertill, a 22-year-old Austrian Nazi storm trooper, shot Dollfuss, who survived the attempt. Murder was part of interwar Austrian politics. In London, the Cabinet was hesitant to help Dollfuss, who aimed to boost the Austrian economy and needed all the help he could get. The Chancellor presented the British with an offer for a trade agreement 'which would be both of economic and political assistance to the government.' He also made it clear that he would appeal to the League of Nations against Nazi Germany's subversion and propaganda.

The Cabinet, chaired by the Prime Minister, James Ramsay MacDonald, admitted that 'our circumstances did not permit us to give direct economic assistance to Austria.' It was suggested that Italy and France should be urged to do so. Intelligence from Austria showed Dollfuss 'calculated that if he could survive the winter he would benefit by the fact that the season would also discredit the Nazis in Germany, where trade would fall and unemployment rise.' In London, the Cabinet concluded,

> 'This calculation proved false, and Dr Dollfuss, who had a few weeks ago been negotiating unofficially with the German Government for a settlement, has evidently failed to come to terms for he has now been obliged by a recrudescence of Nazi activities to take strong repressive measures.'[76]

The Foreign Secretary, Sir John Simon, issued a prophetic assessment: 'the fall of Dr Dollfuss which is now measurably nearer than in the autumn...there is clearly no one in Austria who would be prepared to take his place and continue the struggle with a victorious Germany.'[77]

A few days later, on 21 November, Earle warned Washington: 'The situation here is extremely hard to analyze. From our tour of Austria, calling on Governors, Generals, and Chambers of Commerce in the nine provincial capitals, Kliefoth, Shallenberger, and myself all felt the Nazi movement had decidedly lost force.' In Vienna, foreign diplomats and the press were certain: 'the Nazis are gaining in strength steadily and that a putsch is imminent.' Rieth declined to attend any reception by Dollfuss and 'will simply wait a few days or weeks for the Nazi putsch to occur'; such attitude was 'typical of the faith of the entire German nation that under the surface in Austria a great Nazi development is going on similar to that in Germany just before Hitler was swept into office.' The Nazi diplomat had told Earle about the policy for the persecution of Jews: 'Rieth assured me in no uncertain words that with the Nazi putsch would come a pogrom such as Europe had never had and that 500,000 Jews would lose their property and be lucky to escape from Austria with their lives.'[78]

The US Chargé d'Affaires, Alfred Kliefoth, replaced Earle, who was granted leave to return to the United States. In late January 1934, Kliefoth reported 'Dollfuss has exhausted almost all possibilities of keeping down the Nazis. I too believe that unless the foreign economic help is announced very soon the chances of the Nazis, because of the German help, are increasing with great speed.'[79]

The escalating confrontation between the regime, socialists and

---

[76] Foreign Office memorandum, 'Austria' 22 January 1934, CAB 24/247/19 TNA.
[77] Ibid.
[78] The Minister in Austria (Earle) to the Chief of the Division of Western European Affairs (Moffat), 21 November 1933, FRUS *1934. Europe, Near East and Africa*, p.4.
[79] The Chargé in Austria (Kliefoth) to the Secretary of State, 26 January 1934, ibid., p.8

communists was a challenge for the US Legation to report accurately. At a period when there existed no US foreign intelligence service, American diplomats in Vienna proved themselves shrewd and careful intelligence gatherers. On 12 February Kliefoth wrote: 'The action of the police in Linz in searching Socialist headquarters this morning resulted in bloodshed and martial law whereupon Vienna's electric workmen called strike in sympathy cutting off electric light and streetcar transportation and industries dependent upon electric power. Streets are patrolled by police armed with carbines. Strike is not spreading and city is orderly, difficulty expected to be settled very soon.'[80] The American diplomat showed Washington the real extent of the Austrian crisis:

> 'While Socialist uprising is a lost cause the stubborn resistance in heavily fortified dwellings has not been completely subdued and may take several days more. Government offered truce to rebels at 11 o'clock last night up to noon today in hope of obtaining surrender of last strongholds. The unusual feature of the revolt was the extent of the armaments of the Socialist military organizations. In one center there were 60 machine guns and other armament which is equivalent of five American peace regiments. Such resistance necessitated artillery action and veritable assault methods to overcome it.'[81]

Dollfuss had offered his opponents a truce to gain more time. Kliefoth and infantry Colonel Martin C. Shallenberger, the US military attaché in Vienna, continued intelligence gathering, concluding that Dollfuss's peace offer boosted his standing in the eyes of public opinion: 'Due to the Chancellor's offer of truce, practical peace and order reigns everywhere and uprising definitely ended except for pursuit of armed individuals who will now resort to acts of sabotage, particularly against members of Heimwehr. The truce and lenient treatment of rebels was anticipated by the public and opinion again favoring the Chancellor.' No doubt the American diplomats had taken a risk, but it had paid dividends:

> 'Military Attaché and I have personally seen several fortified strongholds and discreetly interviewed inhabitants of dwellings. Women informed me they were locked in their

---

[80] The Chargé in Austria (Kliefoth) to the Secretary of State, 12 February 1934, ibid., p.10.
[81] The Chargé in Austria (Kliefoth) to the Secretary of State, 15 February 1934, ibid, p.14.

apartments by Socialists so that their presence could be used as screen against attacking forces. They were furious against their own leaders, but not the socialist movement, for the futile armed uprising.'[82]

The Austrian officials informed Kliefoth that 'all new military supplies of Socialists lately acquired were received from Czech sources which fact may be used to arouse public opinion against that country.'[83]

According to the government the troubles led 239 people to lose their lives: 102 police and military and 137 civilians. 658 were wounded on both sides.

Kliefoth and the military attaché continued 'discreet examination of witnesses on both sides' and reported that 'every form of persuasion and warning maneuvers (on behalf of the government) were used before attacks were started. In each case investigated firing was started by the revolters.' At that moment, Dollfuss's political standing was great and 'his use of force has impressed the Nazis'.[84] Kliefoth concluded his dispatch "organized Jewry continuing their support of Dollfuss by offering him service of Jewish war veterans and money donations.'[85]

George Earle returned to Vienna and commended the reporting of Kliefoth. He also questioned eyewitnesses in the rebel districts of Vienna, and Colonel Schallenberger continued collecting secret intelligence. Earle wrote to Washington:

> 'In the midst of negotiations by Chancellor Dollfuss to win over to him the Moderate Socialists who are a great majority of that party the Heimwehr leaders learned of the heavy importation of rifles and machine guns from Czechoslovakia and the placing of these in strategic positions by the small militant communist element of the Socialist Party. Fearing an attempted *putsch* the Heimwehr and Government forces initiated a series of raids to seize these arms. This was the immediate cause of the uprising. That only a very small fraction of the Socialist Party was in sympathy with resistance of any kind to the Government is clearly demonstrated by the refusal of the great majority of

---

[82] The Chargé in Austria (Kliefoth) to the Secretary of State, 16 February 1934, ibid, p.16
[83] Ibid.
[84] The Chargé in Austria (Kliefoth) to the Secretary of State, 17 February 1934, ibid, p.17-18.
[85] Ibid.

labor to respond to the call for a general strike issued as the fighting began.[86]

Dollfuss, the survivor of the brief civil war, proclaimed the new constitution, and the parliament duly approved it on 1 May 1934. Hitler feared that Dollfuss would side with fascist Italy and France, isolating Germany. Indeed, the Austrian Chancellor was scheduled to meet with French and Italian officials. Earlier, in autumn 1933, Mussolini had initiated war plans for an Italian intervention in Austria to counter any German invasion. Nonetheless, the Italian general staff remained hesitant because of the Austrian public's hostility towards Italy and the limited resources of Italy for such an endeavour.[87]

In March 1934, the Servizio Informazioni Militari (SIM) warned of the military potential of Austrian Nazi formations in South Tyrol. In April 1934 Mussolini met with Dollfuss – both agreed on a framework of agreement for the security of Austria. SIM reported to Mussolini that this meeting made Nazis furious; Dollfuss was accused of betraying Germanism to Italian strategic interests. SIM warned of rumours in Vienna, Berlin, Munich and Innsbruck of a planned German show of force, a vast display which would demonstrate the public's support for Hitler. Italian spies reported that the signals traffic directing Austrian Nazis to demonstrations against Dollfuss originated in Budapest, Maribor and Ljubljana in order to hide the complicity of Nazi propaganda originated in Berlin. Curiously 'the Soviet radio in Leningrad vilified the Austrian Socialists for their failure to support the uprising.'[88]

The Nazis escalated their propaganda and subversion campaign against Dollfuss by early May. Kliefoth reported on Nazi bomb attacks against government buildings and propaganda against Dolfuss.[89]

George Messersmith, a seasoned diplomat who had also served in Belgium, Antwerp and Buenos Aires, was transferred from the US Consulate in Berlin to head the US Legation in Vienna. He was already known in the press for being the consul who granted a visa to Albert Einstein to flee Nazi persecution. In Austria, the bombing campaign concentrated on railways and tourist centres. The Nazis sent the Vice Chancellor's office four pounds of explosives. Messersmith assumed it was a strategy to create a pretext for a Nazi invasion of Austria:

---

[86] Ibid.

[87] Mallet, Robert, 'The Anschluss Question in Italian Defence Policy, 1933-37', *Intelligence & National Security*, Vol.19, No.4, (Winter 2004), p.685.

[88] The Chargé in Austria (Kliefoth) to the Secretary of State, 2 March 1934, ibid., p.21.

[89] The Chargé in Austria (Kliefoth) to the Secretary of State, 11 May 1934, ibid., p.25

'...That outrages follow well-directed plan and are not isolated action indicated by fact that night of June 10th bombs exploded on all six of the main rail lines leading to Vienna. The damage so far small and general attacks directed toward terrorizing population and interfering with travel. Government taking new measures but just as concerted action in Berlin was necessary last August to stop first wave similar outrages and threat to appeal to League in January to stop second wave so similar action may be necessary to stop this third wave which up to now gives no indications of letting up.'[90]

At 1240 hours, 25 July, the government radio in Vienna surprised its listeners by announcing that Dollfuss had resigned and Anton Rintelen, currently the Austrian head of Legation in Rome, was appointed as the new Chancellor. Messersmith realised that a crisis was in progress. A couple of hours later, he was informed that 'a group of some 300 persons disguised as security forces had seized the official radio.' The announcement was a part of a Nazi putsch, but details were not known at that moment (1700 hours) when Messersmith sent his cable to the State Department. The rumour spread that all cabinet members were prisoners.

Three hours later, after frantic intelligence collection by Messersmith, Earle, Kliefoth and the military attaché, the details emerged. Nazis had raided the Chancellor's officer and shot Dollfuss. Colonel Emil Fey and and a cabinet member, Karwinski, attended the wounded Chancellor. Dollfuss was shot in the neck without warning as he was walking through the corner room between his office and the Ballhausplatz to the congress hall. He fell and started bleeding.

The assailants gathered around him and demanded he resign. Two officers of his guard who were prisoners were allowed to help him and desperately tried to stop the bleeding. Dollfuss fainted. He recovered consciousness and asked what had happened to the government departments. The Chancellor pleaded for a doctor, but the Nazis refused. They again insisted that he resign. Dollfuss was clear: he said he wanted Kurt Schuschnigg, the Minister of Education, to succeed hm. Dollfuss died of his wound at about 4 o'clock.

Austrian Nazis took up arms against government forces in Carinthia, Styria and Upper Austria, attacking police and military stations. The

---

[90] The Minister in Austria (Messersmith) to the Secretary of State, 12 June 1934, ibid. pp.26-27.

authorities quelled the coup.

The other cabinet members not taken prisoner met under the chairmanship of Schuschnigg and commenced negotiations with Nazis holding the Ministry of Foreign Affairs building. The Nazis threatened to shoot their prisoners if all the cabinet did not resign. Eventually, the police were ordered to raid the building by using tear gas. Meanwhile, in the Tyrol, the Nazis shot dead a police commandant and occupied some government buildings in Styria, but after some hours they surrendered.

Messersmith was informed by the Mayor of Vienna that Dollfuss had died of his wounds and Schuschnigg had taken over as acting Chancellor at the request of Wilhelm Miklas, the President of Austria.

Next day, President Roosevelt wrote to Miklas:

'It is with horror and deep regret that I learn of the assassination of Engelbert Dollfuss, Minister of Foreign Affairs and Chancellor of Austria. I extend through you to the Austrian people sincere sympathy in my own name and on behalf of my fellow countrymen.'[91]

Meanwhile, the Italian Military Attaché told US diplomats that troops on the Austrian-Italian border were on stand-by to intervene in case of a German invasion.

The Nazis made a failed attempt to revolt in the afternoon of 26 and 27 July in some Austrian cities. There was a 'small battle' at Leoben but by the evening of 27 July, the Nazis had lost. The government forces numbered 78 dead and 165 wounded; Nazi casualties were not published to avoid provoking Berlin.

Messersmith spoke of the German complicity:

'According to the information which has now developed…it seems definitely established that this putsch was not only made with the knowledge of the German Government but engineered by it. On June 29 Goebbels told Cherruti, the Italian Ambassador in Berlin, that there would be a Nazi Government in Vienna within a month. On the evening of July 24, a pamphlet appeared on the streets of Berlin, of which the Berlin Embassy has copies, from which it was obvious that there was full knowledge of what was planned in Vienna. An attempt was made to suppress it, and

---

[91] President Roosevelt to President Wilhelm Miklas, 26 July 1934, ibid., p.31.

its contents got into only a few of the German papers on July 25, but the articles which did appear in the German papers of the day of the putsch showed that they had information as to the time it was to take place. I am informed by my English colleague here that London is convinced that Hitler had knowledge of the putsch planned and was entirely in accord with the action, but on the 23rd he is supposed to have called it off, fearing the time not propitious.'[92]

The Nazi Austrian Legion had gathered on the borders and was about to invade Austria. Messersmith concluded 'the evidence is already accumulating in definite form that the movement was stopped when it was found the circumstances were not propitious.' Curiously, also, Dr. Rintelen, the Austrian Minister in Rome, 'was in Vienna for no official reason whatever, and the evidence already accumulated indicates that he was here to be on the spot to form a new government.' There was no doubt 'the key to Rintelen's character is his ambition, which was to be Chancellor, and he really had grown to hate Dollfuss, whom he felt was the only real obstacle in his way.' Rintelen was arrested on the evening of 25 July and attempted suicide, but survived.

Messersmith did not hide his surprise at any of this:

> 'The intervention of Rieth was one of the most extraordinary things I have ever heard of...The fact is that when the besieged found their position hopeless and made the agreement for safe transport under the protection of the military to the German frontier, they insisted that Rieth must be a witness to it. It was only when the besieged Nazis insisted, that Major Fey telephoned to Rieth and gave him the message. Fey says that he transmitted it merely as the message of the besieged, and I think he is telling the truth. All the circumstances point to that. Rieth came, and after talking to Minister Neustädter-Stürmer, had a long conference with the leaders of the besieged Nazis. I admit that he was in an impossible position, but it was only a guilty conscience and the full knowledge of the circumstances which could have enabled him to take the action which he did.'[93]

---

[92] Ibid.
[93] ibid., p.40.

Berlin telegraphed Rieth to return to Germany on the morning of 26 July; his stay in Vienna was an embarrassment. The veteran diplomat von Papen would take over but initially the Austrian government refused; they did not want von Papen to appear at Dollfuss's funeral. The Austrian officials 'are thoroughly familiar with Papen, and while they recognize that he has done much to rehabilitate himself during the last few months, they know that it was his palace intrigue which brought in the Nazi Government in Germany.' The Austrians 'know that for his ambition he sold that fine old figure Hindenburg, who treated Papen as a son. They fear, knowing that type of German as they do, that Papen would not be above using his position here to endeavour to bring Austria into the lap of Germany as a satisfaction of his personal ambition.'[94]

Messersmith assigned Mussolini a key place in the Austrian crisis. Mussolini protested Hitler's complicity in the murder. For some time, Italian Intelligence, the SIM (Servizion Informazioni Militari), had already been supplying the Austrian army with weapons to counter any German offensive. The Italian dictator had put two army corps on standby. Messersmith wrote:

> 'This action and Mussolini's telegram to [Vice Chancellor Ernst Rüdiger Camillo von] Starhemberg undoubtedly did more to have Hitler take energetic action to stop any invasion by the Austrian Legion than the fear of a triple démarche, of which the papers were so full. It now appears there is some reason to believe that Hitler had already taken action before the 25th to stop participation by the Austrian Legion, but if he had not taken this action before, it is clear that it was taken on the afternoon of the 25th, after the determined attitude of Italy.[95]

The American diplomat feared a war provoked by fearful Yugoslavia, whose leaders were nervous about events in Austria ('with the state of mind that they are in') and the involvement of Czechoslovakia.[96]

Messersmith warned that Austria was not safe for the near future:

> 'I had too intimate contact with the real people who conduct Nazi policy to have any illusions. I know what blood they had on their hands, what sinister motives they

---

[94] ibid., p.41.
[95] ibid., p.42.
[96] ibid., p.42.

nourished, and what execrable acts they were capable of. National Socialism is a disease which attacks many worthwhile people and has some strange results. It is a disease which has to be eradicated if Germany and Europe are to be saved. For the moment, the pressure is being exerted on this little country, and what I wish to emphasize is that these good people here [the government under Schuschnigg] with the best will in the world and with the firmest intentions to maintain their traditions and their independence, are helpless without the support of England, France and Italy.'[97]

The Austrian Court of Justice declared invalid the agreement for safe passage to Germany: it was concluded under duress while it was not known that Dollfuss had died; the whole agreement was based on the premise that no-one was to be killed. The thirteen men who murdered Dollfuss were executed. About 4,000 Nazis were detained and there were 100 Nazi casualties.

In his turn, Goebbels kept a diary of the Nazi deliberations. On 22 July he wrote: 'Sunday: at the Fuehrer's [in Bayreuth]...Austrian question. Whether it will work? [the putsch] I'm very sceptical.'[98]

On 25 July, as Nazis stormed Dollfuss's office, Goebbels wrote in his diary: 'At the Fuehrer's: alarm from Austria. Chancellery occupied...great suspense. Horrible waiting.' Once the news had reached them, he added 'Dollfuss dead. Then an honourable retreat by the insurgents. Then victory for the government. Lost!'[99] In his turn, Mussolini directed the SIM to work together with French secret military intelligence to counterbalance any move of Hitler against Austria.

Moreover, on 26 July a German courier was arrested by Austrian police in Kollerschlag and on him was found a document of instructions for the Nazi-instigated mutinies. The typewritten instruction sheet No 10 issued by the SA-Obergruppe XI was found hidden in the tie of the courier, who was armed with a pistol. He was arrested by a member of the Austrian border guard and a customs officer. He was led to the police station at Kollerschlag, where it was confirmed that he carried no identification papers, and he refused to say anything about his mission or identity. He was transferred to Linz and resisted interrogation. His written

[97] ibid., p.44.
[98] Goebbels' diary entries quoted in Kurt Bauer, 'Hitler und der Juliputsch 1934' in Österreich' *Vierteljahrshefte für Zeitgeschichte*, Heft 2, April 2011, pp.208.
[99] Ibid., p.212.

instructions contained code phrases, e.g. 'the old cutlery is broken' meaning Dollfuss is dead, and 'the old cutlery is not broken' meaning Dollfuss is free. The courier had to deliver the instructions to an industrialist who in his turn would deliver the instructions to a loyal Nazi in Vienna. The instructions under the code name 'Summer Fest' entailed mass unarmed Nazi marches in Austria in support of the coup in Vienna. The demonstrators would have their arms hidden in caches. The second phase would have the demonstrators taking over public buildings. In case of government resistance, the Nazis would proceed to the 'Italian Night', a code name for armed mutiny to win over the government before the intervention of the Heimwehr. The Vienna SIS station informed London about Rieth, who was named an ambitious Nazi official and propagandist. According to the intelligence file of Rieth, he 'is said to have been instrumental in smuggling the Nazis out of Austria into Munich after this murder [of Dollfuss] and it is alleged he set up an organisation of fifth column propaganda which contributed to the ultimate downfall of Austria.'[100]

Rieth arrived in the United States on 24 March 1941 on a flight from Mexico City, having visited Latin American countries, including Argentina, for coordinating the setting-up of intelligence networks. He was arrested by the FBI on 30 May and waited in custody for deportation; he was charged with fraudulent entry into the United States. Records showed that he had visited in 1928. The Justice Department characterised him as the 'No 1 Nazi now in the USA' and on 1 August he was deported. Messersmith continued reporting on Austrian and German politics, and soon warned Washington that Schuschnigg:

'Just as he is Catholic and Monarchist by tradition, so he is mildly anti-Semitic. This attitude has not made itself strongly felt, but it is definitely realised in Jewish circles in Austria that this attitude exists. The Jews of Austria are largely concentrated in Vienna where they are powerful. Schuschnigg does not like Jews...'[101]

---

[100] 'Kurt Heinrich Rieth', memorandum 23 May 1941, KV 2/3573 TNA UK.
[101] Messersmith to Moffat (State Department), 20 September 1934, Available at: <http//udspace.udel.edu/bitstream/handle/19716/6393/mss0109_0420-00.pdf> accessed 3 January 2019.

3

The Admiral

Admiral Wilhelm Canaris, the chief of the Abwehr, had noticed something. In his discussions with military and Nazi party leaders, Hitler avoided narrating his life in Vienna with the exception of blaming the Jews of the city. He arrived in Vienna in 1908 with an aspiration to enter a fine arts academy, but after taking the examination twice, he did not pass. In 1971, Helene Hansfstaengl (in whose Munich apartment Hitler lived in the early 1920s) commented: 'He was really very cagy about saying what he really did [in Vienna].' Hitler insisted that he arrived in Munich from Vienna in 1912. In fact, he was not in Germany until 1913.

In Vienna, Hitler led the life of a homeless person for many months, either in shelters or cheap hostels, trying to make a living as a porter and street artist. The Viennese police kept information on all persons; everybody was required to register their address. Hitler wanted to avoid conscription into the Austrian army and left for Germany in 1913. The meticulous Viennese police and military records documented Hitler's various residences and thus his poverty, as well as the fact that he avoided the Austrian draft. While he was an Austrian subject, he exhibited obsessive hatred towards his own country. On 18 February 1938, in a meeting with Chancellor Schuschnigg, he shouted: '...the Austrian Government had prohibited me from entering. Once, some years ago, I was in Vienna at night, and afterwards I secretly visited the grave of my parents. That is how I am treated by Austria.'[102]

Evidently, Nazi spymasters feared information about Hitler's past in Vienna and did not underestimate the intelligence collection of the Staatspolizei and the Evidenzbureau. Thus, once the annexation of Austria to Nazi Germany (the Anschluss) was proclaimed, Canaris and Reinhard Heydrich, the chief of the Nazi intelligence service the Shicherheitsdienst (SD), and his young, eager protégé, spymaster Walter Schellenberg, rushed to hit the Austrian secret archives vaults. In this contest for taking and keeping secrets Canaris won because of his contacts in the Austrian general staff. He had been preparing the ground for Austrian co-operation. From 1937 German and Austrian military attaches started limited

---

[102] Quoted in Schuschnigg, Kurt, *Austrian Requiem* (London: Victor Gollancz, 1947), p.25.

intelligence sharing on Eastern European countries. The Austrians proved more astute, as this chapter shows. Major-General Franz Boehme, head of Austrian military intelligence, appointed Major-General Erwin von Lahousen Edler to 'prepare the reports on Czechoslovakia wanted by the German side.' Lahousen was to become one of the closest associates of Canaris.

In his memoirs, Chancellor Schuschnigg described the security situation in Austria:

> 'Towards the end of 1937 the Nazi underground terror was again in full swing. Telephone booths exploded, tear-gas bombs were thrown, and mass demonstrations were arranged in order to induce the Austrian police to intervene.'[103]

In January 1938, the Staatspolizei made notable arrests. A Nazi network was discovered: they planned to murder Schuschnigg and organise a mass revolt in the spring. The Nazis had instructions signed by Rudolf Hess, Hitler's second in command. The Austrian police stormed a secret Nazi office on 25 January; it belonged to the 'Nazi Committee of Seven'. Leopold Tavs, the deputy to the Nazi Gauleiter for Austria, was arrested and charged with high treason. Berlin, in panic, put strong pressure on Schuschnigg not to publish Hess's name regarding the plot. Austrian police detectives uncovered the fact that Nazis were planning an attempt against von Papen, the German ambassador, so that Hitler had a pretext for invasion. Schuschnigg decided to go public with the evidence.

Eventually, Hitler agreed with the frantic calls from Goering to invade Austria to secure raw materials, mines and cash reserves to support the re-armament of Germany. Ambassador von Papen was against an invasion and on 12 February, in a vain bid, he accompanied Schuschnigg to a meeting with Hitler in Berchtesgaden. The Austrian Chancellor feared for his life and gave clear instructions to Richard Schmitz, the mayor of Vienna, to take over his position in case he was murdered. According to an order he issued, if he did not return by 9pm the borders with Germany should be sealed. In their meeting Hitler shouted at Schuschnigg and showed himself hating Austria, his own country: 'Every national idea was sabotaged by Austria throughout history; and indeed, all this sabotage was the chief activity of the Hapsburgs and the Catholic Church'. Hitler boasted about Nazi Intelligence:

---

[103] Quoted in Schuschnigg, *Austrian Requiem*, p.18.

'I am telling you that I am going to solve the so-called Austrian problem one way or the other. Do you imagine that I don't know that you are fortifying your border against the Reich? You have made rather ridiculous efforts to mine the bridges and roads leading to the Reich...Listen. You don't really think that you can move a single stone in Austria without my hearing the most accurate details about it the very next day, do you?...I have only to give an order, and in one single night all your ridiculous defence mechanisms are blown to bits. You don't seriously believe that you can stop me, or even delay me for half an hour, do you? Who knows? Perhaps you will wake up one morning in Vienna to find us there just like a spring storm. And then you'll see something. I would very much like to save Austria from such a fate, because such an action would mean blood. After the army, my S.A. [Sturm Abteilung] and the Austrian Legion would move in, and nobody can stop their just revenge - not even I. Do you want to make another Spain of Austria?'[104]

Hitler surprised Schuschnigg:

'Why don't you try a plebiscite in Austria in which we two run against each other? You just try that.'[105]

Schuschnigg was warned that no European power would come to his aid: not Italy under Mussolini or Britain under Chamberlain. France was too weak and did not resist in the taking over of Rhineland. [106]

Hitler demanded that a Nazi Austrian be named Minister of the Interior responsible for the police, and that all Nazis imprisoned be freed. General Alfred Jodl, who attended the meeting, remarked in his diary of 'the heaviest military and political pressure' put to Schuschnigg who, eventually, signed the protocol at eleven o'clock at night.

Next day, at General Wilhelm Keitel's flat, a conspirators' meeting was held between General Keitel himself, Canaris, Jodl and Goebbels, where they discussed how to intimidate Vienna. They sought to have military manoeuvres on the borders by 15 February (next day) but they had nothing yet as an actionable plan. Hitler gave the 'green light' in a

---

[104] Quoted in Schuschnigg, *Austrian Requiem*, p. 23.
[105] Quoted in ibid., p. 22.
[106] Quoted in ibid., p. 24.

phone call during the meeting. For Goebbels, who had witnessed the July 1934 coup failure, the anxiety raised by the hour. Afterwards Canaris flew to Abwehrstelle in Munich. Jodl claimed in his diary: 'In Austria the impression is developing of serious military preparations in Germany' - but he was wrong.

Canaris and Keitel coordinated the deception that Germany was preparing to invade. Ostensibly the VII Armeekorps 'had cancelled all leave'; in Munich railway stations, railway trucks were assigned to troops and war materiel 'for the south'. Orders were issued that all German frontier posts were to be reinforced. Nazi propaganda leaked that the German military attaché in Vienna had been recalled to Berlin. The secret orders of Canaris and Keitel aimed to deceive the Austrian general staff and scare Chancellor Schuschnigg - they did not aim for an actual invasion. 'No actual preparations were to be made by Army or Luftwaffe.' [107]

Meanwhile, the SIS station in Vienna reported the increased German military activity. London had been informed of German military movements by the Czech military intelligence. SIS officer Nicholson wrote: 'the Czech officials remained very secretive and almost hostile until the mid-30s when the German occupation became a certainty. Then their attitude changed and they gave us every consideration.' [108] Nonetheless SIS Air Section officer Frederick Winterbotham was suspicious enough: 'The Czechs had taken advantage of close Anglo-French links to try to penetrate the British Secret Intelligence Service, and had even been reported as watching the house where "our man" in Paris lived and where I used to stay when in France. Added to this the Czechs had some kind of intelligence tie-in with the Italians.' Winterbotham feared that Czech Intelligence might leak information to the Italians, and they in turn to the Nazi Intelligence, about his role in gathering intelligence on the Luftwaffe.

Hitler wanted Schuschnigg to dismiss Feldmarschalleutnant Alfred Jansa, the chief of the general staff. He feared Austrian resistance. Jansa had reorganised the Austrian military and argued convincingly in his memoirs that in case of war Austria could repel the Germans: the Austrian people were willing to resist. The protection of the borders could be fulfilled within hours, and a general mobilisation needed four days; all reserves would be ready in six. The Germans had at their disposal two army corps – four infantry divisions, an armoured division, 4,000

---

[107] Quoted in Mueller, *Canaris*, p.121.
[108] Quoted in Whitwell (Nicolson) *British Agent*, p.33.

policemen and a powerful air force. Austrian forces were deemed adequate: in the Tyrol, an infantry division and militias with 50 artillery pieces; between Inn-Salzach and Traun, 5,000 would be deployed in defence positions and more than 100 artillery pieces, to be reinforced by six infantry divisions, a rapid reaction division, a mountain brigade, an artillery regiment with 284 light artillery pieces, 24 medium field guns and 300 anti-tank guns. The Austrian Air Force could fly 72 fighters and would bomb invading forces. Jansa assumed that a protracted Austro-German war would bring the downfall of Hitler. He concluded that Hitler's crawling to Mussolini proved Germany's military weakness in case of a war.

Hitler was hiding his fear beneath his shouting: he knew he was weak. First, politically, if Schuschnigg called Otto von Hapsburg to lead Austria, restoring monarchy, and, second, militarily, Hitler's generals did not have an actual workable plan to invade Austria; the deception of Canaris was just deception. And the Austrian general staff was not persuaded. General Lahousen later told Canaris: 'we were not deceived by this bluff.' In fact, the head of the Nazi Austrian Legion, Hermann Reschny (who commanded about 15,000 Austrian Nazis), feared that the Austrian military would resist, and told Hitler about it on 10 March. Reschny knew about failure; in March 1934 he drafted the operational plan for the coup against Dollfuss which took place on 25 July - Dollfuss was murdered but the Austrian Nazis involved were eventually executed. The people did not revolt on the Nazis' behalf. An Austro-German war would have compelled London, Paris, Rome and Moscow to act; by default, the British Prime Minister, Neville Chamberlain, and Lord Halifax would have to re-consider British policy.

Nonetheless, the fearful Schuschnigg was not at the mental stage to get hold of himself, process secret intelligence provided by his intelligence services and take an efficient counter-strategy against Hitler. General Keitel was ordered by Hitler to attend the meeting. In front of Schuschnigg the Führer asked the General how many divisions they had at the borders and what kind of resistance they expected. Keitel boasted that the resistance was 'not worth mentioning, my Führer.'[109] Hitler did not have enough power at his disposal and thus aimed for a theatrical performance: 'In tanks, planes and motorised vehicles we are the leading power today. It would be completely irresponsible and unjustifiable merely from a historical point of view not to use a magnificent instrument

---

[109] MacDonogh, *1938*, p.23.

like the German Wehrmacht.'[110] The truth was that at that time (early 1938) the German panzers were light and not as formidable as they were years later – the same applied to the Luftwaffe's fighters and bombers.

Schuschnigg did not want an Austro-German war and had no stamina for resistance. Nonetheless the Austrian secret intelligence service and the general staff showed themselves capable for years of tracking Nazis and their brutal espionage tradecraft. When the Chancellor returned to Vienna, he persuaded President Wilhelm Miklas to appoint the key Nazi Arthur Seyss-Inquart as Minister of the Interior and free all Nazis from prison.

On 20 February, Hitler declared at the Reichstag: 'I am glad to say, however, that the Austrian Chancellor has shown insight and a satisfactory agreement has been reached with Austria'.[111] A few days earlier, on 14 February at the annual state reception, while talking to foreign dignitaries, amongst them the French ambassador, Schuschnigg realised that they knew about his secret agreement with Hitler. Gabriel Puaux, the French ambassador, a self-declared supporter of Austria, told Schuschnigg key details of his own meeting with Hitler. Schuschnigg wrote also in his memoirs of the 'rumour' that British Intelligence was informed from the German side of the meeting; the source was the entourage of the Führer. [112] Most possibly the Germans would have told something to the Foreign Office. Kendrick and the SIS could not have been informed by Austrian or German officials; there is no evidence to support Schuschinigg's allegation that contributes nonetheless to the contemporary myth that British Intelligence was always informed of events.

Meanwhile, in the Vienna streets, freed Nazis paraded and organised festivities. Then Schuschnigg decided to surprise Hitler, and on February 24 called for a plebiscite declaring for "Rotweissrot bis in den Tot" ("Red-white-red until we are dead," a reference to the flag colours of the Austrian republic). The Chancellor needed the public's support but for years he had hunted down socialists and trade-unionists. Hitler's and Goebbels' fear was the monarchy: Otto von Hapsburg. The restoration of the monarchy could unite Austrians against the Führer. Hitler feared also that Mussolini might again side with Vienna as in the 1934 crisis.

In Vienna 'some ten thousand people demonstrated their approval of the speech' for the plebiscite. Berlin remained silent; Hitler (who had given Schuschnigg the idea of the referendum during his rage) was confused.

---

[110] Ibid.
[111] Ibid., p.26.
[112] Schuschnigg, *Austrian Requiem*, p.33.

A messenger arrived at the Chancellor's residence. He brought a letter from Otto von Hapsburg sent by messenger from Belgium begging Schuschnigg to appoint him Chancellor to unite the people against the Nazis. Schuschnigg lost the precious opportunity. On 5 March Seyss-Inquart and Edmund Glaise-Horstenau were appointed cabinet members. Seyss-Inquart was eager to have access to police personnel files to organise Nazis inside the state.

The Austrian government and Schuschnigg's party machinery worked quickly to support with propaganda (e.g. flyers, broadcasts and even aeroplane banners) the plebiscite for 13 March. Mussolini and British Foreign Secretary Lord Halifax characterised Schuschnigg's plebiscite as an 'error' and 'foolish and provocative'. General mirrored Hitler's real fear: he wrote in his diary that the plebiscite 'would bring in a strong majority for the monarchists who were backing Otto Hapsburg.'[113]

On 11 March at 5.30am, the Austrian chief of police, Michael Skubl, called Schuschnigg on the phone informing him that the borders were sealed at Salzburg. A few hours later incoming reports indicated that German forces had mobilised in Bavaria. Schuschnigg asked where Nazi minister Seyss-Inquart was. No one knew. It was an indication that something was going on. He assumed that it was crisis time:

> 'I rang police headquarters and asked them to take preparatory measures for a cordon around the inner town and the Government buildings, in case this should become necessary during the day. By now the Cabinet Ministers had been alerted and were arriving at their offices. Only Seyss-Inquart could not be found anywhere. The Foreign Minister came to me with a telephone message from our consul-general in Munich: the German divisions stationed in Munich had been mobilised. Presumable destination: Austria.'[114]

> '...The minutes crept by. I went to the window and looked down to the square before the Chancellery. Across the park I saw the mighty structure of the Imperial Castle...If somebody were to put up a spy-glass on the terrace of the near-by sky-scraper he could see me sitting at my desk. This accounts for the bullet-proof shutters that Kirsch, my faithful

---

[113] Ibid., p.33.
[114] Quoted in Schuschnigg, *Austrian Requiem*, p.44.

secretary, had put on the windows.'[115]

Seyss-Inquart arrived, bringing Goering's demand to postpone the plebiscite. Nazi theatrics ruled: 'If he[Goering] has not heard from Seyss-Inquait within one hour he will assume that Seyss is prevented from telephoning and will act accordingly.'

The Graz police informed the Chancellor's office by telephone that Nazis had been broadcasting that the referendum was postponed and he had resigned. Schuschnigg called the chief of police who told him: 'So far everything is quiet…I must point out that since the general amnesty which restored many Nazi policemen to their jobs complete reliability cannot be expected.' Schuschnigg did not call the general staff:

> 'I did not bother to make such an inquiry at army headquarters. I knew that the leadership of the army was absolutely dependable and that the army obeys unflinchingly. But I also knew of the dilemma when duty and inclination are opposed to each other, as was the case with many a soldier in the army…I was sure of one thing: Never again a war against Germany as in 1866, and never a civil war.'[116]

On 11 March, Canaris informed Abwehrstelle chiefs that Hitler had decided to resolve the crisis by force if necessary. Hauptmann Paul Leverhuhn, later Abwehr head in Istanbul, claimed: 'the seriousness of the situation and the Admiral's deep concern were unmistakable for everybody at the discussion.'[117] Canaris was receiving information from Vienna, from 'the little, busy attaché, Lieutenant-General Muff, who had already for some time been actual chief of the intelligence and information centre which was still officially called "German Embassy",' Schuschnigg wrote in his memoirs. [118]

Hitler was in a state of anxiety, realising that failure was a real possibility. Goering took over the task of giving orders by phone from the Reich Chancellery's switchboard. At 9.30 he ordered Seyss-Inquart and his fellow Nazi minister Glaise-Horstenau to go to the Austrian Chancellery. Goering told them Schuschnigg had to resign and the plebiscite must be postponed. Upon hearing this Schuschnigg asked the head of the police if it was possible to defend Vienna from the Nazis; the

---

[115] Quoted in Ibid., p.45.
[116] Quoted in ibid., p.46.
[117] Mueller, *Canaris*, p.122.
[118] Quoted in Schuschnigg, *Austrian Requiem*, p.49.

reply was negative. Too many Nazis had been freed and joined the police. At 14.45 the Chancellor announced that the plebiscite was postponed. Seyss-Inquart called Goering. Hitler was still nervous of the outcome.

Goering insisted that Schuschnigg had to resign. Seyss-Inquart was to be named Chancellor, otherwise German forces at the border would invade. Meanwhile the Austrian general staff had called for a partial mobilisation, increasing the Nazi fear of war. The general inspector of the Austrian army, General Sigismund Ritter Schilhawsky von Bahnbrück, assumed the resistance 'pointless'. Austria could not count on the European powers. Nazis started parading in some cities. The Chancellor resigned and Nazis stormed the offices of his party.

The general staff issued orders at 20.45: army units were to move to the east and not to pose resistance to German units. At 22.30, Hitler was reassured by Mussolini that he would not intervene. Neither would Czechoslovakia, as minister Mastny told the Führer. In Vienna, Colonel Otto Skorzeny (the infamous SS commando chief) and his men arrested President Miklas and later the same day Mayor Schmitz.

At 05.00 on 12 March, Himmler's plane landed in Aspern. Austrian police chief Skubl and an honour guard greeted him and his party, amongst them Reinhard Heydrich, Karl Wolff, Kurt Daluege and Walter Schellenberg. Himmler took up residence in the Hotel *Regina*. The Gestapo officials opened shop at the Hotel *Metropole*. Following the Nazi intelligence reports and the just-confiscated Austrian police records Himmler and Heydrich arrested between 50,000 and 76,000 in March.

In the relentless hunt for secret documents, it seemed that Canaris had won: he went to the general staff building and Major General Lahousen and the rest of the high command entrusted him with secret files on Hitler, Himmler, Heydrich, Goering and others – the intelligence work of the general staff. These Austrian generals had been burning papers all day. Schellenberg arrived later the same day. Lahousen and Ronge (the old spymaster) refused to accept his proposal to join the SS. Schellenberg sounded disappointed: 'The [secret] papers that I found were not very up-to-date, though there was some interesting material on deciphering codes.' He had no time to study the archives; a bomb threat while Hitler's motorcade was approaching Vienna compelled him to abort the hunt.

In his turn, Himmler needed glory; he arranged for the journal *Die Deutsche Polizei* (The German Police) to report of the 'bold coup by Reichsführer-SS Heinrich Himmler', by which 'this revolution, one of the most epoch making in the history of the world...was carried out without a single shot being fired and without any blood being spilt.' Goebbels hit back: he ordered his ministry to confiscate the journal on the grounds that it betrayed the secrets of the Anschluss. Himmler declared that 800

Austrian SS would guard the new government under Seyss-Inquart and on 18 March he ordered the official establishment of Gestapo headquarters in Vienna. Austrian Nazi Gestapo chief until then, Hermann Müller was named Inspector of the Security Police in Austria.

Hitler himself flew from Berlin to Munich accompanied by General Keitel. At about noon his motorcade reached the borders. He crossed at his birthplace, Braunau am Inn. The mayor and a jubilant crowd greeted him.

Meanwhile in other cities Nazi party members hit the streets and houses, looting to the extent that on 17 March Heydrich warned Nazi Commissar Bürckel to discipline Austrian Nazis, otherwise a special Gestapo unit would take over. Himmler was also angry with Austrian Nazis. Later, General Lahousen claimed that Canaris, who by 13 March had been watching for international reactions to the Anschluss, was fully supporting Hitler's policy in uniting Austria with Germany. Hitler called for a referendum on 10 April which he won with 99 per cent of the vote. In the eyes of the excited Nazi leadership, Canaris enjoyed his part of vainglory; on 1 April he made a speech to the Wiener Neustadt War Academy. He declared, 'We are all now standing under the heart-lifting experience of the development of greater Germany, it was dreamed of, worked for and found its fulfilment in the plebiscite of the 10 April...' It was 'sabotage and crime' if a soldier did not support the Führer and the National Socialist state.

Canaris would turn now against Kendrick, the SIS station chief in Vienna. It was a great opportunity for the Abwehr to show the SS and Gestapo that they were the masters of espionage.

Since mid 1937, Jews had been evicted from Czechoslovakia and reached Vienna. They sought immigration visas to England. The Passport Control Office under Kendrick (who by 1938 had been in Vienna for eighteen years) needed to act. With the Anschluss, Austrian Jews realised that they faced a lethal danger. Nazis roamed the streets and harassed them. Looting and violence was a daily reality. Long queues of people wanting to apply for visas formed along the street outside Kendrick's office; the staff (devoted to administering secret intelligence reports) had to cope with processing visa applications.

In early April 1938 over 7,000 Austrian Jews were arrested: 'Jews walking in the streets are approached by SA or SS men, asked if they are Jews and then taken off to prison. The whole process is senseless and inhuman...' [119] In Berlin Frank Foley, SIS station chief, maintained

---

[119] Quoted in Fry, *Spymaster*, p.107.

'cordial' relations with the Gestapo anti-communist service as he was trying to issue visas and passports to escaping Jews. Adolf Eichmann, a young SS officer, set up an office for Jewish immigration in April in Vienna; Kendrick met Eichmann, who pressed for Jews to emigrate to Palestine; according to British legislation the immigration quotas of Jews for Palestine were very strict, due to Arab protests. Eventually a thousand visas for Palestine were signed by Kendrick.[120] Possibly the Germans did not arrest him not only for providing 'chickenfeed' via a secret agent named Tucek (as we will explore in this chapter) but also because they might have assumed that Kendrick could issue many visas to Jews - thus facilitating Nazi policy.

In April the British Embassy was downgraded to Legation and thus Kendrick, now a Vice-Consul, would have to report to the British Ambassador in Berlin. The Passport Control Office moved to the Legation premises at 8 Wallnerstrasse.[121]

Kendrick frantically issued visas to Britain, having concluded that once in Britain Jews would not be turned over to Nazi Germany.[122] The SIS station chief admitted to Sir Hugh Sinclair, the chief of SIS, that intelligence reports sent were 'somewhat scrappy and badly collated' because of the work pressure of the visas.[123]

Meanwhile, Canaris plotted carefully to unravel SIS presence in Austria. Back in 1937 Kendrick asked Siegfried Richter, the manager of the premises of the consulate, to recruit a spy to report on the Italian navy. Richter, who was eager to recruit spies for Kendrick (though the latter had turned down spy candidates of Richter), met with Karl Tucek, an ex-foreman of a construction machine firm. Richter walked into a secret minefield and took Kendrick with him.

Karl Tucek was a secret Nazi party member and a personal friend of Ernst Kaltenbrunner, who would be the only Austrian to rise to the head of RSHA in wartime. Briefly, in January 1934 Kaltenbrunner was charged by the Austrian police for conspiring against the Dollfuss regime. He led a hunger strike and eventually 490 Nazis were released. Next year he was again jailed on charges of high treason but the charges were amended. He spent another six months in prison for conspiracy. Upon his release in mid-1935 he was named the chief of the SS Abschnitt VIII in Linz and many assumed he was the leader of the Austrian SS. He became a spymaster feeding intelligence to Himmler about Austrian events. In

---

[120] Ibid., p.115.
[121] Ibid.
[122] Ibid., pp.110, 135-140.
[123] Quoted in Jeffery, *MI6*, p.301.

return, he would receive money for the clandestine Nazi organisation. Kaltenbrunner would use trains and ships to Passau to reach his comrades in secret. The resourceful Austrian police arrested him in 1937 and charged him with being the illegal Nazi leader in Oberösterreich. He was freed in September 1937 - and a couple of months later was contacted by his friend Tucek. After the Anschluss, Kaltenbrunner was appointed State Secretary for Public Security; later he promoted the establishment of the Mauthausen-Gusen concentration camp near Linz.

Tucek was not a professional intelligence operative prior to the operation against Kendrick. Tucek had invented a concrete breaking machine and a hand-held concrete rammer, and he needed money and connections to sell his invention. He wanted to present it to foreign firms.

Richter got to know Tucek better and was more interested in him when the latter told him that he had served with the Austrian navy. Tucek seemed to need money urgently. [124] Tucek would meet his friend SS-Führer Kaltenbrunner in Berlin and disclosed the approach of Richter. Kaltenbrunner informed him about the German Legation in Vienna; initially the military attaché called Mueller would be the secret channel of information for Tucek. Surprisingly Kaltenbrunner did not seek to direct the whole operation against British Intelligence but allowed the Abwehr to handle Tucek (and thus Canaris to claim a coup). [125]

The Abwehr officers gave Tucek the task of finding the residence of the 'Englishman' who was employing Richter. Richter was telling him that the Englishman did not live permanently in Vienna but came to Vienna from London 'every 2 or 3 weeks.' The mission of Tucek was to 'bypass' Richter and arrange to see directly the British Intelligence officer.

Richter was described as an employee of the British Legation in Vienna. Richter had approached Tucek to spy on Italy in return for money. [126] Kendrick had been informed by Richer that Tucek, a prospective spy, was a communist and naval engineer. Tucek had offered Richter some technical drawings. Kendrick reviewed them; they looked authentic. In a subsequent meeting Richter told Tucek that he would work for an SIS man in Vienna and should give him his navy record. Tucek obliged and added in his offer: he had a friend who was employed at the Schichau-Werke shipyard based in Elbing, East Prussia, and Tucek, if he found work there, could report on German U-boat construction.

In January 1938, Tucek met Richter. The Abwehr handlers had

---

[124] Activities of Ast Wien', KV 3/116 TNA.
[125] Ibid.
[126] Ibid.

directed Tucek: 'Visit Richter in a disguised manner and bring up his suggestion again, with a hint that you must shortly make a business journey to Germany.' Tucek asked Richter for a cash advance for his planned journey. Richter 'jumped at it' and immediately proposed a meeting 'with the English employer in Vienna.' Kendrick remained hesitant and the meeting was postponed 'again and again.'

Richter still showed himself over-eager to recruit Tucek, who had some professional connections in Dusseldorf with Knorr-Bremse AG Berlin (a known manufacturer of braking systems for rail and commercial vehicles) and a 'great friend' working in ship construction at Elbing. Tucek was careful not to give Richter his friend's name in Elbing.

The Germans were careful in constructing Tucek's bona fides; after the suggestion of the German military attaché in Vienna a telegram was sent to Tucek on 28 February 1938 with the sender named as the firm Knorr-Bremse - they wanted Tucek to visit them. Dutifully, Tucek showed this telegram to Richter together with the correspondence which followed upon it. Richter took possession of the documents and showed them to Kendrick.[127]

Kendrick was finally convinced that he should see in person Tucek, who had asked repeatedly for this meeting, as directed by his handlers. An Englishman appeared in the apartment of Tucek at 52 Favoritenstrasse, Vienna. The Germans were well prepared: 'The Legation was notified in time and Tucek says he saw our attache's E-men (the surveillance agents) shadowing the Englishman after the meeting. We must await information from Vienna as to whether the Englishman's identity has been established.' Tucek described the Englishman as 'over 1.80 tall, broad and heavy, heavy walk, hair combed back, thick upper lip, blue eyes, well dressed, could be an officer, speaks extraordinarily broken German.'[128] In any case the Germans did not arrest Kendrick; they wanted to pass British Intelligence their 'chickenfeed'.

Kendrick spent about half an hour with Tucek, handing him an intelligence requirements questionnaire. Tucek had to learn the questions by heart and then destroy it. Kendrick gave him specific instructions: Tucek would travel via Prague to Germany. Tucek argued that he should travel via Passau, and eventually Kendrick was persuaded. Kendrick allowed for Tucek to spend up to four days in Berlin dealing with the firm Knorr-Bremse and then to go to Elbing find his friend and try to work in Schichau-Werke.

---

[127] Ibid.
[128] Ibid.

Tucek, who had searched for a job in Germany earlier, was aware of the procedure: according to the regulations it would take up to 12 days for an application by a foreign national to work as a specialist in German industry to be processed. Kendrick told Tucek to return to Vienna after three weeks, claiming to his employers that he had to see his ill wife. Richter gave Tucek 1,000 schilling and tickets.

Soon, Tucek reported to his handlers all about the meeting with Kendrick. The Abwehr heads of department IIF and IIB agreed to plot the game further: Tucek gave them Kendrick's questionnaire and started piecing together answers. He was informed that while in Knorr-Bremse's offices in Berlin, Abwehr officers would meet with him. Tucek would travel to Elbing and there he would be taken under the Abwehr station: 'They (the Abwehr station) provide a man to play the part of Tucek's friend in case of possible English observation of meetings in Elbing.'

After a few days' stay in Elbing, Tucek would go to Berlin, where he would receive his final 'answers' for the questionnaire. Then he would return to Vienna, telling Kendrick that he was not hired but 'he obtained the material from his own observation and from friendly conversations with his friends who trusted him completely.' Also, 'he let it be perceived [by Kendrick] that he took a pleasure in the work and would be ready for similar tasks. The extent of his pleasure would depend on the rate at which the Englishman paid him for the material.' Tucek was ordered not to visit the German Legation in Vienna. In case Kendrick asked him to go to Germany, the German Legation would inform the Knorr-Bremse offices in Berlin; they would reach the Abwehr. [129]

In Berlin on 10 March, Tucek had a meeting with Major Rohleder and another officer of the Abwehr in the cafe Berlina at the Bahnhof Alexanderplatz. Together they were to see Regierungsrat Reinhard of Knorr-Bremse. Tucek had 'made an anxious and over-nervous impression.' The Abwehr officers showed him a draft plan of the Schichau-Werk in Elbing and a report on the Schichau-Werk to give Kendrick. Their aim was to persuade Kendrick of the real potential of Tucek as spy. Tucek was ordered to go to Switzerland and ask there for a meeting with British Intelligence; they believed that they could uncover the SIS officer meeting there with him.

Tucek returned to Vienna on 19 March 1938. On 22 March, Richter and Tucek met in the Mondl pub at the Favoritenstrasse. Richter asked Tucek to give him the answers to the questionnaire. Tucek (now in possession of 'chickenfeed' provided by the Abwehr) declined, telling

---

[129] Ibid.

him that now he was a German subject in Germany, and that he could release the secret information he acquired in Elbing on neutral soil. He was *interested* in going to Switzerland and there would give British Intelligence the information in his possession. He claimed that he had information of submarine production in Elbing, Königsberg, and Danzig. He insisted that he had technical details he could share only with an expert, not an intermediary like Richter. Tucek also said that he could find a job at Wilhelmshaven - and passed a question to which he knew the answer: whether British Intelligence were interested in what had been going on in Wilhelmshaven. Kendrick was not pleased with the report of Richter on his meeting with Tucek. Tucek and Richter met again; Richter informed him that he had been waiting for the reply of a British firm on the invention of Tucek. It was a ploy to reassure him. He added that Tucek could go to Switzerland, as he had asked.

Kendrick had asked for instructions from London. SIS assigned the Bern SIS station officer to meet with Tucek. Richter gave Tucek a third-class return ticket to Zurich. Tucek agreed. On 28 May he met Brandon (the SIS officer) in Interlaken. There he revealed all details of information he'd acquired on Elbing, Königsberg and Danzig. Brandon asked him several questions and Tucek replied confidently. Brandon handed over 150 Swiss Francs and asked about Tucek's expenses staying in Wilhelmshaven for four to eight weeks. Tucek asked for 400 Reichsmarks. Abwehr identified Brandon as an intelligence officer but it is not clear if Abwehr agents watched his meeting with Tucek.

Tucek reached Vienna on 29 May and two days later he met Richter, telling him that everything went well in Switzerland. Kendrick gave Richter 600 RM (440 for expenses) for Tucek's Wilhelmshaven mission. Tucek assumed that he had to secure information about warships exceeding 35,000 tones. In Wilhelmshaven he found an engineering job. On 12 June Tucek returned to Vienna. Kendrick, via Richter, informed him of his monthly 600 RM salary paid by SIS. Tucek (as directed by the Abwehr) claimed to Richter that he was given an entry pass in the dockyards because he worked in the submarine and torpedo boatyards.

Kendrick and Richter were interested in intelligence of the battleships *Scharnhorst* and *Tirpitz* under construction. In particular, Kendrick was interested in armour, keel construction, horsepower, speed, and fuel consumption. On 17 July, Richter and Tucek met to discuss the final details for his mission in Wilhelmshaven.[130] In June and July 1938, the Abwehr station head in Wilhelmshaven, Korvetten Kapitain Sokolowski,

---

[130] Fry, *Spymaster*, p.155.

was handling a secret agent known as Tull who would give British Intelligence 'chickenfeed' of the naval shipyards at Wilhemshaven and also the Schischau-Werk. 'Tull' was an abbreviation of the name Tucek-Tullinger.[131]

Now was the moment of Canaris's strike. On 13 August, Richter and his family were arrested by the Gestapo, as he had locked the British consulate building. For the Foreign Office he maintained double nationality; he was a German subject, and despite the pleas of his wife, was not to receive any help. He stood trial in 1939. Tucek testified; Richter was sentenced to twelve years for helping Kendrick. In February 1943 he died in Auschwitz.[132]

On 17 August, Kendrick was arrested, just about to reach the border with Switzerland with his wife. He was kept for about four days in the Gestapo building under interrogation. Eventually, after London's pressure, and given that the Anglo-German and French contacts were leading to the Munich agreement on Czechoslovakia, Kendrick was released and deported. On 22 August he reached London.

SIS's spy ring was in disarray, and London had to rely on Czech Intelligence sources. One of them, shopkeeper Josef Kellner from the small South Moravian town of Wostitz (now Vlasatice, Czech Republic), made trips to Vienna and gathered military intelligence on behalf of Czech Intelligence. Kellner was arrested on 13 April 1939 in a refugee camp where he had found shelter, and transferred to Dachau and Flossenburg. In March 1941, he was sentenced for five years for spying. He was not executed because his offence had taken place before the start of the war.[133]

Kendrick's second-in-command, Kenneth Benton, and his wife, were ordered to leave Vienna in 24 hours. The secretaries of Kendrick, Mary Holmes and Betty Hodgson, escaped unnoticed by the Abwehr and the Gestapo.

Canaris had scored a victory against SIS. The Gestapo sealed Vienna to British Intelligence and Nazi spymasters continued feeding British Intelligence 'chickenfeed' about German troop movements. Between December 1938 and August 1939, the Abwehr station in Vienna employed the agent under the code-number E 10006 against the SIS. Other secret agents working on the same task were: E or GVE 1006, GV 1011, GV 1005, E 1002, E 1014, GV 1017 (alias Weber), GV 1007 (alias

---

[131] Activities of Ast Wien', KV 3/116 TNA.
[132] Fry, *Spymaster*, pp.178-79.
[133] Neugebauer, Wolfgang, *The Austrian Resistance, 1938-1945* (Vienna: Steinbauer, 2014), p.247.

Gast) and GV Toni. Weber had a single meeting through Gast with British Intelligence officers in Holland on 5/6 June 1939. Weber offered 'chickenfeed' to start the British getting interested in and immersing themselves in the game (Spiel) the Abwehr had plotted.[134]

Weber reported later: 'My employer at the Hague the former Czech intelligence officer Major Starkenberg and the English intelligence officer Loewe have learned from me verbally: "I was formerly in the service of Ast (Abwher station) Köln; I was later handed over to Ast Wien. While with Ast Wien I collaborated with Major Achtelstatter's office which is to be found at the well-known address of the firm Dobler & Raios". I mainly have to do courier work I fetch and carry documents to and from different barracks in the protectorate.'

Weber was in direct contact with the British, being the courier for E 1002. Both operatives are first mentioned on 28.1.1939 in a letter from Ast Wien to IID (Oberst Dr Schaefer). E 1014 was working in Bucharest. In late June 1939, he handed over to the British a training manual for flak units. On 20 July Ast Wien gave him some 'chickenfeed' for the British station in Bucharest, information about the strength and disposition of troops in Vienna. In another deception scheme, on 5 July 1939 the Abwehr station in Vienna gave secret agent E 1014, the courier to secret agent codename GEL, material in rolls of film, namely a booklet 'Directions for Training in Reserve Units' issued 1.6.36. The aim of the Abwehr was for the operative to transmit the information to the former Czech Intelligence officer Palecek, named 'the old', residing in Paris.

In April 1939, another secret agent controlled by the Abwehr station in Vienna, GV 1005, passed military and war production information: 'Small quantities of c[hicken]f[eed] were passed at the rate of about one report a month.' In August 1939, secret agent E 1006 passed his chickenfeed to secret agent GV 1011 to be handed to the SIS; it was military intelligence on Austria. 'Deliveries [of chickenfeed] continued spasmodically until August 1939 sometimes by E 1006 or by GV 1011. GV 1011's contact was George Palmers - they had met in Zurich on 10 July' an Abwehr report read. The German spymasters concluded that Palmers was a British Intelligence officer in place.[135] A post-war conclusion of the SIS read:

'By 1939 the Abwehr had developed the practice they tried out in 1938 of basing chickenfeed on the personal

[134] Activities of Ast Wien', KV 3/116 TNA
[135] Ibid.

observations made by their *GV Men*. The advantages of this if the information was sufficient to satisfy us [British intelligence] were presumably a GV Man would not give himself away if questioned verbally on a written report; b) his information would confirm any sent in by a real agent c) on the whole chickenfeed would be founded on what should be seen by any passer-by.' [136]

After defeating the SIS in Vienna, Canaris started working against his enemy, Hitler.[137] The secret game of Admiral Canaris in Vienna against Nazi Intelligence will be explored in chapter 5.

---

[136] Ibid.
[137] 'Canaris Secret Organisation' (Interrogation of General Lahousen), p.1, KV 2/173 TNA.

4

The Man from the Gestapo

Some onlookers noted, near the village railway station, close to the tracks, three idle workers in their rather shabby outfits waiting at a corner. Suddenly, they jumped at an unsuspecting pedestrian. He was a man in his early thirties in a heavy dark brown coat and hat. They surprised him and dragged him to a corner. A black sedan drove up and stopped. In a couple of seconds, he was thrown in. The car left at full speed.

Watching from a window of a nearby house, whose occupants stared at him, silent and fearful, Johann Sanitzer, the Gestapo spymaster in charge, was happy that any loss of life was avoided; he was anxious in case this Comintern agent parachuted into Austria last night would open fire on his agents. They had been ordered to be in workmen's outfits in their operations. The arrested secret agent would be given new clothes at the first stop and the Gestapo would search thoroughly what he had been wearing for secret messages or a suicide pill. Gestapo agents were usually dressed as rail-workers, cable-layers, or civilian air-raid protection groups 'so to avoid loss of life on both sides' as Sanitzer repeated to his section members.[138]

The OSS officers who interrogated Sanitzer after the war described him as of heavy corpulent build, about 1.8m tall, black hair brushed back, dark brown eyes and one or two gold teeth in his left upper jaw. His appearance was 'Mexican, had soldierly gait, throws out his stomach when walking; tends to spit while talking'. He had 'full lips' and spoke 'quickly and nervously with an authoritative voice', being fluent in Latin, Greek and Hebrew.

Back in the mid-1920s, Sanitzer was a student at the Faculty of Philosophy at the University of Vienna, but had to drop out because he could not support himself financially. He started working as an assistant chemist and managed to earn some money to study chemistry. Eventually, he could not afford the fees and was compelled to abandon this endeavour. In January 1928, he joined the Viennese police as a constable and two years later he was appointed to the technical department (Technische Abteilung) because of his background in chemistry. Sanitzer

---

[138] Detailed interrogation report of Johann Sanitzer, Gestapo, Vienna Section IV2, July 1945, p.30 KV 2/2656 TNA.

worked on the development of anti-riot tear gas, and with the introduction of wireless communications in the police service he started getting more interested in radio, which was also under the authority of the technical department. He was trained as wireless operator. In 1931 he joined the Nazi Party in secret. In 1934 he was appointed acting head of the technical department.

In March 1938, at the time of the Anschluss, he was transferred to the Gestapo Referat (Department) IIV under Dr Hubert Kern. In September, Sanitzer became a Gestapo assistant, the equivalent of police inspector. He gained a reputation as an investigator after discovering an SD secret agent who stole Goering's wife's fur coat while in Vienna. The Gestapo leadership sent Sanitzer to Berlin to be trained in criminal investigation for two years. He attended the Fuchrerschule der SD and was trained in criminology, criminal tactics, criminal technique, police law, Weltanschauung (world affairs), criminal psychology and criminal medicine.

In April 1941, Sanitzer returned to Vienna as Kriminal Kommisar for the Gestapo, working against 'rumour-mongers', and in August he was named head of anti-communist operations. In February 1942, he was selected to head the Gestapo security operations covering sabotage investigations, the protection of high officials during travels, weapons and ammunitions and forged papers. In May 1942, his section was given the designation Gestapo Department IVa2. More responsibilities were added: industrial counter-espionage and wireless counter-espionage operations. Sanitzer, a policeman turned spymaster, realised that no industrial sabotage was taking place in Austria; all fires in factories were caused either by accident or negligence. Once the Gestapo building in Vienna was bombed, Sanitzer moved his department to the villa of Franz Messner (an agent of the OSS who would be executed; see chapter 9) at 61 Hasenauerstrasse in Vienna XVIII Bezirk (district).

The Gestapo spymaster commenced his 'radio games' (Funkspiele) against Soviet, American, British and French Intelligence. This chapter, based on the interrogation of Sanitzer by the OSS, focuses on the tactics and tradecraft of these secret operations which led to the arrest of Allied secret agents in Austria. For the OSS interrogation team Sanitzer:

> '...has shown a complete willingness to talk about his former activities. He seemed to display a certain professional pride in the thoroughness of his work. He repeatedly emphasised that all major decisions were entirely of his own and that as far as the activities of the Referat are concerned only he could be made responsible and that he was ready to

suffer the consequences, if any, resulting from them.'[139]

In May-June 1942, the SD received reports that Russian agents had been parachuted into East Prussia. One of them, named Koenen, was arrested. In fact, Koenen was a well-known communist deputy of the German parliament, the Reichstag. He had witnessed the fire set by the Nazis on 27 February 1933 and blamed on the communists. Koenen was known to Nazi Intelligence and it is beyond understanding why he was selected by the Russians to be parachuted into a suicide mission in Germany.

Koenen's wireless operator was shot by the Gestapo during their arrest. Agents' documents were discovered; a signal plan together with the wireless apparatus was found. Koenen, after torture, revealed that agents were already dropped and some were about to be parachuted, amongst them a certain Panndorf and a Joseph Boerner. The Gestapo arrested Boerner in Vienna. Sanitzer was the one who took over the investigation. Boerner had on him a signal plan but insisted that he had hidden his wireless set somewhere in East Prussia. Sanitzer compelled him to co-operate and together with some other Gestapo officers took Boerner to East Prussia to show them the cache. Boerner led them directly to where the wireless was kept. Sanitzer had escorted Boerner to East Prussia because 'he did not want to give the impression to his subordinates of sitting behind his desk and sending them out on dangerous missions.' Boerner told Sanitzer that his mission was to gather military and political intelligence and weather reports.[140]

The RSHA headquarters in Berlin cleared Sanitzer to commence a play with Boerner against Soviet Intelligence. Boerner proved himself helpful. This operation was named *Quartiermacher Eins*. Kriminal Direktor Horst Kopkow, head of the IV2b section of the RSHA, began, with the help of Koenen, another play under the code name *Quartiermacher Zwei*.

The aim of the Germans was to deter the Russians from parachuting more agents into areas the Russians had assumed were safe for them. In parallel, the plays would lead the Soviets to parachute agents where it would be easy for the Gestapo to arrest them. The Gestapo would assess all that the NKVD wanted to know from their agents.

Kopkow was over-eager and started his play immediately. In contrast, Sanitzer plotted his moves cautiously. He wanted to find and interrogate

---

[139] Ibid., p.14.
[140] Ibid., p.4.

74

Panndorf, who had accompanied Boerner, because he feared that the first could leak something to his Russian handlers. Boerner had told Sanitzer that the NKVD orders were standard: to contact them on the 5th, 15th and 25th of the month with a 'cut-out' he would meet in a forest near Chemnitz in East Prussia. Sanitzer rushed there and on one of the dates set by the NKVD arrested the messenger, a woman who had with her three prepared postcards addressed to safe houses in Berlin. The Gestapo in Berlin raided the houses and eventually found Panndorf.

On 1 August 1942, Sanitzer, with the help of Boerner, who feared for his life, commenced the play with Soviet Intelligence. During the transmissions Boerner was watched by an officer of the Polizei Funkstelle (police radio communication station) who knew about transmissions. The Abwehr Abteilung IIIF in Vienna gave Sanitzer military intelligence to transmit to the Russians. The Germans were willing to share with their enemy so-called 'cold' information of troop movements. Sanitzer had to provide political intelligence as well. As he later admitted to his interrogators, he 'dreamed up' political intelligence and then submitted it for approval to Gestapo Directorate IV A 2b in Berlin. Sanitzer sought to establish a 'good cooperation' with the Russians and scotch any doubts of Boerner's bona fides. Thus, he eagerly submitted weather reports for transmissions.

But the spymaster took a great risk with Berlin. Once it became known that he had given weather reports to the NKVD, he 'was severely reprimanded for this as this constituted a case of high treason.' True, Sanitzer could have been put on trial and executed, but Berlin was reassured by his superiors that he could not be a Soviet secret agent. Sanitzer proved himself fearless in 'playing' the NKVD.

Boerner was ordered to contact the NKVD twice or three times a week. The atmospherics compelled the operator to conduct lengthy transmissions: about four to five hours for a few hundred groups of characters. Meanwhile, Sanitzer ordered the direction-finding units based in Vienna to locate any other secret agents' transmissions. He was in contact with the Funkuberwachungstelle of the OKW under Captain Johannes Bauer; his unit was based in a villa at 13 Maxingstrasse in Hitsing.

After orders from Sanitzer, Boerner radioed the NKVD informing them that he had lost contact with Panndorf. In October 1942, NKVD radioed Boerner that they would dispatch a secret agent to meet with him; his name was Emil Kammler. Kammler was a professor at the Leningrad Higher Institute of Physical Culture and he was recruited by the NKVD along with his mistress, Viola Sandroos, a Finnish subject; she had returned to her native Latvia from the United States in the company of her father. Kammler and his girlfriend had completed a mission for the NKVD in Latvia before 1941. A few months before the German invasion of Russia, the couple had settled in Reichenberg on another spy mission maintaining contact with the Soviet Legation in Berlin.

Kammler was a German subject, so he was soon recruited to the Wehrmacht. Viola Sandroos remained in Reichenberg. Eventually, Kammler deserted to the Russians and reached the NKVD in Moscow. After brief training, the NKVD sent him back to Germany. Kammler was parachuted into East Prussia and reached Sandroos in Reichenberg. He had to go to Vienna to meet Boerner, whom he assumed was free. Sandroos was directed to keep the wireless set Kammler had brought from Moscow.

Sanitzer was shadowing Boerner, who was trying to set a meeting date with Kammler. Moscow agreed with Boerner that the meeting was to be arranged at a certain date and at 1700 hours. But there was a mistake; the Russians had assumed that the time of the meeting was 0700. Sanitzer's agents missed the appointment. But once they realised that Moscow meant 0700, they arrested him in a subsequent meeting.

Sanitzer played Kammler against his girlfriend. He contacted her and persuaded her to come to Vienna. She agreed and was arrested by the Gestapo. The ever-cautious Sanitzer assumed that the current plays were enough for the Gestapo in Vienna and thus sent Sandroos to the Gestapo station in Prague, where after torture she was compelled to start a radio play with Soviet Intelligence.

Sanitzer drafted a new play. In February 1943, two NKVD agents were arrested: a man named Koehler (alias Konrad) and a woman known as Emilie Boretzky, the wireless set operator.

Koehler was known to Nazi Intelligence. He was the chief organiser of the Communist Party in Austria between 1938-39; after the Anschluss he had fled to France and then to Russia. Sanitzer began the operation *Burgenland*. Koehler was parachuted from an RAF plane. It seemed it was a joint SOE-NKVD operation. The secret agent had taken with him a small bottle of cognac and while landing it spilled over his uniform, so it was easy for Sanitzer's German bloodhounds, who were lurking in the area (as he was forewarned by the NKVD-Boerner radio communication), to find Koehler. Boretzky was also located and arrested by the Gestapo.

Sanitzer knew all about Vienna, a city he had been living and working in since the 1920s. The Russian-made wireless sets needed alternative current to operate; there were very few apartments in Vienna with this type of current and it was very easy for the police to have informers there. Boretzky was arrested and tortured; she was compelled to work for the Gestapo in radio transmissions to the NKVD under the operation *Burgenland.*

Sanitzer's intelligence coups were based on Moscow's mistakes; they had been employing known Austrian communists or their adult children. In April 1943, the Gestapo arrested the first Schutzbund children; their parents had been killed in February 1934 by the Dollfuss regime and they had been adopted by the Soviet Union. Now, after being trained by the NKVD, they were sent back to spy. Austrian police and immigration authorities had kept detailed records, available to Nazi Intelligence post 1938.

Ernst Dorfegger (alias Kernmeyer) turned up at the Vienna railway station. He was 21 years old, holding a member's card for the Hitler Youth. Police checked his identity and referred him to the Gestapo; he was too old to be a member of the Hitler Youth. Sanitzer interrogated him and soon discovered his mission, and compelled him to play a radio game with Moscow to be codenamed *Alpenrose.*

Meanwhile, the play codenamed *Quartiermeister Eins* was transferred to Munich Gestapo station because Sanitzer believed that the Viennese Gestapo would not be able to handle many games at once without something being compromised.

Boerner and Boretzky began communication with each other and Moscow in order to make the Soviet Intelligence understand that something was wrong. The result was to increase Moscow's suspicions of their transmissions; and thus operations *Quartiermeister Eins*, *Quartiermeister Zwei*, *Burgenland* and *Krone* collapsed. Moscow had received a clear warning from a female NKVD agent. She was arrested in Frankfurt. Sanitzer was informed, and persuaded the Gestapo in Frankfurt to 'talk' to her about the plays directed in a bid to 'persuade' her to work for them. He wanted to take her under his control. The woman agreed to collaborate and was assigned a Gestapo officer expert in communications to start transmitting on her behalf to Moscow. In June 1943 she managed to seduce him and he dropped his guard, allowing her to slip a warning to Moscow. Only the operation *Alpenrose* survived this Soviet secret victory over the Gestapo.

Sanitzer placed confidence in the results of operation *Alpenrose,* which lasted until the end of the war. Through the transmissions and Moscow's replies to their 'agent', Sanizter disclosed the existence of a Russian agent, Oberregierungrat Dr Major Lebouton, who was on the staff of Reichsttalter of Poson. *Alpenrose* led also to the arrest of another Russian agent, codenamed Fr. NZ.

The Comintern worked in parallel with the NKVD to deploy agents in Austria. In August 1943, three agents led by an Austrian communist leader who fled to Moscow in the 1930s, Gregor Kersche, and two women wireless operators, Louise Soucek and Hidegard Nraz, were parachuted into Poland. They hid their radio equipment and moved to Vienna. There, they started building radio sets with spare parts from their friends in the city. They soon contacted Moscow. The German direction-finding units intercepted the Russian recognition signals. Sanitzer started searching the police files for communists who had fled in the 1930s and on 2 January 1944 he made his move, arresting the agents. He planned to play a game against the Comintern under the codename *Lindwurm*.

Meanwhile, in London, Guy Liddell, the MI5 director of counter-espionage, recorded his frustration with Russian agents being parachuted by the RAF into Austria:

> 'The people sent over here appear to us to be of a pretty low mentality and our efforts to get them dropped have on the whole been somewhat disastrous. An aeroplane carrying two had to return owing to bad weather conditions and crashed on landing. All the occupants were killed. Another one was destined for Vienna which under any conditions was an extremely hazardous flight. One of our best wing-commanders insisted on doing the job himself and has never been heard of again.'[141]

After torture, Kersche and the two female agents admitted that they were secret agents and had hidden the radios in Poland, but Sanitzer could not go there, because by then Russian troops had been deployed. So the spymaster used a Russian radio-set in reserve and compelled the agents to start transmissions to the Comintern. Sanitzer was more than happy upon his 'agents' receiving messages-directives from Georgi Dimitrov, the leader of Comintern. He informed Berlin about this intelligence coup at a time many believed that the Comintern had been dissolved.

Kersche's mission before his arrest was to report political intelligence and organise an Austrian workers' resistance group in Austria. A number of secret intermediaries ('cut-outs') would help him in these tasks, but they were arrested by Sanitzer, who started a radio play with Moscow employing one of the women arrested with Kersche. The Comintern ordered her to inform the other (now arrested) woman to go to Graz to gather political intelligence. Sanitzer put pressure on the Gestapo in Graz and in Vienna to give him political information to 'feed' the Comintern.

---

[141] Diary entry for 14 August 1942, West, Nigel, ed. *The Guy Liddell Diaries: MI5's Director of Counter Espionage in World War II, Vol.1: 1939-1942* (New York: Routledge, 2005), p. 289.

Usually the NKVD was cautious, acknowledged messages and gave some intelligence requirements. The Comintern proved eager to work with their secret agents, boosting Sanitzer's chances of continuing the 'game' in his own terms. Comintern signalled Kersche; there was an Austrian Legion organised by Marshal Josip Broz Tito, the communist resistance leader in Yugoslavia. Sanitzer rushed the intelligence to Berlin.

The spymaster hit back at the Comintern. Kersche (under the direction of Sanitzer) radioed the Comintern that he'd had contact with a communist-inclined group of Wehrmacht officers. He asked for directions. Moscow sounded suspicious; they sought to check the identity of the sender. 'Tell me the name of the grandfather of your wife.' At this very moment Sanitzer had to rely on Kersche, who eventually answered correctly. The Russians continued to communicate with Kersche. Once their troops approached Vienna in March 1945, they demanded more information. As the Third Reich collapsed, in the ensuing chaos of Nazi officials fleeing, Sanitzer had to make up information for the Russians. Kersche claimed in his communications that his associate was sick and later that he was called by the police to register.

Sanitzer had initiated yet another game. Two Austrians were parachuted in mid-1943 and it seemed that they belonged to another section of the NKVD. They were discovered because of bloodstains on a banknote they had with them. Their mission was not intelligence gathering but sabotage and assassination of Nazi officials. The wireless operator had instructions to signal the Director of the NKVD. Sanitzer remembered that other NKVD agents he had arrested and used were directed to contact the 'Centre'. These new agents had a signal plan. They were in German army uniforms. One had been trying to find an apartment and he visited his father's house. An informer reported his appearance to the police and the Gestapo raided the house, arresting him. The other agent tried to flee to Switzerland but was arrested at the frontier, trying to shoot a Gestapo officer. The harsh interrogations led to the revelation of the existence of a cache with explosives, which soon was uncovered. After torture the agents confessed that their task was to kill leading Nazis, designated by numbers by the NKVD; Hitler was number one, and Goering was number two. Baldur von Schirach, the leader of the Hitler Youth, was number four; but at that time, Schirach was Gauleiter in Vienna (responsible for deporting 65,000 Jews to concentration camps). These agents would recruit their associates amongst Austrian communists who were veterans of the Spanish Civil War and amongst former republican Schutzbund members defeated by Dollfuss back in 1934.

The combination of torture and promises employed by Sanitzer turned them into his doomed allies. Under Sanitzer's directions, the head of the NKVD was informed by his agents that they had found some members of the Schutzbund and were preparing a sabotage operation. Sanitzer was looking for something - anything - he could offer these agents to claim a success. At the ammunition factory in Enzefeld there was a fire. The investigation showed that the cause was negligence, but Sanitzer directed the agents to report to Moscow that they were the ones responsible. Surprisingly, the NKVD was not thrilled. They replied that they wanted 'number 4' (Schirach) dead. Sanitzer informed the RHSA Berlin. The chief of the RSHA, the notorious Kaltenbrunner, an Austrian Nazi, blocked the publication of the plot to kill Schirach. He did not want to boost the man's popularity as a target of the Soviet Union.

The NKVD demanded that the agents should not send any signals unless Schirach was dead. So Sanitzer had to abandon this game. In January 1944, the leading agent committed suicide. Sanitzer let an article be published that a Russian agent was killed while handling explosives for a sabotage mission. Moscow asked for the article, and under Sanizter's directions, the wireless operator transmitted it. Moscow ordered him to hide for a while. Berlin did not want to continue with this game and ordered Sanitzer to execute the wireless operator who had shot at a Gestapo officer during his arrest.

Sanitzer had now become an expert of the game. In November 1944, the Russian army parachuted reconnaissance agents into Hungary. The group was composed of three men; the leader, in a Russian major's uniform, was Werner Unbehauen. He had been a Wehrmacht Oberfeldwebel (staff sergeant) and had served as divisional wireless operator in France. He was 'the best w/t man'; Sanitzer had noted he could receive and transmit 120 groups easily. Unbehauen had been transferred to the Eastern Front and during the siege of Leningrad he was taken prisoner of war. After interrogation he offered to work for the NKVD; proving his bona fides he undertook some dangerous missions behind German lines. Other agents arrested by Sanitzer told him that in the NKVD training camp they thought that Unbehauen was a Russian major. After the end of the war, Sanitzer surprised his American interrogators by telling them that Unbehauen had revealed to him that his next mission (assuming he survived the one he was arrested for) would be to spy on US forces together with a lieutenant colonel.

Sanitzer had no trouble getting authorisation from the RSHA in Berlin to begin a radio play against the Russians. Unbehauen signalled to the NKVD that he had a German signals plan; in fact, the Wehrmacht had printed one only for Sanitzer's operation. Sanitzer directed Unbehauen to tell Moscow that they needed to send a secret agent to get the plan. Vienna was the place for the secret meeting. The Russian agent arrived but it was New Year's Eve and all Gestapo personnel assigned to arrest the man from Moscow had 'drunk took much and missed him.' Sanitzer returned to Vienna and was informed about it. The Russian disappeared.

The Gestapo spymaster tried to persuade Moscow to get interested after this setback. He directed Unbehauen to contact Moscow: he could give them a new German-made gas mask filter. Sanitzer had been given one by the Wehrmacht, and his plan was to lead Russian industry onto a wrong track in the development of their own new gas mask. The reply was negative. The NKVD was not interested in sending a secret agent to get the mask.

The NKVD contacted Unbehauen; he was to send his own agent into the Russian front lines and he gave them a special piece of information, where he could safely penetrate the lines to avoid being shot by Russian soldiers. The Wehrmacht Ic (Military Intelligence) was clearly not willing to risk a life of a man for Sanizter's games with Moscow. Eventually they agreed to sacrifice a 17-year-old Slovak but Sanitzer declined to proceed with the plan. After all, it was March 1945 and everything was collapsing around Vienna.

Since 1944, an order was issued by the RSHA for the Gestapo to build up teams to penetrate the Russian lines and from there to transmit deceptive intelligence to Russian reconnaissance teams. Sanitzer had to set up four teams with his arrested agents (amongst them Unbehauen and Kersche), whom he directed to send messages to Moscow.

At one time, about forty-five radio plays were conducted by the various Gestapo and Abwehr stations based in Germany and in occupied Europe. The majority of these were against the Russians. Plays against Polish resistance, Czech resistance, British, French and US Intelligence were also planned and carried out. A dozen members of the Polish organisation named 'Stragan' operating in Vienna were arrested by the Gestapo in March and April 1943, crippling the intelligence gathering of the Polish 'Home Army' (Armia Krajowa). Amongst the arrested were Austrians, like teacher Karl Englisch (in his 60s), the lawyer Robert Milata, the head of the Vienna group, Johann Mrozek, and Lutheran pastor Gustav Ozana. Eighteen members were executed in February 1944.

The plays against the Russians were leaked by a Gestapo officer from section IV2b of the RSHA under Kopkow who fell in love with a woman in Berlin. He revealed the plays to her. She was a secret agent and managed to reach the Russian Embassy in Sweden and inform the NKVD. Sanitzer was informed about this episode.

He had been studying the Russian intelligence requirements as communicated to their 'agents' under his directions. The NKVD was interested in political and military intelligence. The head of the Austrian section was a woman about 30 years old, married to a Viennese Schutzbund member; her section replied in the plays codenamed *Quartiermacher I* and *II, Burgenland, Alpenrose, Hanshauerfelf, Rote Mauer*, and *Stalingrad*. Another section of the NKVD was planning sabotage and assassinations and the messages had to be communicated to the Director. The NKVD trained the agents in 'agent-lure', making a caché, establishing a secret letter box, 'shaking the tail' of hostile surveillance, selection and execution of secret meetings, diversionary methods, sabotage, handling of explosives and hand weapons.

The Comintern dispatched agents separately from the NKVD; once they were captured, they were compelled to send messages according to the direction they had received, addressing Dimitrov, the secretary general. The agents of the Russian military reconnaissance units were led by a Russian and composed mainly of Germans or Romanians, Hungarians and Serbs. Between December 1944 and March 1945, the Gestapo arrested five groups. Sanitzer worked out that the toughest and more experienced operatives were selected by the NKVD; they were veterans of the Spanish Civil War. The NKVD recruited Austrian communists who had immigrated to the Soviet Union since 1934 and German deserters and prisoners of war, members of the National Committee Freie Deutschland. The Comintern employed mainly Austrian communists and the Red Army. At NKVD training Camp No 27, secret agents were also taught courses in the political and economic situations of their target country, 'world political situation', Marxism and Austrian and German history.

Communists in Vienna showed the Nazi regime that they were active. A bomb was placed and exploded in the entrance of the Hofburg palace; Kopkow remarked the attack 'was presumably a demonstration against Gauleiter Schirach by the Viennese population and [another sabotage attack was] the attempt at blowing up the railway bridge over the River Sieg, a tributary of the Rhine.'[142]

The Gestapo had concluded that:

> 'in Austria, the preparation for sabotage action by communist groups were much further advanced [in comparison to Germany] and reached the stage of action; willing helpers had been found among Austrian railway workers. Altogether there was a series of attacks on railways, against which fairly large-scale Stapo (Staatspolizei) counter-

---

[142] Field interrogation report on Horst Kopkow, p.16, KV2 /1500 TNA.

measures were initiated. However, from the Stapo point of view the danger was never disposed of, and the transfer of SS Stub[annafuehrer] Straub from Brussels where he had been Leiter IV to Vienna, where he took up the post of KdS in autumn 1944 was an indication of the seriousness of the situation.'[143]

'...most cases of sabotage in Germany occurred in Austria. It was always a group of railway employees who joined together to carry out the acts of sabotage. They were exclusively communists who were dismissed after the unrest of February 1934 and who were trying to make themselves noticed after the annexation of Austria...it was noticed only in Austria that the extreme Left-Wingers were receiving orders from abroad for acts of sabotage.'[144]

In May 1943, the Gestapo arrested a Russian agent. During his interrogation, Sanitzer was informed about the existence and activities of the NKVD Camp 27, which had three zones. First, the German prisoners were screened, then they were promised better treatment if they spied on the Wehrmacht or undertook propaganda missions. Parachute training for NKVD agents was located outside Moscow. Usually, the Comintern did not train their agents in parachuting, despite their being dropped. Document examination by the Gestapo, and Sanitzer in particular, proved that the Russians meticulously prepared false documents for their agents, amongst them the Soldier's Pay Book (Soldbuch).

Nonetheless, the Gestapo in Berlin (section IVa2 of the RSHA) warned Sanitzer that the Russians had made some mistakes in issuing false Soldier's Books: 'When the Soldbucher (plural) were printed at the printers and before they received their cardboard wrapper, they were accounted by the military inspector'. He drew an indelible pencil line along the binding to make the counting easier. Even after the book was wrapped with cardboard and used for a while, 'the indelible pencil mark would show up faintly through the binding'. Therefore, books without this mark were considered forgeries.

The NKVD agents were armed with a German-made pistol, dagger and hand grenades. The military reconnaissance agents carried machine guns with silencers. A key weakness of Russian radio equipment was that some made by a US manufacturer needed alternative current to operate,

---

[143] Fourth Interim Report on Stubaf Horst Kopkow, p.4, KV 2/1501 TNA.
[144] Ibid., pp.15-16.

making it easy for the Gestapo to pinpoint the Viennese apartments and houses where such current was available.

The Russian agents carried a signal plan in microfilm the size of a postage stamp. They hid it in their clothes and they could easily destroy it if captured, while waiting interrogation. For example, on one occasion when a Russian agent was arrested, he took the microfilm out of his necktie and threw it into the latrine under the very eyes of the Austrian gendarmes before the arrival of the Gestapo.

NKVD agents carried hard currency, up to 20,000 Reichmarks and 500 US dollars; Comintern agents carried less money, up to 200 dollars. The NKVD agents had concentrated food on them for eight days and a large number of forged ration coupons. They had concealed poison tablets in a rubber wrap. Sanitzer studied and updated files of German deserters on the Eastern Front, believing that they would be employed by the NKVD. Also, the hospitals in Vienna and other cities were warned to report any patient presenting with injuries indicating a parachute drop.

The former Philosophy student who had to drop out and the Viennese police constable turned Nazi spymaster had no difficulty in tracking secret agents in the city. He concluded that the majority of the Russian spy missions had failed because the spies could not find safe apartments. The NKVD had been giving them some safe addresses, but they were out of date, having been listed before the Anschluss; the communist sympathisers had abandoned these places and new residents had moved in. The persecution of Jews, communists and socialists had led to a change in the network of safe houses - something unnoticed by the NKVD - because, simply, there were no spies alive to report to Moscow.

Sanitzer did not underestimate the ingenuity of his Russian opponents. He had noted a trap of theirs during his various plays. Occasionally, Moscow would signal their agents to repeat a certain previous message, claiming that they could not decipher it. Sanitzer, watching the sequence of signals closely, had concluded that Moscow had successfully deciphered the message. Moscow tested the agent: if he/she sent the message again that would mean that he/she was under the control of the Germans.

Sanitzer was aware of the NKVD standing order to their agents to destroy their messages after they had sent them. Sanitzer was careful in his reply to Moscow: he paraphrased the message sent earlier, enciphered and sent it adding a note that the exact message requested was destroyed in accordance with the standing order. He 'could not remember' what he had sent Moscow earlier as the exact text. This ploy assured Moscow that their agent was free.

Sanitzer's strategy had two stages. Firstly, the agents would receive

84

and respond to Moscow's intelligence requirements; in the second phase, the agents would try to 'dictate' to Moscow. For example, Sanitzer suggested that Moscow transfer the agent (under his control) from Graz to Vienna. Moscow accepted this since for some time they were receiving interesting intelligence from the agent in question.

Sanitzer was thinking and planning as if Russian spies shadowed him and his Gestapo officers. For example, he sent a Gestapo agent to register a house address with the police authorities in the name a Russian agent who was in Sanitzer's custody. If Russian agents operated in Vienna, they would report that their comrade must have been free after checking his house registry. In the majority of cases, Sanitzer offered the Russians real 'cold' military intelligence provided by the Abwehr station in Vienna and the Ic of the Army Command XVII; the RSHA gave him final clearance for every piece of information.

The Gestapo said of the NKVD:

> 'one of the most outstanding features of the Russian I[intelligence]S[service] was the mass employment of agents [this was intensified after the outbreak of war]. The Russians intended to achieve their ends through the large number of int[elligence] missions they initiated, and whilst they must obviously have taken into their calculations that this mass employment must result in heavy losses, they failed to realise that such methods could only result in their whole org[anisation] becoming known to the enemy and being effectively countered.'[145]

> '...It is hard to understand why the Russians never considered checking the genuineness of the keying of the WT operator. With present-day tech[nical] knowledge, this would not have been difficult, and it would certainly have defeated a major part of the "turning" that was done by the Germans, for in the majority of the cases of "turned" agents, a German operator had to be put to work the W/T and imitate the keying as best he could. The danger of allowing the agent himself to pass the traffic was too great, and even keeping a close watch on him while he was operating provided only a very limited safeguard...The Russian IS was consistent in its policy of dropping its agents in places far distant from where

---

[145] Fourth interim report on Horst Kopkow, p. 13 KV 2/1501 TNA.

they were to operate; thus, agents for Western Germany were dropped by Russian aircraft in East Prussia, agents for the Berlin area in the territory of the General Government. Captured Russian agents repeatedly confirmed that they had not reckoned with such strict travel control within the Reich.'[146]

The Gestapo looked for the usual mistakes of the NKVD:

'The Russian agents were on the whole well equipped with forged documents; these were printed by the state printing works in Moscow. Good ration cards, however, were a great difficulty to the Russians after the Stapo had ordered these to be changed frequently. German travel ration cards were watermarked and the Russians never succeeded in copying these. Agents were supplied with a considerable amount in USA dollars; this idea proved a failure, for unless the agents had connections in the Black Market, which only a very small number of them ever had, this money was useless in the open market. Strict currency regulations provided for such harsh penalties for persons found to be in possession of foreign currency that no one was willing to take any chances in this respect.'[147]

Kopkow described the evolution of Soviet secret operations in Germany. In the first phase, in 1939-1941, 'the Russians apparently suspended both their use of agents in the military espionage and sabotage activities. However, in the political intelligence field the Russian IS used this period to create a foothold within the Reich for future activities.' The NKVD was more interested in industrial espionage. In the second phase, in 1941-1942:

'The agents who were landed by parachute lacked any long term training. The selection of these agents was not made with any discretion. The great majority of them were compelled to taken on the work against their will. Thus it was no uncommon thing for the agents at that period to be threatened with being thrown out of the aircraft while over

[146] ibid.
[147] Ibid., p. 14.

the sea or to be told that they would be liquidated instantly if they failed to carry out their missions. It often happened that these agents gave themselves up voluntarily on landing. The technical equipment for the use of agents was often out of date, and in no way suitable for the tasks in hand. The Russian agents at that point were not sent to Germany itself, but to Bohemia and Moravia, Poland, Ukraine, Romania and Bulgaria...these agents proved to be easy enough game, even for the relatively backward Balkan police forces.'[148]

In the third phase, from mid-1942 to mid-1943, the NKVD 'changed aims and methods'. Indeed, Nazi Intelligence realised that they confronted hard-trained NKVD agents: 'the best agents NKVD could produce'. These agents were highly motivated: they hated Nazis and 'really felt that they had to fulfil the tasks which had been given to them and thus make a contribution to the Soviet victory.' The agents' mission in Nazi Germany was espionage, not sabotage. The Germans recruited, trained and parachuted in were selected from immigrant communities in the Soviet Union. The NKVD took interest in their local German dialect and deployed them in specific areas. Kopkow also concluded that the agents' technical training 'reached a very high standard...they were really outstanding and were able to keep up W[ireless] T[ransmitter] contact under the most difficult circumstances.' Indeed 'never again did the Russian IS have such good agents to serve them as during the second half of 1942 and the spring and summer of 1943.' He added:

'The only weaknesses in the activities of the Russian IS
(Intelligence Service) during this phase were:
a. The WT control stations did not function properly; thus it was possible to turn captured agents and thereby investigate the build-up of the Russian IS in the Reich itself.
b. In spite of their improved tech equip, these agents, who were admittedly far superior to those previously employed, failed largely because of their ignorance as to the actual conditions in Germany. Many of them were Germans who had left Germany in 1933, and when they were dispatched they were told that they would easily be able to get in touch with Communist groups in the Reich who would

[148] Seventh Combined Interim Report on Stubaf Horst Kopkow, Stubaf Harre Andreas Wilhelm Thomsen, Ostubaf Gustav Adolf Nosske, 2 October 1945, pp.1-2, KV 2/1501 TNA.

help them in their work. In actual fact, conditions in Germany had altered considerably since 1933, and the contacting of Communist groups had become almost impossible.'[149]

In the fourth phase, in 1943-45:

'...It may be said to have been really successful from the middle of 1944 to 1945. It consisted in the employment on a very large scale of parachute agents, WT agents working alone and WT agents working in groups. The number of transmitters and agents captured was very considerable, but in spite of this, WT monitoring in the European area showed clearly that from the middle of 1944 there were sufficient transmitters in operation, to provide the Russian IS with a wealth of valuable information.'

The agents in the last phase of NKVD operations were German prisoners of war (mainly social democrats and communists) on political intelligence missions. Many took the missions merely to escape the Russian prisoner of war camps.

Meanwhile, Sanitzer's unit had been intercepting US and British communications; their officers and missions reported problems with Tito in anti-Axis operations. Also, intercepted messages revealed that a group of Austrian agents of the SOE were operating in the Vienna area only on 'letter boxes'; these agents were assured by their headquarters that they would receive a wireless transmitter soon. The intercepts later showed that no wireless was ever transferred to the secret agents in Vienna.

In one episode of the secret war, the Gestapo spymaster was about to arrest a British agent. He intercepted a signal which read 'Mac and Harry had been dropped blind in the Kor-Alpe'. It was the mission of British Captain Mac Cranford and Rudolf Stuhlhofer. Sanitzer used Mac's wireless to start a play - codenamed *Thonse* - against British Intelligence.

A British agent, Paul Poemmerl, had already been parachuted in. The Gestapo arrested him in the Laibach area (Ljubljana had been under German occupation since 1943). Sanitzer read the intercepts bulletin: circuit No 51 contained an emergency warning to all other agents. It was assumed that these were agents whom Poemmerl had known. SOE headquarters in Bari ordered 'all agents to cease all activities and

---

[149] Ibid., pp.2-3.

disappear'; there was a fear that Poemmerl would give away their whereabouts during interrogation.

In the summer of 1944, Sanitzer was informed of the arrest of a British captain by the Landwacht (rural emergency/reserve police). He had on him identity papers in the name of Mac Cranford and during interrogation admitted that he was a wireless operator. His set was found near the place where he landed, in Graz. Sanitzer assumed that the Gestapo in Graz was not capable of commencing a play and had Cranford transferred to Vienna. The RSHA in Berlin gave the green light for a play against British Intelligence, but Cranford sacrificed himself; he took a cyanide pill he was hiding in his clothes.

Sanitzer was trying to piece together anything that could help him launch the play; he knew that this agent employed a double transposition cipher system on the basis of an English school song. But Sanitzer could not grasp the method of building the recognition groups and their place in the enciphered message. At this stage he asked for help from the cipher experts of the Funkuberwachung Abteilung of the OKW, and they offered some useful advice.

Sanitzer felt confident to start a play of 'preventive' strategy; he had to deter the British from parachuting agents into areas he did not want them in. He had to be cautious: he did not know Cranford's mission, or if he had an associate. The latest intelligence received was that parachutes and bundles had been found near Hartberg. Gestapo officers concluded that British agents had landed in the area. Sanitzer assumed that the equipment was for Cranford's mission.

Frantically, he started studying intercepts for some clues on how to pretend to be Cranford in his radio communication with the British. He took note of the intercepts of circuits '51' and '58' employed by the SOE. The Gestapo officer made an educated guess: Cranford was to collect political information on the existence of Austrian resistance groups. Sanitzer could signal something to the British; at that point he had no military intelligence available to give away.

But there was another problem. Sanitzer did not speak English. He had to write the message in German and get an expert in the Funkoberwachungstelle in Vienna to translate it. The translator was a German businessman in Britain prior to the war. The Bari SOE station replied immediately. Sanitzer and his staff rushed to decipher the message. It took a while and they acknowledged the signal. The British signalled back:

> 'God dam! Is this message really from you? It is
> absolutely illegible! If it really originates from you, then you

have placed the recognition groups at the wrong places and built them erroneously. This is the way you should have built them ...'[150]

Sanitzer claimed in his post-war interrogation that the British helped him immensely when they sent this angry message. In fact, he also played the angry card, showing some nerve; usually secret agents were not cipher experts. He wrote the message in German, which was duly translated to English. His signal to SOE in Bari read:

'To hell with the damned cipher. You know quite well that I am weak in this sort of thing. Thanks for the lesson and will try to do everything correctly from now on. Have arrived well. Have made good connections with a priest and some French pows [prisoners of war] from whom I expect many advantages in my future work...'[151]

The SOE's reply confirmed that Sanitzer was playing the game excellently. The SOE radio operator signalled 'Harry' that his headquarters were happy to receive the signal from Austria. He divulged the operatives (under Sanitzer's control) were the only ones for the time being in Austria.

Sanitzer wanted to know who this 'Harry' was. He went to Graz and started studying all police and Gestapo records. He noted the file of a workman named Rudolf Stuhlhofer from St Peter near Graz. The Wehrmacht had reported that he was taken prisoner by the British on the Italian front. Earlier, he had a criminal conviction in Austria for vagrancy and theft. Sanitzer deduced that this one had to be Harry, recruited as a prisoner by the SOE. This man was Cranford's associate.

Sanitzer, pretending to be Cranford, sent a signal to Bari:

'I am now in Harry's company. Have been separated from him but met him at the pre-arranged meeting place. The addresses given by him are not to be used as Harry possesses a very bad reputation and nobody wants anything to do with him.'[152]

In another Gestapo operation, section IV3 (counter-intelligence)

---

[150] Ibid., p.37.

[151] Ibid., p.38.

[152] Ibid., p.38.

employed an informer under the codename 'Pilot'; he was sentenced because he had attempted to contact Allied Intelligence. In prison, he met a Yugoslav aristocrat, Okbith Slavetish, imprisoned for resistance and high treason. 'Pilot' played the Yugoslav, telling him that he was an Allied wireless operator. The Yugoslav confessed that he was a member of the Austrian resistance government which sought recognition from the British and asked if 'Pilot' could contact anyone outside the prison. 'Pilot' keenly agreed to help and soon informed his guards about it. Then Sanitzer was called. He was confident that he could use the story of the Yugoslav as a sub-plot in his radio deception plays. 'Pilot' informed the Germans that the Yugoslav had asked him to contact SOE and the phrase 'The rose will bloom again' was transmitted in the Austrian broadcast of the BBC.

Sanitzer was cautious. The play with Bari with Cranford's name was still in its initial stages and SOE might grow suspicious. This special phrase had to be transmitted via another play but the refusal of other Gestapo officers to undertake this compelled Sanitzer, as 'Cranford', to ask Bari to arrange for the transmittance of the phrase 'The rose will bloom again' by the Austrian broadcast of the BBC - the 'signal' that this group was to be recognised by London.

Bari agreed but warned 'Cranford' not to approach civilian circles but 'to moot some specialists'. Already 'Pilot', now free, had contacted some communist groups after the directions of the Yugoslav. The informer had to be careful; a communist group seeking recognition as a resistance government for themselves antagonised the organisation whose member was the Yugoslav count. This group asked 'Pilot' to arrange with Bari to transmit the phrase 'bombs fall from the sky' if recognition was granted by the British. Again, to please them, Sanitzer as 'Cranford' asked Bari to arrange for this message to be transmitted by the BBC.

Sanitzer realised that 'Pilot', the petty informer of the Gestapo, had turned into a key member of a small resistance group operating an illegal print shop. The Gestapo noted that the Swedish consul in Vienna, who earlier had tried to contact a Russian wireless agent in communication with Moscow, had now tried to contact 'Pilot'. The Gestapo IVIa interfered and they raided the safe house of the Yugoslav's group; this group planned to assassinate Brigadeführer Fuber, the commander of SIPO-SD in Austria. The Gestapo turned against the commander of the security forces in Vienna. He was a suspect - in case of a British air-landing he would shoot eleven of his officers and join the British. It was a groundless fear.

Sanitzer had received the signal from Bari for Cranford: he was to move from Styria to Vienna. There were no secret agents in the city but a contact could help him. Sanitzer wanted to make Bari reveal something about this contact. Eventually, Bari told him that the contact was in a village near the city. But at that moment, the Red Army had advanced into the area.

Sanitzer shadowed French-directed intelligence missions into Austria. In the later hours of 4 April 1945, a Luftwaffe detachment reported to Sanitzer's office giving him a parachute and a bundle dropped that same afternoon outside the village of Neusieil near Nousiedlersee. It contained a letter from a girl addressed to a certain Josef Sasso; another letter was addressed to a Brezin. Sanitzer ordered a police files review on these two names. Two hours later, the SD station in Nieder Neustadt informed him that they had the file of Josef Sasso from Wunzendorf Kreis Wiener Neustadt. Back in 1940, he had been imprisoned for being a communist and afterwards sent to a penal colony in North Africa. There, it was reported he had deserted to the British. The files had the address of Sasso's father's house. Sanitzer went there with two men. Sasso was with his parents. On seeing the Gestapo detail, he opened fire, killing one of Sanitzer's officers. He made a bid to escape and was arrested after a chase.

The interrogation was on the spot and maltreatment was harsh. Sasso had to confess that his associate was Karl Brezina and Sanitzer raided the latter's house in Vienna the same day. Brezina admitted that he had deserted and been interned in a camp in Suez, Egypt. He was recruited into the French Military Intelligence by a Foreign Legion veteran, probably a German. Together with Sasso, he was trained in espionage in Algiers before being handed over to the RAF to be parachuted into Austria on 20 March 1944. These secret agents had lost their wireless transmitters. They told Sanitzer that they had been directed that in such an event they should post prisoner of war postcards to themselves (i.e. their home addresses in Austria).

Sanitzer started a play with French Intelligence. He directed Sasso to write a card: 'Marie, a common friend, was unfortunately drowned during a boat-ride in the Nousiedlersee'. It was posted to a safe address in Austria. The reply came. He was about to be conscripted into the German Army and so Sasso should write to another address until the 'friend' would be able to reply.

Once Himmler was informed of the incident with Sasso he ordered him executed. Sanitzer, seeking to build the basics for a play, wanted to save Brezina, who had co-operated, and pressed for the RSHA in Berlin to authorise him to use Brezina for a play against the French. Berlin concurred.

The Gestapo had reported the arrest a year before (June 1944) of a

92

Wehrmacht non-commissioned officer, Justus Gutterman. He was wounded, decided to surrender to the gendarmerie and was brought to Sanitzer's office. He admitted that he was parachuted in by the RAF and was wounded while landing. He had on him a forged Soldbuch, 60,000 RM and a wireless set.

Sanitzer felt that Sasso, Brezina and Gutterman must have known each other. He brought Guttermann to the interrogation room with Sasso and Brezina and it was clear that they recognised each other.

Guttermann was also interned in Suez and had been recruited by the French to spy in Austria. He told Sanitzer that his mission was espionage:

> '…against British, Americans and Russians which was
> only to be activated after the end of the hostilities. Until then
> he was to send from time to time some report on his activities
> and only send actual reports when they concerned objects of
> the highest importance, for instance, new weapons etc.'[153]

Sanitzer concluded that he was presented with a story that could not be proved. Probably Guttermann was 'playing' with him. Guttermann insisted on telling him that while in Suez he met another prisoner, a German medical officer, who planned to join the French Intelligence in order to go back to Germany. Sanitzer demanded the name of this officer. A frantic search in Wehrmacht personnel records confirmed that this medical officer was exchanged with the Allies and had returned to Germany. The first Anglo-German exchange of prisoners took place in autumn 1943. This medical officer was approached by the Gestapo and admitted that Guttermann had told him that he was to join the French Intelligence.[154]

During a harsh interrogation, Guttermann revealed that he had recruited Sasso and Brezina. Sanitzer still did not have much intelligence but could not help himself starting a radio play with French Intelligence. He first contacted the French in the name of Gutterman. The French, in early 1945, were interested in intelligence on the Russian advance in Burgenland and the German defence; how long they could hold out? Sanitzer directed Gutterman to ask for a parachute drop of supplies. Nonetheless his men went too late to the drop zone in the night and could not find it. Sanitzer asked for another drop, but by that time the drop zone was occupied by the Red Army.

---

[153] Ibid., p.35.
[154] Ibid., p.35.

Sanitzer had turned against the OSS. Back in August 1944, they had launched their first mission into Austria from Italy. The mission was under the codename *Orchid*. Of the three operatives only one survived and was evacuated to Italy. US Navy Lieutenant Jack H. Taylor led the OSS *Dupont* mission manned with Austrian former prisoner of war volunteers. Taylor looked 'an oddly chilling guy'; 'a perpetually tense man with a remoteness in his eyes, forever flicking his tongue over dry lips.' He was 'a humourless loner…forever disciplining an inner impulsiveness through stony self control.'[155] Taylor and his three volunteers were parachuted on 13 October 1944, their aim being to contact their trusted friends and relatives in Vienna. They were soon discovered. Taylor described his arrest and interrogation by Sanitzer:

> '…We climbed down from the loft about 1900 as usual for supper in a tiny room next to the manger. I had just finished shaving and unfortunately had shirt, tie and coat on, but not my field jacket. The watchdog barked; we snapped the light off as usual (Kaufmann [the owner of the house] had many visitors) and remained quiet. We heard the front gate open, followed by the door to the house. In a few minutes we heard someone come to our door, but as it was usual for one of the family to come and tell us when the "coast was clear," we thought nothing of it. Suddenly, the door was thrown open and eight plain-clothes men rushed in. We grappled for a few seconds, but I was forced back in the corner, beat over the head with a blackjack and while groggy had my arms pinioned behind my back. My left arm was then twisted backwards until the elbow joint was torn loose; such as you would the joint of a chicken leg. Four men were on each of us, and I realised the futility of further struggle. Blackjack taps on my head continued while my wrists were chained together behind my back, painfully tight, and locked with a padlock. The same had been done to Underwood [Austrian OSS operative] who was held down under the table. He was bleeding profusely from several cuts on his head. Outside were two more men with Tommy-guns.'[156]

---

[155] Quoted in ibid., p. 124.

[156] J.H. Taylor 'DUPONT Mission' (October 13, 1944-May 5, 1945) available at: <https://www.scrapbookpages.com/DachauScrapbook/DachauTrials/JackTaylorDebriefing.html> accessed 1 July 2019.

The Germans realised that Taylor was the head of the mission: 'As soon as we ceased to struggle and our captors had a good look at us, one of them said to me, "*Ah, ein offizier,*" as he saw my collar insignia.'[157] The OSS operatives were taken to the Burgermeister's office in Schutzen, their arms 'still chained behind'. Taylor reported later:

> 'We were slapped and kicked while being questioned. Although in opposite corners of a large room with our backs turned to each other, we could hear what was happening to the other. Kriminalrat Sanitzer, who directed the raid, did the questioning and intimidation. He pointed to my collar insignia and inquired what it was. "Hauptmann" (Captain), I answered, and received a heavy slap in the face coincident with the word: "falsch" (false). This was repeated several times including kicking but each time I was questioned, I repeated the same. As I learned later, they were trying to make me admit that I was a civilian in uniform as they said the British used frequently. When Underwood was asked his name, he replied "Underwood," but after the same treatment for some time he gave his true name, and the Kriminalrat immediately stopped, saying "that's better" or words to that effect, apparently knowing both our names beforehand...'

Taylor was transferred in this state to the Gestapo headquarters in Vienna at the Hotel *Metropole* on 1 December 1944 and locked in cell no.5:

> 'I was not allowed to lie down, not to sleep, nor was any food or water allowed. Very strict guard control was exercised...Later in the day, I was brought to the 3rd floor to Kriminalrat Sanitizer's office for interrogation but I refused to answer any questions until they returned my uniform. They threatened to "give me the works," but aside from twisting my already painful left arm and slapping me around, no real torture was instigated. Sanitizer's assistants, none of whose names I ever heard, although I will positively remember their faces, did the intimidation...After about three hours, they returned me to the cell and I had a pan of watery beet-soup, the first "food" in 24 hours. At this time, I never

---

[157] Ibid.

expected to live another day and consequently slept very little.'

Sanitzer was interested in interrogating Taylor further:

'The next morning I was again brought to Sanitizer's office and after a few minutes verbal sparring, they brought me my uniform, dog tags and shoes, which were heel-less from searching for a secret cipher or poison. I put the uniform on immediately and their whole attitude changed. They inquired about my arm and said they would have a doctor see to it but they never did. They offered cigarettes and brandy, both of which I declined, and tried to be friendly. I asked to be reported to the International Red Cross but they said it would have to "wait a little"…The interrogation lasted most of the day with a few hours lost due to an American air raid during which time we were chained in our cells. They [Sanitizer and his assistants] showed a remarkable knowledge of OSS including names and had a diagrammatic relationship of OSS Theater headquarters to Washington. They were particularly interested in northern Italy and told me several things about the organisation, which I didn't know, such as the establishment of a detachment at Cannes. Communications questions were mainly on procedure as they were very familiar with one-time pads and I had destroyed my 99 D.T.[radio set] They brought out a 99 D.T. and asked me how it worked but I denied all knowledge of it and questioned their claim that it was American. I noticed, however that it had 'HOUSEBOAT' (the name of the mission) printed at the top, and I remembered that we had such a mission but couldn't place it geographically. They then proceeded to correctly explain the principal of the 99 D.T. In fact, they seemed eager to show me how much they knew. During this interrogation, I suffered no intimidation or torture although threatened several times. I requested better food and told them I expected to be treated the same as a captured German officer. They promised better food.'[158]

Taylor was released by Allied forces in the Mouthausen concentration

---

[158] Ibid.

camp in May 1945.

By intercepting communications and playing deception games Sanitzer and his lieutenants had crippled two other OSS missions: the *Dillon* mission under Lieutenant Miles Pavlovich and the *Dawes* mission under Holt Green. The *Dillon* mission was parachuted into the Villach-Klagenfurt area in Carinthia for military intelligence and liaison with resistance groups. It was a five man team parachuted in on 27 December 1944.

A member of the team, an Austrian volunteer, was found to be unreliable and executed by the team, who assumed that he had betrayed their mission. Soon the Gestapo, with the help of intercepts as well as of informers, located the team members and raided a house in which Pavlovich was hiding. He was killed during a firefight on 19 February 1945. The *Dawes* mission was led by Lieutenant John Holt to liaise with Czech resistance fighters in Banska Bystica. Between 6 November and 26 December fifteen operatives were hunted and arrested by the SS and the Gestapo and led to Mouthousen concentration camp. The captured American and British operatives, amongst them Lieutenant Holt, were executed on 26 January and the OSS aborted further missions into Slovakia by the end of the month. Their operatives were presumed killed. This was confirmed through German communications with Berlin intercepted by Allied Intelligence. In February 1945 mission *Greenup* was launched: the OSS dispatched three operatives by parachute in the Innsbruck area.

The OSS mission *Deadwood* was launched but the single operative, an Austrian volunteer, was arrested in the train from Innsbruck and compelled to cooperate with the Gestapo, thus giving them vital clues for deceiving the OSS in Italy.

Sanitzer survived the war, and as we will explore in chapter 11, he was offered protection by US Intelligence in their confrontation with the NKVD.

5

The Spymaster Plots

In Vienna, Gestapo spymaster Johann Sanitzer was initiating deception plays against Allied agents, gaining the applause of Berlin. But the Gestapo leadership did not know that the Abwehr Aussenstelle (station) was conspiring against the Nazi strategy throughout the war. Since 1938, Admiral Wilhelm Canaris, the chief of the Abwehr, had been building a secret organisation that survived countless counter-intelligence operations by the Gestapo and the SD. Gestapo officer Hans Gisevius plotted with Major-General Hans Oster, deputy chief of the Abwehr, against the Nazi regime from 1934. Upon the appointment of Canaris as chief of the Abwehr on 1 January 1935, Gisevius vividly remembered:

> 'Oster whispered hopefully to me, [Canaris was] an officer who was absolutely reliable and to whom I could safely talk with entire freedom...Canaris was in fact extremely understanding. From the time of that very first meeting he never abused my confidences. Toward me he always acted more upright that I had any right to expect.' [159]

Austrian General Ervin von Lahousen disclosed to his British interrogators: 'The meaning of the "confidential mission", given to me by Canaris, was as he himself often pointed out, to co-operate in sabotaging a German victory.' Lahousen was appointed head of the Abwehr Abteilung II (sabotage) responsible for the feared Brandenburg regiment. In early 1939, he commenced the 'counter-activity' within the guidelines set by Canaris. He was an Austrian officer of the old school who was promoted ahead of other German officers. Lahousen was certain that he could not find friends in Berlin. Early on, Canaris had been hiring non-Nazis in his organisation while ousting, discreetly, Nazis. Lahousen remembered: 'At the time of my entry on service in the OKW in May 1938 General Oberst Beck revealed to me that my specially favoured assignment to the Abwehr had taken place on the basis of information given him by Admiral Canaris in regard to my political attitude. Beck, in any case, was very anxious for

---

[159] Gisevius, Hans Bernd, *To The Bitter End* (Boston: Houghton Mifflin, 1947), p.187.

me to stay in the Abwehr. For the rest I should receive from Canaris exact instructions and directives as to how this service was to be carried out in the situation which at the time was extremely critical for Germany and Europe.'[160]

Initially Lahousen served in Abwehr Abteilung I. Canaris had absolute trust on him and confided his fears:

> 'After the (unfortunately) smooth and all too easy occupation of Austria Hitler was now resolved to attack Czechoslovakia and to dismember it by opening the Sudeten German question. This would mean a European war... [we] must try to prevent this war which would be a misfortune for Germany and all Europe. It this sense he was imparting to me the following secret directions for the handling of incoming Abwehr I material on Czechoslovakia.'[161]

So, Abwehr Intelligence staff should over-emphasise and over-evaluate any reports received about the strength of Czechoslovak defences, forces and people's morale. Also, the estimates drafted should warn of the serious probability of Western intervention against Germany and the spark of another European war. The Abwehr should produce reports warning of a Soviet air force intervention since the Soviet Union was close enough to Czechoslovakia. The Foreign Intelligence Section of the SD was giving Hitler and the rest of the Nazi leaders 'optimistically coloured, editorialising reports' (Zweckberichtestattung) 'based on pure Nazi ideology.' In effect the Abwehr had to scare Berlin in order to deter Hitler from any adventurism.

Canaris had directed Lahousen not to recommend any Austrian Nazi to the OKW and the Abwehr. Canaris was a born master of deception. Secretary of State Enst Von Weizsäcker wrote in his memoirs:

> 'One cannot pass over this phenomenon...Canaris had the gift of getting people to talk without giving anything away himself. His watery blue eyes gave nothing away. Very rarely, and only through a small chink, one saw his character, clear as a bell, the ethical and tragic depths of his personality.'[162]

---

[160] Ibid.

[161] Ibid.

[162] Quoted in Mueller, *Canaris*, p.134.

He was sarcastic towards Nazis: 'That is a kidnapper,' he would confide to his trusted assistants, after meeting a high-ranking Nazi bully. In his austere office, he retained a picture of Greek Admiral Konstantinos Kanaris, a fire-ship captain during the Greek War for Independence. Kanaris was a fearless fighter but there was no blood relationship to Canaris.

The Admiral confused his superiors for a reason. In autumn 1939, after the invasion of Poland, he stopped SS atrocities. His lethal antagonist was Reinhard Heydrich. General Keitel was briefed by Canaris who had 'phrased his objections to the plans for murder and extermination in such roundabout language that Keitel asked Obersleutanant Nikolaus von Vormann who had been present during the discussion what Canaris had really wanted, but Vormann could only confirm that he did not know either.'[163]

Back in early autumn 1938, some general staff officers planned a coup against Hitler to avert a war with Czechoslovakia and escalation into a general war in Europe. Canaris did not want the assassination of Hitler, but his arrest and trial after his forced resignation. He was not close to the conspirators, who planned for a coup in mid September 1938. Ironically it was the visit of the British Prime Minister Neville Chamberlain which averted the coup, and with the Munich agreement handed a precious diplomatic victory and also precious time for Hitler to prepare for war.

Canaris had received general orders for preparing the Abwehr - espionage, sabotage and propaganda for a possible invasion in Poland. He was sure that the SS units under Reinhard Heydrich would commit atrocities. On 23 August 1939, after Hitler's secret speech the day before, Canaris feared that a general war was coming.

Hans Gisevius, the Gestapo officer attached to the Abwehr (who leaked Gestapo information to Major Hans Oster of the Abwehr), remembered:

> 'His [Canaris's] voice trembled; he felt he had been witness to something huge. We were both of the opinion we must preserve for the world this document (the notes of Canaris of Hitler's secret speech) and therefore we made a copy that Oster added to his document collection.'[164]

Major Helmuth Groscurth of the Abwehr sabotage group in Abteilung

---

[163] Quoted in Mueller, *Canaris* p.165.
[164] Quoted in ibid., p.144.

II, one of the high ranking men in the early resistance against Hitler, wrote in his diary entry of 24 August 1939, 'the basis for the war is to be provided by 150 concentration camp inmates, who will be dressed in Polish uniforms and sacrificed! This is Heydrich's doing. WC [Canaris] has done everything he can do to stop it, Army declines, etc.'[165]

Canaris and General Ludwig Beck, the chief of staff of the Wehrmacht, were both surprised on being informed of the 1939 'non-aggression pact' between Nazi Germany and the Soviet Union. It was signed by Foreign Secretaries Joachim von Ribbentrop and Vyacheslav Molotov. Canaris spoke of the 'cold calculation' of Moscow which gave a victory to the Nazi leadership, making them confident to invade Poland and divide the country with the Soviet Union. Gisevius, with Major Oster, Reichsminister Hjalmar Schlact and General Georg Thomas planned for a coup while the invasion of Poland was about to commence. Canaris was not informed about it. His deception game was always personal and untraceable by the Gestapo and the SD.

Throughout autumn 1939, Canaris was against the assassination of Hitler after General Franz Halder implied this should be undertaken by the Abwehr. Gisevius wrote about it:

> 'Canaris reacted angrily and forbade [Major] Oster or me to take on the task. We regretted it but somehow we cannot say that Canaris was wrong to decline. The admiral informed the chief of staff that whether he wanted to discuss that kind of high-political subject, he should do him the favour of seeing him personally. Moreover he insisted that Halder assume responsibility unequivocally and that all possibility of a straightforward military coup had been exhausted beforehand.'[166]

The one who had the mental and physical stamina to plan the assassination of Hitler was a 36-year-old carpenter, Georg Elser. He worked meticulously planning a bomb attack on the Munich beer hall where Hitler was to make his speech on the evening of 8 November. Hitler made his speech before leaving in a hurry for Berlin. Only thirteen minutes later, the bomb went off; the ceiling collapsed, killing eight Nazi members. The surprised Gestapo assumed that Elser was a member of a large organisation and that British Intelligence was implicated in this

---

[165] Quoted in ibid., p.150.
[166] Gisevius quoted in ibid., p. 175.

101

attempt. The truth was that he was alone. Elser was interned in a concentration camp until his execution in 1945.

In autumn 1939, Canaris looked depressed after being informed of the insistence of Hitler to start a war against Belgium, Holland and France. In Gisevius's eyes Canaris was a 'vibrating bundle of nerves'.[167]

Back in the early 1930s, Major Fechner was an official of the paramilitary Wehrbund supporting Dollfuss and opposing Nazis in Austria. He was an old friend of Lahousen. In 1938 Fechner was dismissed by Berlin and was under fear of persecution. He asked Lahousen for help. The Gestapo had already arrested his father; 80 years old and a Catholic, he had once been a colonel in the Austrian army. Lahousen did not worry: he enlisted Fechner in the Abwehr to protect him from the Gestapo. Canaris agreed.[168]

In January 1939, Lahousen was named head of the Abwehr Abteilung II (sabotage). The secret orders and directions given to him by Canaris, as Lahousen explained, were as follows:

'1. Limitation to purely military tasks and absolute non-participation in political actions.

2. Sharpest rejection of all methods that were customary with the SD and the Gestapo. The struggle is to be carried on within the boundaries that have been maintained in past and present by all participants in the war, even in this special sphere.

3. No collaboration with SD and Gestapo.' [169]

Canaris confided to Lahousen 'the other great powers will not be caught this time by the political sleight of hand tricks of this pathological liar.' His secret orders for Lahouse's policy in Abteilung II included:

'1. Formation of a secret organisation within Abwehr Abt(eilung) II and the Brandeburg Regiment, with the purpose of embodying the anti-Nazi forces and preparing them for all illegal acts that might be possible in the future against the system.

2. Gradual but systematic removal of fanatical Nazi or SD spies from the section.

---

[167] Gisevius quoted in ibid., p. 176.
[168] Report by General Major Lahousen on Canaris' Secret Organization, Part I, pp.2-3, KV2/ 173 TNA.
[169] Ibid., p.3.

3. Passive conduct of Abwehr II work, with external show of apparent very great activity.

4. Failure to carry out enterprises whose execution can be avoided in any way.'[170]

Canaris put strong emphasis: 'Absolute prevention or failure to follow orders for kidnapping, assassination, poisoning, or similar actions related to the methods of the SD.'[171]

After the invasion of Russia, Abwehr officers who had received these secret orders understood that the third and fourth order did not apply in the Eastern Front. Lahousen tried to reassure his interrogators post war that the policy of the Abwehr for no atrocities and employment of SD methods had been implemented, though there was no doubt that Canaris was 'anti-Bolshevik'. Lahousen would also try to alleviate 'the hardships created by the brutalities of the Nazi regime as far as the possibility for this is given in the sphere of influence of the section' (Abteilung II). Lahousen assumed that the secret strategy of Canaris would help set Austria free.

Other orders of Canaris included the secret collaboration with military attachés of neutral countries and contact with 'anti-Fascist elements' while liaison was not to be maintained with allies to Nazi Germany such as fascist organisations like the Spanish Phalange, Arrow Cross and Iron Guard. It was Canaris's aim for the military attachés of neutral countries to have an alternative source of military information to the 'consciously deceptive and coloured information of the Wehrmachtfuehrstab'.

The Gestapo, the SD, the Intelligence service of the Auswärtiges Amt and the NSDUP were the enemies of the Abwehr. Any SD informer or 'active' Nazi Abwehr officer had to be quietly transferred. Major Fechner purged Nazis working alongside other high ranking administrative officers of his station. Lahousen remarked: 'this secret task [was executed] with great cleverness and with characteristic intelligence.' Dozens of Nazi officers were removed:

'Captain Dr Hippel 'a somewhat confused, very activistic (sic) adventurer. An old South-African who already during the First world war had been in English captivity. No Nazi. Most recently was leader of the Arab legion in Tunis

[170] Ibid., p.4.
[171] Ibid., p.4.

and was taken prisoner by either the English or Americans; Major now General Bebert. An old E-officer, vain, limited and obstinate Nazi; Regierungsrat Dr Petzold, SS member suspected of acting for the SD; Rittm (Rittenmeister, cavalry officer) Spies. Intellectually unimportant but a convinced and fanatical Nazi. Suspected of working for the SD. Captain Fleck. 1939 Ast (Aussenstelle) Breslau former Austrian officer. Illegal fanatical Nazi who was proud of his dynamite operations in Austria. Removed by me from the Abwehr even before the French campaign. Captain Rudolff 'research activist', over-bearing Prussian, was removed by me (I believe in 1940) but turned up later in Abw III in Africa, last in Tunis. Captain Weinert Formerly Austrian officer. Sudente-German SD type. Took part in hangings and torturing of the Russian civilian population in the East (interrogation methods of the SD) not by order of the military posts. Witnesses present. Is a war criminal. Makor Hotzel. Limited, ambitious Nazi. Was in the Abteilung (I believe in 1941-42) as group leader in the west. Was transferred to an Abw II Kommando in the East'.[172]

Lahousen managed to use Nazis and kept his enemies close, one of them his deputy General Stolze, who had already served with the Abwehr for thirteen years. Lahousen was always ultra-cautious: 'In the "counter-activity" I could use him [Stolze] only with limitations and, even then, only with the greatest care. At times he was a heavy drawback for me. Stolze was a moderate Nazi, with lines out to the Prussian reactionaries. Within the narrow limits of his Prussian mentality, he intrigued against me as the Austrian who had been advanced ahead of him.'[173]

Lahousen went on to serve in the Eastern Front where he was wounded; this saved him from suspicion of conspiring against Hitler.

Canaris had introduced his confidantes into the 'the principle of passive leadership...under a pretence of the greatest apparent activity.' The apparent activity of the Abwehr entailed the production of large volumes of reports claiming the warnings given and intelligence coups against Allied Intelligence. Careful editing of the intelligence reports ensured success. Over-eager Nazi leaders would be confused with the details. The passive leadership entailed the secret personnel policy of

---

[172] Ibid., p.3.
[173] Ibid., p.4.

Canaris:

> 'Anti-Nazi sentiments were to come before specialist
> qualifications. The younger, intelligence and technically-
> qualified people were to be taken and placed in leading
> positions only when they could be used for our purposes. By
> and large, the old, experienced ('the good old Santa Clauses'
> as he [Canaris] expressed it) should be retained and allowed
> to continue their work. A few Nazis should be used as cover
> and protection against the RSHA.'[174]

The success reports of the Abwehr were custom-made for Nazis.
'Any other head of the OKH than General Keitel and any other military
leadership would have recognised and seen through these, in themselves
"daring" exaggerations and falsifications. But in a system built on lies,
self-deception and over-weaning self-confidence, this part of the counter-
activity cost the least effort of all' Lahousen emphasised.[175]

He provided some examples. Abwehr listed 'astronomical figures'
(e.g. 500,000 tons damage) on ship sabotage in the Black Sea and the
Mediterranean. 'This immensely angered the Navy (Kriegsmarine) who
indeed saw through the deceptions but drew the wrong conclusions as to
the motive which inspired them. Furthermore, the responsible Referent
(director) of the Abteilung, who had been placed in Romania, Kapitain
Lieutenant Fetzer, was well-known in the Amt and the Abteilung for his
dunderheadedness, and for his ambition quite other than for a successful
career in sabotage ("a faithful, good sailor, but with latrine outlook!" to
quote Canaris, who recommended him to me as the best qualified for
carrying out this task).'[176] The actual counter-activity 'meant neglecting
enterprises which had been ordered and the non-execution of any orders
which involved atrocities. Finally, all forms of sabotage of the war
effort.'[177] Effectively Canaris employed the tactic of the 'useful idiot', a
term wrongly attributed to Lenin.

Studying the memoirs of Walter Schellenberg, the loyal protégé of
Heydrich and later of Himmler, we conclude that the head of the Abwehr
was a master of deception as he succeeded in recruiting Schellenberg, a
fanatical Nazi, as his secret source.

There is no doubt that Canaris hated Heydrich and Heydrich hated

---

[174] Ibid.
[175] Ibid., p.5.
[176] Ibid., p.6.
[177] Ibid.

Canaris. For Heydrich, Canaris was an 'old-fox' who claimed authority over the Nazi Intelligence machine. After the Great War, Heydrich joined the Kreigsmarine and served aboard the cruiser *Berlin* as officer cadet. The captain of the ship was Canaris. Later as a junior officer Heydrich was reprimanded: 'because of his personal conduct and especially his affairs with women he had to appear before an officers' Court of Honour and was forced to apply for his release from the service' Schellenberg wrote. He added:

> 'Penniless and unemployed, he at last succeeded in 1931, through SS friends in Hamburg, in obtaining an introduction to Himmler, who in order to try him out assigned to him the drafting of a plan of organisation for what was to become the Party's security service (SD).' [178]

Canaris had noted in his diary that Heydrich was 'a brutal fanatic with whom it will be difficult to have an open and friendly cooperation.' [179] In 1935, after a quarrel with Gisevius, Heydrich said 'with a grin', 'Just you wait. You'll see the day, ten years from now, when Adolf Hitler will occupy precisely the same position in Germany that Jesus Christ has now.' [180] Schellenberg described Heydrich having:

> '...an incredibly acute perception of the moral, human, professional, and political weaknesses of others and he also had the ability to grasp a political situation in its entirety. His unusual intellect was matched by the ever-watchful instincts of a predatory animal, always alert to danger and ready to act swiftly and ruthlessly. Whatever his instinct pinpointed as useful, he adopted, exploited, and then, if necessary, dropped with equal swiftness. Whatever seemed redundant or to offer the slightest threat or inconvenience was thrown out. He was inordinately ambitious. It seemed as if, in a pack of ferocious wolves, he must always prove himself the strongest and assume the leadership. He had to be the first, the best, in everything, regardless of the means, whether by deceit, treachery, or violence. Untouched by any pangs of conscience and assisted by an ice-cold intellect, he could

---

[178] Schellenberg, Walter, *The Labyrinth: Memoirs Of Walter Schellenberg, Hitler's Chief of Counterintelligence* (New York: Da Capo Press, 2000), p.12.

[179] Quoted in Bassett, *Hitler's Spy Chief*, p.99.

[180] Gisevius, *To the Bitter End*, p.189.

carry injustice to the point of extreme cruelty. Towards his assistants and colleagues and toward the higher Party leaders, such as Rudolf Hess, Hitler's deputy, Martin Bormann, chief of the Reich Chancellery, and the Gauleiters, he operated on the principle "divide and rule", and even applied this to his relations with Hitler and Himmler. The decisive thing for him was always to know more than others, to know everything about everyone, whether it touched on the political, professional, or most intimate personal aspects of their lives and to use this knowledge and the weaknesses of others to render them completely dependent on him, from the highest to the lowest...he was a master at playing antagonists off one against the other, feeding each one, under an oath of strict secrecy, with detrimental information about his rival...' [181]

Heydrich was extremely dangerous. Alfred Naujocks, a die-hard Nazi, one of the operatives of Heydrich, revealed that he 'was anxious to form a "bacteria" section with the object of liquidating (by "illness") all persons antagonist towards the Nazi regime.' [182] Of course he could employ bacteria (had he had them available) against his own antagonists in the party, the SS and the Wehrmacht.

Canaris had decided to recruit Schellenberg as his source inside Heydrich's camp. Schellenberg played the game, reported back to Heydrich, but a close reading of the memoirs of Schellenberg shows that he was leaning to Canaris's side and could not imagine Canaris's secret strategy against Hitler's war plans. Canaris always remembered the animosity of Heydrich and in due date would take his revenge. One could never discount the fact that Canaris was shaped by the experience of escaping a Chilean island where he was interned as a junior officer in 1915, and enduring the journey through the Andes to Buenos Aires and then to Berlin to rejoin the Imperial Navy. In contrast Heydrich did not have wartime experience, to cope with the fear of death or capture. The Nazi spymaster's mindset was shaped by his political affiliations with Himmler in the early 1930s.

In early 1940 Canaris and Schellenberg met daily, both enjoying horse riding: 'Every day I went riding with Admiral Canaris...as we rode we discussed problems of mutual interest with a view to co-ordinating the

---

[181] Schellenberg, Walter, *The Labyrinth*, p.13.
[182] Reference to Naujock's revelation in Memorandum Camp 020, 29 December 1944 KV2/163 TNA.

work of our respective agencies' Shellenberg wrote in his memoirs.[183] Canaris showed that he liked to discuss matters with the young, resourceful and over-ambitious SD officer. Indeed, it was curious for an admiral to converse with a Nazi officer well below his rank who could be his son. No doubt Canaris manipulated him. This is evident in Schellenberg's account:

> 'Hitler must have arrived at his vital decision by the middle of December 1940. This came to my knowledge in the following way: Admiral Canaris had become worried about my health and had arranged for me to be thoroughly examined by Professor Zahler, Goering's personal physician. Zahler having discussed the results of this check-up with Heydrich, I had been ordered to go to Karlsbad for a rest cure. This was shortly after Molotov's visit to Berlin.'[184]

Heydrich told Schellenberg, 'it may interest you to know that recently the Führer has been concerned almost solely with information concerning the Soviet Union.' Hitler was reviewing war plans for the 'Eurasian spaces'. On 18 December 1940, Hitler signed the order No. 21 to start planning Operation Barbarossa. There is a distinct possibility that Canaris wanted Schellenberg out of the way for some time, recuperating, as Canaris was arguing against the invasion.

The chief of the Abwehr was also aware of the weakness of the Abwehr to protect conservative officers known to Nazis. Gisevius, who had argued with Heydrich, was taken over by the Abwehr. But as he put emphasis in his memoirs:

> 'Canaris...took advantage of the fact that the victorious Wehrmacht was at this time riding high. He appointed me [in June 1940] to fill a post in the consulate-general at Zurich which was at the disposal of his counter-intelligence service...Abwehr was so organised that neither the admiral nor his chief of staff was empowered to make special assignments. Only the section heads of counter-espionage or information could cover up an off-colour affair.'[185]

Meanwhile, the admiral had persuaded Schellenberg that he had no

---

[183] Ibid., p.98.
[184] Ibid., p.139
[185] Gisevius, *To The Bitter End*, p.457.

intention of antagonising the SD and Heydrich. Gisevius had described Canaris as 'a man who was craftier than Himmler and Heydrich put together.'[186] Heydrich asked Schellenberg if the reorganisation of the Abwehr would cost the SD. Schellenberg explained: 'I replied that was a problem which would have to be dealt with at another level, a problem of the relative political influence of Heydrich and Canaris. But, on the whole, it seemed to me that Canaris had enough to do with his own problems, and that if any encroachment was to be feared, it was Ribbentrop (the Foreign Minister) rather than Canaris that I would worry about. Heydrich agreed with this.'[187]

Throughout 1941, before the invasion of Russia, intelligence on the Soviet military and industrial capabilities was the subject of continuing quarrels. Canaris was trying to dissuade the Wehrmacht and Hitler and offered confusing assessments. Schellenberg elaborated: 'Another point of disagreement arose because Canaris claimed he had documentary proof that the industrial centres round Moscow and in the northeast, the south, and near the Urals, as well as their chief centres of raw materials, were linked only by single-track railways. My department had received different information. However, Canaris claimed that his had been verified, while we possessed no means of checking the accuracy of ours.'[188]

> '[In spite of Canaris's inclination] to underestimate Russia's technical progress, later conversations with him were dominated by fears that we would now become involved in a two-front war, with all its inherent dangers...Heydrich's own theory, which Himmler and Hitler shared, was that military defeat would so weaken the Soviet system that a subsequent infiltration of political agents would completely shatter it. Both Canaris and I [Schellenberg] agreed that the optimism of the military leadership was ludicrous, and Canaris also considered Heydrich's political theories extremely doubtful. Indeed, Canaris's estimate of the political strength of the Russian leadership was quite the opposite of Heydrich's. He confided to me, however, that he had been powerless to persuade Keitel, his superior officer, to this point of view.'[189]

---

[186] Ibid., p.187.
[187] Schellenberg, *The Labyrinth*, p.143.
[188] Ibid., p.191.
[189] Ibid., p.192.

Schellenberg tried to persuade Heydrich who shot back: 'It's curious, Canaris mentioned the same sort of idea to me [that the Soviet system would not collapse after an invasion] just a few days ago. You two seem to be developing some remarkably negative notions on your morning rides together.'[190]

Canaris confused Hitler, who was complaining to Himmler: 'the Abwehr always send me a batch of individual, undigested reports. Of course, they are all of great importance and come from the most reliable sources, but it is left to me to sift the material. This is not right, and I want you to instruct your staff to carry out their work quite differently.' [191]

Schellenberg assumed that Canaris was depressed:

> '[His] great nervousness at this time about a two-front war seemed to me an expression of his deep pessimism...Sometimes his remarks were so elusive, so vaguely and obscurely couched, that only those who knew him well could understand what he was driving at. This was especially true of his telephone conversations. Once I jokingly remarked over the telephone that I thought I really ought to tell Heydrich and Mueller about this "pessimistic" line of talk. "Oh dear," said Canaris, "I forgot we were talking on the telephone".'[192]

The truth was that Canaris sought to baffle the Nazi spymaster, who would leak everything he heard to Himmler and Heydrich.

By confiding *some* of his views to Schellenberg, Canaris made him feel that he trusted him, while in reality Schellenberg (having the personal attention of an admiral spymaster) worked to exert influence on Heydrich. Indeed, on 21 June 1941 Canaris invited Heydrich and Muller (head of the RSHA) and Schellenberg for lunch in a fashionable Berlin restaurant with the aim of persuading them to warn Hitler against the Wehrmacht's optimism in the coming invasion of Russia. Schellenberg assumed that he knew the methods of Canaris: 'It was typical of Canaris to choose a seemingly casual luncheon date as an occasion for giving his opinions on a problem that was of exceptional importance to him. He wanted to enlist Heydrich's support against the optimistic attitude of the Wehrmacht High Command.' Heydrich surprised all, telling Canaris that Himmler had phoned him and told him that Hitler (at dinner the previous day) was

---

[190] Ibid., p.192.
[191] Ibid., p.198.
[192] Ibid., p.194.

anxious and not very optimistic about the invasion to take place in a few days.

Heydrich had been gradually and secretly changing his mind. Earlier in 1941 he attacked Schellenberg: 'Stop your hypocritical, small-minded, and defeatist objections' he said, 'you have no right to talk like that.'[193] Schellenberg was closely studying his master:

> 'Yet one never knew what was really in his mind. Thus, one day in the summer of 1941, when we were together at his hunting lodge, he remarked to me, apropos of the direction the war was taking, "The way things are being handled by us, there must be a sticky end. Also it's sheer madness to have created this Jewish question".'[194]

Schellenberg was confused; why did Heydrich mention the Holocaust?

Canaris had been fighting his secret war every single day. Himmler and Heydrich had been pressing for the French General Henry Giraud, captured in May 1940 and interned in Königstein castle in Dresden, to be executed. The French general proved himself a fine operative, planning his escape for two years. In secret, he made a 46-metre rope out of twine and copper wire; he learned German and memorised a map. He informed his family by code letters that he was about to escape. On the evening of 17 April 1942, he descended the wall of the fortress. He had shaved his moustache and wore a Tyrolean hat, and managed to reach Schandau where he met an SOE operative who handed him clothes, money and forged identity papers. He reached Switzerland and was arrested by the border guards and deported to Vichy France. Giraud contacted General Philippe Petain and prompted him to confront the Germans. Hitler was more than furious upon learning that the Vichy government was not interested in handing Giraud back. Prime Minister Pierre Laval entered into negotiations with Giraud to persuade him to surrender to the Germans. Himmler arrested 17 members of Giraud's family as hostages.

General Keitel ordered Canaris to find and kill Giraud. Lahousen remembered that 'the refusal to execute this order likewise and the prevention of its transmittal to the SD was one of the most difficult and dangerous tasks of the active counter-activity.' Lahousen had to be in daily contact with Keitel, who pressed for the operation *Gustav* (the murder of Giraud). The general was reprimanded by Hitler for the delay.

---

[193] Ibid., p.193.
[194] Ibid.

Keitel was now in panic. Lahousen was on his own; Canaris was in Paris. 'But naturally nothing had been planned,' Lahousen remembered. The French general was not to be murdered and the Abwehr would block any attempt by the SD. Lahousen stated 'as a last resort I had taken the precaution to warn Giraud through a member of the resistance in the Vichy embassy in Budapest.'[195]

Keitel wanted Lahousen to brief the RSHA when Canaris would forward the request to the SD to take over operation *Gustav*. Canaris avoided this; General Oster (an old hand in secret resistance and confidant of Canaris) ordered Lahousen to fly to Paris immediately to inform Canaris about Keitel's demand. Lahousen wrote later:

> 'I flew immediately to Paris and discussed the affair with Canaris who was immediately very excited as he realised the danger that menaced him. Suddenly during dinner, Canaris asked me when the Abt II conference in Prague had taken place, and when Heydrich had been shot. After I gave him the desired dates, he appeared a changed man, and in completely good humour. And I soon found out the reason for this transformation. The order of Keitel was dated before the assassination of Heydrich, and before the meeting of Abt III in Prague, Canaris had invited Heydrich to the above-mentioned meeting of Abt III (one of the very clever gestures of Canaris in the fight against his most dangerous enemy). On the basis of this chronology, the order - Heydrich's arrival in Prague - Heydrich's death - Canaris made his plans for the deception of Keitel and Hitler.'[196]

Heydrich was assassinated by two SOE agents, a Czech and a Slovak, on 27 May 1942. In the preceding period, he had been humiliating Canaris, putting immense pressure on the SD and SiPo to continue with their atrocities and take over responsibilities of the Wehrmacht. Himmler did not confront Canaris. The SS in retaliation set ablaze the villages of Lidice and Ležáky and executed all men over the age of 16; women and children were locked in concentration camps.

Schellenberg saw Canaris crying at the funeral of Heydrich. Schellenberg was mystified:

---

[195] Report by General Major Lahousen on Canaris' Secret Organization, Part I, pp.6-7, KV 2/ 173 TNA.
[196] Ibid., p.7.

'The meaning of this reference to the problem of the Jews became clear to me only when Canaris told me after Heydrich's death that he possessed proof of Heydrich's Jewish ancestry.'[197]

Canaris had taken his revenge against his Nazi enemy.

Canaris returned to Berlin and persuaded Keitel that he had planned everything about the assassination of Giraud, and 'he had fully informed Heydrich' at their meeting in Prague 'about which Keitel also knew and Heydrich had already set up a special commando to "liquidate" Giraud.' Canaris told Keitel: 'Heydrich however had emphasised specially the strictest secrecy and had asked him (Canaris) not to mention the undertaking to anybody (not even Mueller [of the RSHA] or the SD Führer in Paris).'

Heydrich, long dead, could not confirm Canaris's claim. For Lahousen the ploy 'was based on the purely intellectual superiority of Canaris over Keitel.' Canaris had gained precious time; his 'preparations' for operation *Gustav* were complete but Giraud had escaped to North Africa to lead the French forces.

German ambassador Rahn and General Zeitzler (at that time chief of staff of the Army Group West) based in Paris knew of the order to kill Giraud. Rahn had attended the secret negotiations with Giraud to surrender. Lahousen remarked:

'When Hitler learned that Giraud had not been immediately arrested at this meeting of Wehrmacht representatives he exploded in one of his habitual rages especially against older officers who had never understood the meaning of the national socialist revolution and who clung to out-worn ideas of justice and honour.'[198]

Canaris talked his way out of Nazi quarrels and suspicions. But someone plotted his assassination: it was Kim Philby, working in the Iberian section of SIS. Intercepts and decoding of the German cypher system called Enigma uncovered Canaris's Spanish travel plans. Philby kept his Soviet handler fully informed; the dates, hours and the names of the hotels to be visited by Canaris were known. Besides, Phiby was in Spain during the civil war and knew the countryside. Canaris was

---

[197] Ibid., p.193.
[198] Ibid.

scheduled to stay at the Parador hotel at Manzanares, a village between Madrid and Seville. Philby suggested that his SIS superiors plan the assassination of the spymaster. Yuri Modin (his Soviet handler in the late 1940s) wrote: 'His plan was carefully prepared: there was every chance that it would succeed, given that the British knew the exact date of the visit, the layout of the Parador and ways to escape once the assassination had been carried out. The only element lacking was the number of the admiral's bedroom, but this could easily be obtained on the spot. Philby even arranged a hideout where the killers could lie low after the attack. This was highly acceptable to Kim's immediate superiors, particularly Felix Cowgill. All that was needed was the assent of the head of MI6 (SIS), Stewart Menzies.' The British spymaster was clear, and angry: 'I forbid you to lay a finger on Canaris...Don't even think about it! Leave the man alone!'[199]

Philby and some other officers at his section were surprised. Philby and the Soviets wrongly interpreted Menzies' rebuke as hiding a far-fetched secret Anglo-German conspiracy. Modin remarked that Philby

> '...had no proof whatever, but in his report to us he drew the NKVD's attention to the possibility. The Centre took this warning very seriously and ordered a detailed investigation of Canaris's youth, career and friendships. We deduced from this that the Nazi admiral had always had close ties with the British, knew them well and had many English affinities. Nobody had imagined it before, but after analysing all the facts we concluded that contacts between Canaris and MI6 were perfectly possible, even probable.'[200]

Some other British Intelligence officers concluded that Menzies was afraid of a German retaliation against his life.

Back in Vienna, Canaris's secret organisation had been active since the autumn of 1939. 'During the following years, the organisation was able to direct innumerable orders into completely different paths' in accordance with the secret orders of Canaris, Lahousen wrote in his memoirs. He mentioned as an example the order to whip up revolt and commit sabotage in Yugoslavia, which the Abwehr in Vienna 'turned into a purely passive enterprise consisting in the defence of railroads and material.' Many orders from Army Group South after 'thorough'

---

[199] Modin, *My Five Cambridge Friends*, p.62.
[200] Ibid.

examination were deemed 'infeasible' by the Abwehr officers under the resourceful Major Fechner. On other occasions, the Abwehr station complained that there was not material available for daring missions ordered. The Luftwaffe demanded action 'but the Vienna group was successful especially in hindering or at least limiting the execution of commands given by the Air Force.'[201]

Another example of Abwehr intervention was the mission of organisation for the defences of the Danube. Abwehr procrastination made sure that it would remain a 'passive' defence structure and not 'an active sabotage group'. Despite orders and in spite of the fact that it would have been perfectly feasible, they never undertook one real sabotage action, from the beginning of the war until they were taken over because of their inactivity by the SS Jagdverbande in 1945. The leader of this organisation, Korveten Kapitain von Weihs, an Austrian, was absolved of a charge of suspected treason, Lahousen remembered.

Major Fechner had to manage the Ukraine nationalist groups. It was yet another delicate task:

> 'Cooperation which had been ordered with the organisation of the Ukrainian nationals was carried out mostly by Vienna in the early days of the war. The leader in that area of the combined organisation Oberst Jary a former KuK officer of Ukrainian origin was an old school friend of mine [Lahousen] and Fechner. Thus there existed a relationship of mutual confidence…The unexampled (sic) unjust and unfair attitude taken by the responsible Nazi posts towards the Ukrainians had soon provoked a strained atmosphere, passive resistance and finally direct enmity which at the end of the war showed itself in the attitude of the Ukrainian Revolutionary Army.'[202]

The OKW in Berlin demanded that the Ukrainian Nationalists form into special fighting groups. This order was 'indeed so far as appearances were concerned carried out by the Vienna post [Abwehr station] in grand style; a few hundred Ukrainians were actually made ready, training camps were built and great activity was apparently developed.' Lahousen added:

> 'The actual mission [of the German-trained Ukrainians]

---

[201] ibid.
[202] ibid.

however both against Poland in 1939 and against Russia in 1941 was dragged out interminably and thereby prevented in practice. In both cases, the formations set up by the Vienna post were finally brought in to the operations area in the rear, but in such case, mainly because of their belated arrival, they found there was no longer any fighting taking place.'[203]

Fechner was in contact with Austrian resistance circles 'and supported them in every possible way...in time the extensive and very active counter-activity carried out by the Vienna Group which was also numerically quite strong led to the cropping up of certain suspicions which...developed into actual reports about what was going on at the post.'[204]

A certain Captain Reinhardt grew suspicious of the Abwehr in Vienna. He had asked to be provided with transmitters required for an operation. The station delayed in helping him. He reported this to the Army Group South. An SS officer named Kops reported this directly to Otto Skorzeny.

Major Fechner was about to confront the most serious danger for him and Canaris. After an SS raid on a partisans' headquarters in Slovenia, documents were found. Dr Repp, a Nazi serving as a soldier-interpreter in Abwehr, deciphered coded documents found and concluded that they contained the names and addresses of partisans' connections in Vienna. Amongst the names were those of Austrian resistance members. There were also names of intelligence officers of neutral countries in Vienna. A Lieutenant von Mesov took an interest in the claims of Repp and together with the Nazi interpreter and an aide visited Fechner and demanded 'by reason of the great significance of these captured documents, that rooms (in the Abwehr building) should be made available in order to carry on further action'; investigating the whole affair in Vienna.

Fechner concluded that if an investigation was begun by Mesov in Vienna, his links to the resistance would be exposed. He kept his nerve and ordered Mesov back to Slovenia, claiming Mesov had no authority to start such an investigation. Mesov did not argue but filed a report to Army Group F claiming that Fechner was rude to him. The head of the Ic (Military Intelligence Bureau) of the Army Group F, Oberst I.G. von Harling, a well-known Nazi, forwarded the report to the RSHA in Berlin. He requested an investigation against Fechner. Berlin approved this, but

---

[203] ibid.
[204] ibid., p.16.

116

the war situation helped Fechner: the continuous bombings in Austria and Germany disrupted official mail services as well as rail communications. The investigation was not the first priority for the RSHA and was not concluded by the end of the war.

6

The Recruiter

George Eric Rove Gedye, the leftist journalist who had worked for the SIS station chief in Vienna back in the 1920s, would become the key SOE recruiter for spies destined for Austria. After the Anschluss he fled to Prague – only to stay for a while, until the Gestapo and the Wehrmacht invaded the country. He escaped again with the help of the British Legation. Eventually he sought to go to Moscow to become a correspondent for the *New York Times*. After a year he asked to be recalled and once in London agreed to work for the SOE in propaganda. Leads of his life under the NKVD surveillance in Moscow are hard to find.

In Vienna in 1934, Gedye was introduced to young Kim Philby and was aware that Philby had been helping the communist cause. Philby even asked him for clothes for communist refugees. During the Spanish Civil War, Gedye, reading the pro-Franco articles of Philby, passed a message via a trusted female courier: 'Tell him [Philby] I am sorry to find him in such bad company.' Philby replied via the same messenger: 'Tell Eric not to be misled by appearances. I'm exactly what I've always been.' [205] Gedye kept this secret when in 1951 Philby was accused of being a spy for Moscow. He also did not challenge Philby after his famous interview in 1955, when Philby stated that the 'last time *he* spoke to a communist knowing he was a communist was back in 1934' ; the communist was Philby himself.

Istanbul was Gedye's base for SOE operations in black propaganda. In early 1941 SOE planners tried to put together the strategy for Austria. Former assistants of SIS station chief Kendrick, Evelyn Stamper, Clara Holmes and Elizabeth Hogson, wrote the first drafts of SOE strategy. Their understanding and proposals were usually at odds with the cautious Foreign Office, and they were influenced by their pro-Austrian feelings and experience in espionage and Central European politics from their Vienna days pre-Anschluss. Together with Gedye, they assigned primary importance to the politico-military potential of the Social Democratic Party – crushed by Dollfuss and Schuschnigg before the coming of Hitler.

---

[205] Quoted in Knightley, Philip, *Philby: KGB Masterspy* (London: Andre Deutsch, 1988), p.66.

It was assumed that loyal Social Democrats were in hiding ready to unite with their long-time rivals the Catholics and take up arms against the Nazis.

Stamper and Holmes wrongly concluded, wrongly, that the Anschluss was 'a model' for SOE action in the days preceding the final Allied victory. Stamper wrote: 'In spite of any statement to the contrary, we were witnesses of the extreme efficiency of the German method in Austria. There was no possibility of resistance – consequently, there was no bloodshed, and the Anschluss was a fait accompli within a matter of hours.'[206] As we have shown in chapter 3 the Anschluss was mainly the result of Schuschnigg's cowardice, not of Nazi planning, which was chaotic. SOE planners listed the tasks for special operations: they included contacting dissidents and prompting populations to revolution, instigating separatist sentiments in Austria.[207]

It was, though, admitted that 'little can be achieved by sporadic acts of sabotage which, in addition to costing the lives of the perpetrators, gives the Gestapo an excuse for a rigid control, thereby making general action at a future date far more difficult. We should rather seek to lull the Nazis into a false sense of security.'[208] *In theory*, Social Democratic Party members (the ones who remained free), Catholics and Monarchists could be the best allies of the SOE. The Social Democrats were deemed 'the best organised and the most virile': 'We [the SOE] have every reason for believing that it still commands a very large following amongst the workers, and that it still disposes of an appreciable quantity of arms.' A vague report from an informer inside Austria read:

> '...There are occasional acts of sabotage, but they are said to be suppressed by the old Social Democratic Organisation so as not to fritter away valuable forces in useless efforts, but to save them up for a decisive coup, when the moment comes...There is no programme for action, but there is the will to act...'[209]

The SOE tried to re-open contact with the Austrian Social Democrats; 'messengers have been despatched (sic) from Yugoslavia to contact reliable Social Democrats in Austria, and to persuade them to go to some neutral countries to confer with our Austrian agents. When this has been

---

[206] 'Austria' 21 January 1941, HS 6/3 TNA.

[207] Ibid.

[208] Ibid.

[209] Ibid.

accomplished, we shall ascertain from them what are the immediate needs of the Social Democrats, and how best we can help. It will not be necessary for our men to cross the frontier at present, because the Austrians will come to them or send agents. The lives of our men must be safeguarded at this juncture.'[210]

In parallel 'Catholic propaganda can be worked both from Hungary and from Yugoslavia. Our main desire now is to establish a whispered propaganda in the village inns through the village priests, which is practically the only method of reaching the peasantry…There are ample supplies of sabotage material in Yugoslavia, and once the channels have been established, this material is available should police decide upon its use.' Informers seemed to produce useful intelligence:

'According to recent reports, there has been a very large increase in Monarchist support in Austria…we [the SOE] have one of two key men in Budapest, who have already smuggled large quantities of Monarchist propaganda into Austria, and who will be ready to play an active part when the moment comes. These persons own estates on the borders of Austria and Hungary, and can be trusted 100%. We shall, furthermore, soon be in possession of a list of all the Monarchists in Hungary. We intend to use Hungarian Monarchists as contacts between Austria and Hungary.'[211]

The SOE assumed that the key to victory would be 'a special elite corps of saboteurs, parachutists and leaders, to be introduced into Austria twenty-four hours before the crack comes…' The SOE operatives and their Austrian supporters would take over from the Nazis after the defeat of the Wehrmacht.

Interestingly a secret source reported: '…I have seen riots at the *Westbahnhof* in Vienna on account of the forced deportation of Austrian workers to the Reich. This aroused the greatest nationalist feeling among the Austrian workers.' The source claimed of 'a universal feeling' of 'anti-Prussian feeling.'[212] Evidently, this kind of reporting boosted over-optimistic planning in London for some time.

Eventually, reports about unrest in Austria were forwarded to Winston Churchill's Office and Desmond Morton, his long-time trusted secret intelligence adviser. Close examination revealed that the allegations

---

[210] Ibid.

[211] Ibid.

[212] Comments on Propaganda to Austria' 28 January 1941, HS 6/3 TNA.

about unrest were quoted 'in special summaries' submitted to the Committee for Imperial Defence.

Soon it was revealed that the secret source behind these reports was the Brazilian Minister at Berne. He had telegraphed 'that working class circles in Vienna and other places were preparing to rise against the regime as soon as the Allies landed on the continent.' In a minute of 31 December 1942 Brigadier Colin Gubbins, the head of SOE, informed his counterparts that all was 'considered as wishful thinking and irresponsible rumour.'[213]

Meanwhile, Foreign Secretary Antony Eden sensed the complex political landscape of Austrians in exile. SOE had been approaching Austrians in London and New York where the 'Austrian Centre' and the 'Austrian Office' operated; the former was left-wing and the latter right-wing. Eleven other Austrian exile groups existed 'whose main characteristic, as in other parts of the world, has been their marked inability to collaborate amongst themselves.'[214] In early December 1941, these eleven groups agreed to form a 'Free Austrian Movement' for the self determination of the Austrian people. But Eden feared: 'there is a strong possibility that the whole movement may fall under pre-dominantly Communist influence.'[215] He was right.

In early March 1943, the Foreign Office began promoting the policy for an independent Austrian nation-state with no change in the pre-war borders. The British, Russian and American foreign secretaries agreed, in October the same year, on the Moscow declaration: the Anschluss was 'null and void'. A free Austria should emerge after the defeat of Nazi Germany and Austria was 'the first free country to fall a victim to Hitlerite aggression, [it] shall be liberated from German domination'. Nonetheless 'Austria is reminded, however, that she has a responsibility, which she cannot evade, for participation in the war on the side of Hitlerite Germany, and that in the final settlement account will inevitably be taken of her own contribution to her liberation.'[216] It was a vague declaration allowing many conflicting interpretations.

Early in 1942, Elizabeth Hogson went to Switzerland. In Zurich, a place of wealthy expatriates and refugees, she identified a retired high-ranking officer of the Vienna Staatspolizei. The old gentleman worked now as a journalist. He was glad to make the acquaintance of Hogson; he insisted that he retained contact with former politicians, monarchists and

---

[213] SOE War Diary, Germany and Austria, July 1942-December 1943, p.31, HS 7/253.
[214] Eden to Halifax 12 March 1942, HS 6/3 TNA.
[215] Ibid.
[216] Joint Four-Nation Declaration, Moscow Conference, 30 October 1943.

officials in Austria. He was designated secret source 'No.8' and his claims found a willing ear.

No 8 had entered Lichtenstein several times to meet Austrian aristocracy ready to organise themselves against the Nazis. Nonetheless, soon it would be proved that No 8 - his real name was Dr Hans Hollitscher - could be of no use to SOE: 'His disastrous passion for intrigue' had unravelled all his connections to monarchists and Catholics. The SOE officers were frustrated: his efforts to contact his Vienna friends from the Dollfuss time and 'organise resistance in the gendarmerie' were futile.[217]

A promising recruiter of agents was Gedye, who agreed to work for SOE in June 1942. In his early 50s, he 'took up his new task with enthusiasm and unflagging energy.' Since the 1930s, he had maintained contacts with Austrian Revolutionary Socialists. He strongly believed that they had the best chance of fighting the Nazis; he did not mind that they were verging on communism.

The excited Gedye, obsessed with Central European politics, read his SOE instructions: he had to establish communication with wireless transmitters and couriers carrying coded letters and micro-photographs with opposition groups in Austria and Germany. He had to find and recruit workmen, technicians, secretaries and governesses from the Balkans to go to Austria and Germany for work. Secret intelligence was not the sole mission of Gedye; he had to infiltrate by covert means black propaganda into Austria and Germany. His actions would urge people first to passive resistance, then to the sabotage of key targets of communication hubs and industry, and then to general strikes. The transport system of roads and railways were the first priority for sabotage.

The issue was that Gedye was not a man who lived in the shadows, seeking secrecy. The British ambassador in Turkey did not want him in the country; in February, Gedye proved himself a serious embarrassment. Since early 1941, in Istanbul, he had been working under Colonel W.S. Bailey of SOE in black propaganda before he accepted work from the Austrian SOE section. Gedye was directing an anti-Axis whispering campaign, having recruited some agents in the city. In January 1942 one of his French agents leaked a directive sheet to the French military attaché, who informed the British military attaché - the British Embassy was unaware of the propaganda scheme and naturally the ambassador was furious because Gedye was the one who had issued the directive.

A new shock awaited Sir Hugh Montgomery Knatchbull-Hugessen,

---

[217] R. Jelinek 'Work into Austria', HS 7/146 TNA.

the British ambassador. In February 1942, Gedye's agents threw thousands of anti-Nazi leaflets from the house tops of the Grand Rue de Pera, a busy commercial road in Istanbul. Turkish policemen and gendarmes, with the help of their informers, rushed to arrest a total of thirty-two people. Gedye had been noted by police informers. In a cosmopolitan city like Istanbul, secrets were difficult to keep.

He was brought in for interrogation but confused his interrogators and succeeded in evading any connection to the incident. Nonetheless, a policeman found in the boot of one suspect a copy of the directives of the whispering campaign. The now furious ambassador demanded that Gedye leave the country. SOE had to concede, but they did not forget their man in Istanbul, who had to go, for the time being, to Cairo.

The SOE Austrian section needed Gedye; they gradually put pressure for his return to Istanbul. It was the key city for access to Austria through the Balkans. Eventually, the ambassador allowed Gedye to 'visit' the city in January 1943. The visit was prolonged enough and by May 1943 he was stationed there. Knatchbull-Hugessen's reputation would suffer when it was discovered that his valet (during the same period) spied on him and handed over secret diplomatic correspondence to the SD in Ankara. Austrian SD officer Ludwig Carl Moyzisch was the one who handled Elyesa Bazna, the Albanian valet, under the codename *Cicero*. Earlier, the ambassador's butler, called Marovic, was suspected of being a spy for Nazi Intelligence. On 21 November 1941 SIS was warned about it. Moyzisch had direct contact with Naci Perkel, the head of the Turkish Secret Service; the limited intelligence sharing targeted Allied agents in Turkey. Moyzisch received 'regularly' (about every 2 months) from Berlin a blacklist with the names and descriptions of known members of the British Intelligence service in Turkey. The blacklist was compiled by Abwehr Abteilung III and forwarded by SD Amt VI under Schellenberg. The list contained Austrian agents and contacts of the SOE and OSS in Turkey.

After the assassination attempt against von Papen, the German ambassador in Ankara, in February 1942, the diplomat assumed that the culprits were the SIS. Nonetheless, Turkish police accused Russians of the plot to kill him.

SOE assumed that Gedye's identity would be hidden in plain sight: he would continue claiming to be a noted journalist writing freelance, and a member of the British Public Information Office in Istanbul. Gedye, the recruiter of Austrian agents, would have to use a middleman; he could never appear to contact an agent directly. He insisted that Austrian Socialists had to be assigned this task. Karl Hans Sailer was imprisoned by the Dollfuss regime and after his release he moved to the United States.

British Intelligence contacted the FBI and he was found, and he agreed to work in Turkey. Sailer arrived in Istanbul in February 1943. However, 'it was evident that four years of soft living had sapped the fire this man possessed and was useless for SOE work.' Sailer was indiscreet and complained about everything; so he was sent back. Another Austrian socialist, Stefan Wirlander, was recruited as a middleman. He soon proved to be an 'unqualified success', deemed 'enthusiastic, energetic, and skilful.'[218]

Gedye did not fear putting his ideas into practice. He first wanted to infiltrate subversive propaganda into Austria with the aim of urging soldiers to desert and urging civilian disobedience against the Nazis. He pursued the idea of employing foreign workers as agents, but soon abandoned this scheme. He sought information about the drug trade; but soon realised that the drugs (e.g. hashish and heroin) were trafficked from Syria and Turkey to Egypt, not to Germany. Diamonds were a commodity to be exploited but Gedye's informers revealed that illicit diamonds were handed to the German consul in Istanbul and sent by diplomatic bag to Berlin.

Gedye liked black propaganda methods; it was his game. He inserted subversive messages in lottery tickets, cigarette boxes and packing cases destined for Austria and Germany. It was a child's game under the mantle of secret service work: 'Good use was made of "itching" powder which was scattered to good purpose where it could cause the maximum discomfort to the German troops.'[219]

He was fascinated with tricks and games, overestimating their impact on the secret war against Nazi Germany. He arranged for soft soap, sabotage instructions and propaganda in waterproof small bags sealed in tinned fish and exported to Austria and Germany. War-weary, hungry-for-fish Germans and Austrians would find themselves not eating fish but reading sabotage instructions and Allied propaganda. In November 1943, he reported to London that about 5,000 tins of fish would reach Germany and Austria in the following 50 days.

He boasted, 'It will be a very valuable Black offensive going to every corner of Germany and Austria and by a hitherto untouched channel [of propaganda].' He also claimed that up to 1,000,000 anti-Nazi publications had reached Austria and Germany under his instructions.

Nonetheless, Gedye had not earned admirers in the SOE:

---

[218] Ibid., p.4.
[219] Ibid., p.5.

'...whereas he was singularly successful in the infiltration of Black Propaganda, he was definitely less so in establishing contacts inside Austria. When one considers the painstaking and meticulous work involved, the weeks of careful briefing, the documentation, the micro-photography, the concealment articles and the financial outlay necessary for even one courier, we must admit that the results were disappointing.'[220]

The causes of failure were attributed, firstly, to the inaccessibility of Austria - it was a country 'too far'. Secondly, recruiting spies was a doomed activity in Turkey, because of 'the low moral standards of Europeans who lived for some years in the corrupt and enervating air of Turkey.' It was added, 'It will be observed that it is not only the Levantine adventurer type who is venal...Idealism and fanaticism seem entirely lacking in agents recruited in Turkey. Money alone was the driving force.' After all 'It should be remarked that it does not lie in the Austrian temperament to organise active opposition, excellent as they are at all forms of passive opposition...such Austrians as would have attempted to organise some active movement were even prior to the outbreak of hostilities scattered throughout the German armed forces and the Reich. In spite of this we know that the Nazis executed many thousands of Austrians for high treason...'[221] Gedye aimed to recruit secret couriers carrying neutral country passports to reach contacts in Austria. 'He took the risk of a grand chance and lost,' SOE officers concluded.[222]

He was known to be a British agent and was easily approached by Austrians in Istanbul. An Austrian, Kurt Beigl, approached an SOE agent working for Gedye in May 1943. That agent was aware that Beigl worked for SD against Turkey. Beigl asked for help to escape to Syria. He was just 'a traitor,' commented SOE officers, and they did not offer any help.

Gustav Ruediger approached Gedye in early 1943; he was a businessman and a member of a resistance organisation and sought, in exchange for his services, the RAF 'guarantee' that they would not bomb his factory Semperit Rubber. Franz Joseph Messner, the chairman of the board of Semperit, would contact Allen Dulles, the OSS spymaster in Bern, offering intelligence (see chapter 9). Ruediger, in agreement, approached the OSS offering his services.

While staying with SOE, Ruediger was assigned the codename *Star*. In August 1943, he brought fascinating intelligence. The Germans had

[220] Ibid.
[221] Ibid., p.9.
[222] Ibid., p.10.

been developing a 'rocket gun': the V1 and V2 rockets. The SOE reported to the War Office:

> 'This report aroused a great deal of interest and opinions with regard to its value varied considerably. It was submitted to ACSS (Assistant Chief of the Secret Service) who informed us on October 27th that whereas their scientific adviser and section V considered the report as plant, [names deleted; probably the prime minister's office] and MEW [Ministry of Economic Warfare] considered the report most valuable and the internal evidence from the industrial point of view quite convincing. We discovered later that 'Star' had passed the same report to the Americans.'[223]

There was no doubt that the demand for secret intelligence by SOE and OSS created a competitive market for interested people. By March 1944 all SOE connections with *Star* were suspended. Turkey broke diplomatic relations with Nazi Germany and the Turkish police arrested and detained *Star* as a Third Reich subject. SOE noted that he 'talked very indiscreetly about Gedye.'[224]

Gedye would soon fall into the trap of a Swiss serving in the Swiss consulate in Istanbul. He was named Trumpe and was in his late 20s. On 22 December 1943, Gedye informed SOE in London of the plan to employ Trumpe. A hasty search into the archives revealed that Trumpe 'was known definitely on one occasion to have been in contact with the Germans.' Gedye did not discover anything 'sinister', after a 'long weighing up of pros and cons.' He proceeded with his plan. Employing a middleman, he supplied Trumpe with instructions in code and a cover address in Austria.

The SOE report on the affair referred cryptically to a role of the SIS while otherwise it was an SOE mission: 'As 'C' was paying the man [Trumpe] for the trip it was to cost us [SOE] nothing, but Gedye through a 'C' contact offered a premium of 25 pounds if Trumpe brought back the first and last letters of a certain person's name.' The name was 'Franz Novy': the letters were 'N' and 'Y'. A man under the surname Mehlich lived in the cover address; Trumpe should give him the message:

1   I come on behalf of your friend Franz who spent the

---

[223] Ibid.
[224] Ibid., p.17.

night of March 12th with you and with whom in 1930 you spent three days holiday…with whom you made a tour of the mountains in 1931.

2   As proof that I have duly delivered this letter to you, you should give me the first and last letters of Franz's surname.

3   Are you ready to accept another dispatch from me?

4   Do you wish to prepare a message for me to take along for   Franz on my return journey?

Trumpe, posing as a Swede, visited Mehlich's house and talked to his wife; he subsequently visited her, and it turned out that he worked for the Gestapo. Mehlich was interrogated by the Gestapo regarding his British connections but released and was ordered to reveal anything of any future communications with SOE. On 26 April 1944, Gedye himself invited Trumpe to dinner to find out what had been going on. Trumpe played his cards very well: Trumpe was 'best described as a regular dare devil. He says that he himself gets away with murder by having a reputation of being a pretty wild playboy and quite unserious.'[225] Trumpe described his meetings with Mehlich and his wife - Gedye was persuaded of his bona fides. The conclusion of SOE was not kind regarding Gedye's performance:

> '…we can assume that we were thoroughly duped by both Trumpe and his agents; that they were a thoroughly corrupt group of persons, completely ruthless, prepared to betray anybody or anything for gain…Fortunately, as Gedye had worked on a water-tight system throughout it was only this one line that was "blown".'[226]

Post war, Gedye worked as a correspondent in Vienna. As a civil assistant of the War Office, he was appointed a Member of the British Empire. From 1950 to 1967 he was the bureau chief of Radio Free Europe in Vienna.

---

[225] Ibid., p.15.
[226] Ibid., p.19.

7

The Man from the SOE

'This is no life for a gentleman,' SOE Major Alfgar Hesketh-Prichard, attached to the Slovene communist partisans, signalled to Lieutenant Colonel Peter Wilkinson, based in Monopoli, near Bari, Italy. Hesketh-Prichard was the SOE man to go into Austria through the mountains of Slovenia. Since December 1943, he had endured unimaginable hardships and had excelled in battle against 13th SS Police Regiment transferred from Russia. He had inspired the suspicious Slovene communist partisans to stand up and fight, as reported by Major Charles Villiers, who witnessed his leadership.

Earlier, Hesketh-Prichard was the SOE officer who trained the Slovak and Czech SOE agents to assassinate Heydrich. He proved himself a charismatic guerrilla operative, but like his comrades in arms Wilkinson and Villiers, underestimated the growing antagonism of Slovene communist partisans against the SOE. He could not grasp the post war communist intent for Central Europe. Wilkinson and Hesketh-Prichard failed to understand the motives of the Secretary of the Central Committee of the Communist Party of Slovenia, Franc Leskošek-Luka. Both British officers were unaware that the Comintern and the surviving members of the Austrian Communist Party were working to boost communist influence in the partisan groups. A key and lethal variable in the secret war for Austria was the aspiration of Slovenian and Yugoslav partisans seeking to claim part of the Carinthia region of Austria.

Hesketh-Prichard reached the partisans of West Korosko Odred in the mountains south of Eisenkappel on 31 May. In June, Major Villiers arrived there. Both officers started working on building up a partisan team for operations into Austria. From June to September 1944, they arranged for the RAF to drop twenty-five tons of war materiel, much needed for the communist Slovene partisans. The British officers reported back that the partisans numbered 2,000. They raided villages in the Drau Valley. Repeatedly, Hesketh-Prichard tried to persuade them to fight the Germans, but they were more interested in consolidating their forces to claim Austrian territory for Slovenia, once the war ended. The communist partisans sought supplies to survive and strengthen their outpost north of the Drau river. Wilkinson, who had been in constant signals communication with Hesketh-Prichard, remarked in his memoirs that the SOE officer was more than committed:

128

'Alfgar made the crossing of the river Drau his personal responsibility which he pursued with an obsessive single-mindedness, believing it was essential for the development of Clowder's plan [the code name of the mission] in the longer term. This conviction was shared by members of Clowder's HQ staff, who received every encouragement from the Special Operations branch of AFHQ at Caserta. Alfgar was uniquely qualified to carry out this task.'[227]

SOE planners and Hesketh-Prichard based their operations on faulty intelligence. The partisans just tolerated the British officers and the risk-taking Hesketh-Prichard because they needed RAF supplies to survive. Partisans' hopes were boosted by news that the Red Army had advanced into Austria and that Tito was about to confront the British. Eventually, Hesketh-Prichard convinced the partisans of the need to advance and cross the Drau river.

Slovene partisans took offence at the leak of information of one SIS agent attached to the SOE mission and compelled the SOE to parachute agents into Austria without Slovene help on the ground; these were 'blind' missions into the hands of the Gestapo. Wilkinson remarked:

'Germans had woken up to the threat posed by Partisan forces, armed and supplied by air from Italy. They had certainly broken the Slovene ciphers which were elementary and they were probably also monitoring the Clowder radio traffic though the latter, being always enciphered on one-time pads, was reasonably secure. They would also have noted the supply drops of matériel in remote mountain valleys and though no attempt was made to intercept these sorties, raids by border police and militia interfered with the collection, distribution and storage of these supplies. The treachery of the so-called British agent led to a surprise attack resulting in the burning of the house in the Logan valley in which the British staff had been living and a running fight lasting five days in which both Charles [Villiers] and Alfgar [Hesketh-Prichard] distinguished themselves, the latter being credited with the improbable tally of forty Germans to his own gun. (This legend died hard and was repeated to me when I visited

---

[227] Ibid., p.198.

Slovenia forty years later.)'[228]

Austrian operations for the RAF and SOE had to be put on hold. The Italian front was a priority and more human and material resources were needed. The Slovene partisans assumed that RAF support would not be coming in the winter weather. Hesketh-Prichard communicated with Monopoli and with London as proof that help would continue coming. He succeeded in arranging for a drop on 26 August 1944 and distributed the war material. The partisans were impressed. A group of 100 of them, with Hesketh-Prichard, was formed for operations into Austria. But London started worrying. Wilkinson wrote:

'Political objections were raised to the mass deliveries of arms and explosives for the Slovene minority in the Drau valley which, it was pointed out, would be included in the British [post war] zone of occupation. While accepting that guerrilla raids against the Leoben–Klagenfurt railway and German communications generally might be of short-term tactical value and politically acceptable, the massive air support on the scale envisaged by General Luka might be taken by the Partisans as acceptance of their territorial claims and could not be countenanced.'[229]

At that time, the head of SOE, General Colin Gubbins, assumed that the officer on the ground, Hesketh-Prichard, should take the key decisions. Gubbins had concluded that the German resistance was about to collapse. He wrote to Wilkinson early in the summer, 'Vienna is the next stop.'[230]

On 13 July 1944, two SIS operatives, former Austrian prisoners of war, attached to Clowder mission, were ambushed by a German patrol. One escaped. The other was taken. Soon a reliable source of the partisans told them that this SIS operative was 'talking in friendly terms with the Germans.' The operative escorted the German raiding troops to the guerrillas' secret base. About 1,000 German troops reached the area, coming from three sides simultaneously. Hastily, Villiers contacted SOE headquarters in Monopoli:

'Disaster. Night 14th [June 1944] Huns surprised us by attack

---

[228] Ibid.
[229] Major C.H.Villiers, Report on the Clowder Mission, HS 6/17 TNA.
[230] Ibid.

with 2,000 men and Gestapo [from] Klagenfurt. Too late [to] stop plane, we almost caught, got to hills where starved four days, reformed [on] 18th but Huns had found out bunker containing all [Mission code-named] Greenleaves blank documents and stamps...all propaganda as far sent us also spare crystals [for transmitters] and three w/t sets.'[231]

In SOE, panic ruled:

> 'From the list of the papers given to Greenleaves by DM/350 it would appear that not only did they have blank and completed documents, but also certain sections of the Handbook on German Papers. As you know, this Handbook has always been regarded as of exceptional security importance and the possession of considerable parts of it by the enemy would be of great assistance in their interrogations of suspected agents, since they would know exactly what information about documents is given to the agents in the course of their training here.'[232]

Indeed, Sanitzer and the rest of the Gestapo spymasters would take advantage of all SOE documents in their deception operations. On 8 July Villiers returned to their bunker: 'Our safest bunker, which was excellently hidden away from the houses, was empty. It had contained our most valuable, secret and compromising material.'[233]

The role of the SIS Austrian operative 'was investigated very carefully by the Partisans and by ourselves and I fear the greatest suspicion of having betrayed us.' Villiers added: 'We certainly harboured no bad feelings against SIS for this disaster, which was largely my fault, for we well knew the proclivity of ex-prisoners of war to "go bad" under strain. The Partisans were taking no risks and they altered every one of their dispositions and plans. Further, they resolutely refused to have any non-British members of our party anywhere near them in the future, so my remaining three Austrian [operatives] had to be incarcerated at a new signal station which we had constructed in an area never yet visited by the Germans.' Villiers wrote 'the incident was not without benefit, for the [Partisan] Staff took Hesketh-Prichard, myself and Roberts (Radio operators) to live and move with them from that time on. This was the

---

[231] Buxton (Villiers) to Miller, 5 July 1944, HS 6/11 TNA.
[232] X/A2 to X, 11 August 1944, HS 6/11 TNA.
[233] Major C.H.Villiers, Report on the Clowder Mission, pp.15-16, HS 6/17 TNA.

beginning of a close and happy co-operation which lasted till we left Slovenia, and which greatly eased the working out of our plans.'[234]

Villiers described the regional leader of the communist partisans as a 'young red headed Communist, [named] Ahac. His talk is emphatic and original in form…That he is shrewd is shown by his instant appreciation of the use we could be to his ambitions to raise the Slovenes, north of the [river] Drava.' The communist was 'a bon viveur and the occasional delicacies in our gift considerably influenced his dealings with us.' The British officers were informed that some communists of the resistance in Klagenfurt had escaped the Gestapo and some had reached the northern slopes of the Karawaken mountains. The partisans tried to find them and for the time being they could not build up their secret courier system into Austria with the remaining resistance members.

Ahac told Hesketh-Prichard and Villiers that the only hope lay in a paramilitary 'invasion' of Austria, which 'might stir up Austrian resisters.'[235] The partisan leader insisted that former Austrian prisoners of war should not be used by SOE; they were not reliable.

Desperate for information, the British officers and the partisans noted whatever travellers were telling them. But a close examination of their claims, after months of investigations, showed them to be just rumours. Deserters and former prisoners of war 'attached too much importance to individual acts of kindness shown them on route.' Villiers was clear: 'the lowest common multiple of these reports produced the following basis for our calculation as the Austrians are so tired of the war that in some places (especially Graz) it is bad form even to speak of it. Many Austrians are anxious to resist but they have not got beyond talking of resistance within their pre-Anschluss political Groups. There is no sign of communists, Social Democrats, Christian Socialists and Legitimists combining for resistance purposes.'[236]

Villiers and his team, alongside Tito's son, would cope with the hardships of walking the 200-mile mountain track to escape the German troops and reach the Adriatic and the SOE outpost by September 3. Villiers suffered from typhoid fever but he endured. He described Hesketh-Prichard, who stayed with the partisans preparing to enter Austria, looking 'thin, worn and tired, but driven by fanatic determination on what he himself described as a one-way journey.'[237]

The SOE surveyed Soviet propaganda for some clues. Nonetheless,

[234] Ibid.
[235] Ibid., p.16.
[236] Ibid., p.18.
[237] Wilkinson, *Foreign Fields*, p.201.

'the lack of hard news in those [radio] broadcasts indicates that the Russians have no more contact with it than we have.' Villiers and Hesketh-Prichard agreed that Austrian resistance could have 'potential value' to the Allied war effort but for the time being there was no leader and no nucleus organisation.

Hesketh-Prichard was signalling to Wilkinson that his operation into Austria should not be cancelled. On 20 September he sent:

> 'I have no illusions as to the risks involved or the relative importance of Drau crossing or what I may achieve there but feel that even a little first-hand local knowledge and possibly a tiny base free from chores of personal security may be of help to you when you put your final plans into effect. As far as judgment is concerned, day to day Partisan work in the first place is largely a matter of instinct and the longer one does this job the stronger the instinct gets.'[238]

Frank Lindsay, the OSS major with the partisans, remembered Hesketh-Prichard before he left with the guerrillas. 'As he was leaving, he told me he doubted that he would survive because snow was now on the ground at the higher levels, and tracks that could be followed would be left in the snow. But he was determined to make a try.'[239]

Alongside a group of partisans, Hesketh-Prichard crossed the Drau river with inflatable, British-supplied dinghies. The three partisan groups met on 10 November. The Slovene partisans tried to persuade the suspicious and poor Austrian villagers that they were not nationalists. But the Austrians were not willing to take up arms and join them.

Lieutenant Colonel Hans Fleckner, commander of the SS police troops in Carinthia, ordered more operations to ambush partisans in the slopes. The Germans unleashed their hunt on 27 November; the 13th and 19th SS Police Regiments would lead the charge.

On 20 October, Hesketh-Prichard reported that his team had climbed to the top of the Saualpe west of Wolfsberg and asked for an RAF drop of supplies. But extreme weather conditions prevented flying over this region. The partisans badly needed supplies to survive. For six weeks the RAF could not approach the area of operations due to the bad weather. The partisans with Hesketh-Prichard had to ask for food from isolated villagers (Slovenes and Austrians) struggling themselves to survive. There

---

[238] Ibid.
[239] Ibid.

were also armed outlaws in the area and the fear of a coming German offensive persisted. Small guerrilla raids were conducted on the Klagenfurt-Hüttenberg railway.

Hesketh-Prichard recruited some Austrian outlaws and Wehrmacht deserters. But the starving Slovene communist partisans were hostile to these British initiatives. The communists assumed that any tactical action by Hesketh-Prichard could impact on their strategic aspirations. Hesketh-Prichard signalled to Wilkinson that the 100-man group had to be divided to survive the bad weather and the German attacks. Hesketh-Prichard and his team were deployed in the neighbourhood of Eberstein, about 15 miles north-east of Klagenfurt on the western slope of the Saualpe. By mid November SOE concluded that the German collapse would not come. The same was realised by the Slovene communist leadership.

The assessments of SOE concluded with the futility of operating in Austria: 'Although it is possible to organise small resistance groups in Klagenfurt of Austria, it is doubtful whether they will be able to do enough to justify the airlift to maintain them. In any case, due to adverse flying conditions, no serious support can be given until the spring of 1945.'[240] 'There is no active resistance group similar [in Austria] to those which have been operating in the occupied countries.'[241]

On 3 December 1944, Hesketh-Prichard was desperate but committed. He signalled Wilkinson that he was thinking of attacking an airfield and hijacking a Luftwaffe aircraft to escape to Italy. His last signal read, 'This is no life for a gentleman.'

Eventually Hesketh-Prichard was executed by the Slovene partisans in cold blood. For the communists preparing for the post Nazi defeat confrontation with the West, the enemy were the British. His death was kept top secret by the UDBA, Tito's post war secret service. For decades, his SOE comrades assumed that he was killed during a battle with the Germans. In January 1945, Hesketh-Prichard was declared as 'Missing believed killed'. For all his courageous efforts, he was awarded the Military Cross. SOE planners had no other choice but to wait for the spring:

> 'We should aim at establishing in Austria small clandestine groups with w/t communication who, although their role would necessarily be passive throughout the winter, would both form a framework for any subsequent action in

---

[240] Progress report/Clowder Mission, 25 November 1944, HS 6/17 TNA.
[241] Note on Special Operations in Austria in Mid-November 1944, HS 6/17 TNA.

the spring and constitute a valuable source of intelligence.

'Owing to the extreme difficulty of the supply problem the most which can be hoped for at Trigger is the maintenance of a British officer with the Slovene Partisans throughout the winter. The formation and arming of independent Austrian resistance groups is out of the question until the snow melt and flying conditions improve at the end of March.'[242]

Parachute operations into Austria were aborted 'owing to the capture by the enemy of crystals and codes.'[243]

---

[242] Ibid.
[243] Ibid.

8

The Man from the OSS

In Vienna in July 1916, a junior American diplomat, Allen Dulles, born in 1893 and having graduated from Princeton university, started his career in the foreign service. The Great War had raged since August 1914 and for the time being the United States remained neutral. Dulles was mainly employed in the tedious work of reviewing visa applications. In his memoirs, he remarked that he had to read the Legation codebook: '[in the code book] we had six or seven words for "period." One was "PIVIR" and another was "NINUD"...The theory then was - and it was a naïve one - that if we had six or seven words it would confuse the enemy as to where we began and ended our sentences."[244]

In 1917, he was transferred to Bern, Switzerland, shortly before the entry of the United States into the war. He took up a junior advisory role during the 1919 Paris Peace Conference and from 1922 to 1926 served in the Near East Division at the State Department.

Dulles opted to become a lawyer and started working in a prominent New York firm. In parallel he served as occasional adviser to US missions on arms limitation negotiations for the League of Nations. In conferences he had met Mussolini and the Soviet Foreign Minister Maxim Litvinov. By the start of the Second World War he had a background in international negotiations and international finance, with a wide network of international bankers and officials. But he was not a spymaster.

Upon the formation of the OSS, his name was put forward to serve in Switzerland gathering military and political intelligence on Nazi Germany, Italy and nearby occupied countries. Dulles arrived in Bern in late 1942; he was named Special Assistant to the US Minister, Leland Harrison. Until the end of the war he would receive volumes of information from secret sources who volunteered to work for him.

The international finance lawyer started learning the ropes of secret intelligence reporting and espionage, amassing vital experiences for his post war service with the CIA. In January 1951, Dulles was named CIA Deputy Director for Plans; it was an all-powerful position in drafting and implementing Cold War covert operations strategy. Upon the election of

---

[244] Quoted in Dulles, Allen W. *The Craft of Intelligence* (Guilford CT: Lyons Press, 2006), p.67.

General Dwight Eisenhower as President, Dulles was named Director of the CIA. This meteoric rise to intelligence power would not be forgotten by former SD spymasters, amongst them Wilhelm Hoettl, who from the final days of the war established contact with the ambitious Dulles aiming to 'cultivate' him indirectly and secure his support in the Cold War era.

In December 1943, Dulles sent an optimistic cable to Washington on the prospects of armed resistance in Austria:

> 'Through sources that are usually reliable, we have been informed that an anti-Nazi organization with about 5,000 members, mostly communists and leftist socialists, exists in Vienna. We have been in touch with envoys professing to represent this organization. They want to establish contact in order to suggest industrial and military targets, secure instructions as to sabotage and pass on to us secret intelligence. Previously their organization communicated only with Moscow over Prague. They now want a radio transmitter and an operator, and they will notify us when they finish with reception preparations now being made. According to them, two Swedish communists with a radio transmitter parachuted into Austria recently from a plane which might have been Russian, in order to cooperate with their organization.'[245]

Dulles *wanted* to believe that something could come out; but the information of the 5,000 members ready for action was erroneous. Besides, at that time, Sanitzer the Gestapo spymaster had been routing operatives parachuted into Austria.

Throughout his tenure, Dulles did not hesitate to expand on grand strategy - forecasting the strategic antagonism with Moscow - proposing psychological warfare ideas and tactics, and secret operations like creating hyperinflation of German ration cards by printing forgeries and other measures to hit the Deutsch Mark. It is no surprise that financiers are listed in his sources; Dulles was willing to read their reports and views.

Joseph Johan, a financier, informed him that Vienna was encountering a 'food problem'. The financier insisted that the Gestapo was all too powerful and thus Dulles had to cable to Washington: 'open

---

[245] Dulles to Washington, 8 December 1943, Petersen, Neal H. ed. *From Hitler's Doorstep: the Wartime Intelligence Reports of Allen Dulles, 1942-1945* (University Park: Pennsylvania State University Press, 1996), pp.173-174.

resistance or even organization of secret activities is nearly impossible because of Gestapo control over such tendencies.' He added that the pro-monarchists did not enjoy the support of ordinary Austrians. This source mixed political information (that monarchists did not enjoy much support) with street gossip (that young people who were to be drafted took drugs to fail the Wehrmacht medical examination). The financier claimed that the Austrians did not want their country to be tied to Germany any longer and many were in favour of 'a large economic entity composed of perhaps Hungary, Croatia and Czechoslovakia.' [246] It seemed that the Austrians sought the return of an empire.

Dulles felt like a real spymaster when Lanning McFarland, the OSS chief in Istanbul, brought him the services of an Austrian businessman, Franz Josef Messner, and his network. The spy ring was codenamed *Cassia* by Dulles. Remember that Messner worked first for the SOE with Gedye in Istanbul (see chapter 6) before opting to contact the Americans. Dulles was excited: 'I wish to offer my congratulations to Packy [McFarland] for his accomplishments in developing this line [of reporting] 840 [Messner; Dulles met him in Bern] impressed us very favorably. We are convinced that he is worthy of all...' [247]

As the Normandy landings were impending in June 1944, Dulles was informed that Messner had been arrested by the Gestapo. He doubted that he was a Nazi, trying to deceive the Americans all along. In Dulles' eyes Messner was always honest and money was never a motive of his. Dulles explained to Washington:

> 'I feel that genuine opportunities may be lost to us if we are unduly suspicious [towards informers]. As an instance of this, I have the feeling from my dealings with Zulu [the British] that their services, because of the leg-pulling they suffered in gloomy times of 1940-1941, are unaware on occasion of the degree to which the situation has been reversed, even in the field of intelligence. Several of my finest sources would have been lost to me had I pursued their [British] course.' [248]

Claims of powerful resistance organisations were not unheard. British Intelligence was informed of the case of die-hard Nazi Alfred Naujocks, a former SD spymaster. A US infantry patrol arrested Alfred Naujocks on

---

[246] Dulles to Washington, 24 February 1944 in ibid., p.230.
[247] Dulles to Washington, 14 March 1944 in ibid., p.238.
[248] Dulles to Washington, 8 May 1944, ibid. p. 286.

19 October 1944 at 1200 hours, four kilometres from Wirtzfeld, near Malmedy, Belgium. It has to be remembered that a couple of months later, on 17 December 1944, members of the 1st SS Panzer division executed 84 American prisoners of war in Malmedy.

Naujocks was in civilian clothes and told the infantrymen that he carried false papers and was a peace envoy; he needed to report to their headquarters to transfer a message from the Austrian resistance to a certain Colonel Christie of the British Foreign Office. The case of Naujocks reveals to what extent the weak Austrian resistance groups were unable to employ reliable and risk-taking couriers to reach the Allies; thus they needed true Nazis to do this job.

Naujocks showed the US officers who interrogated him the special German pass he used to approach the front area. The pass read: 'Alfred Naujocks has to carry out a mission for the Reichssicherheits-Hauptamt, the RSHA. This mission is top secret. His assignment has to be carried out in the area Roetgen-Eupen. It is requested that all German civil and military authorities protect and assist Naujocks while carrying out this mission. Signed SS Obersturmbannführer.'[249]

Naujocks was 'very tall and strongly built with blue eyes, dark blond hair, small nose, oval face'.[250] Four vaccination marks were noted in his right upper arm as well as an appendix scar. A scar inside the left knee and a bullet wound by the big toe of his right foot betrayed his violent past. He had joined the SS in 1931 and three years later he was appointed to the newly-established SD political intelligence department in Berlin. In September 1939 he personally took part in the staged incidents on the German side of the border with Poland. Executed prisoners from concentration camps were dressed in Polish army uniforms and sprayed with machine gun fire. Hitler would show to the world that the Polish army invaded German soil, before his invasion of Poland. It was a plan of Heydrich executed by his trusted lieutenants, amongst them Naujocks.

On 3 November 1939, Naujocks, Werner Goettsch, a fellow SD officer and nine others, amongst them Walter Schellenberg, kidnapped two British Intelligence officers, Richard Stevens and Sigismund Payne Best, in Venlo, Holland, after an exchange of fire. The SIS officers were deceived and lured to the place of their arrest. Naujocks was one of those who opened fire during the incident.

But in 1940, Heydrich accused Naujocks of corruption; he was demoted and sent to a penal battalion. Eventually he persuaded an SS

---

[249] Naujocks, Alfred, G2, 23 October 1944, KV 2/ 279 TNA.
[250] Interrogation report, Office of AC of S, G02, 20 October 1944, KV 2/ 279 TNA.

commander of his innocence and was transferred to a Waffen SS unit in the Eastern Front, the infamous Leibstandarte Adolf Hitler. In 1942, he was discharged on medical grounds and as a trusted Nazi was assigned to Brussels in the Economy Investigation Service (Wirtschaftlicher Fahdungsdienst), a unit supervising the black market.

The American officers read the secret message Naujocks was supposed to hand over to Colonel Christie of the Foreign Office. It was written in German and the author was a certain Professor Heinrich in Vienna:

> 'It's more than 6 years ago now since we met in the snow covered mountains of Arosa. The walls, established between us, made it up to this date impossible to transmit a sign of life to you. Now I see a possibility which I am exploiting with pleasure. I hope wholeheartedly that this letter will reach you in excellent health. The bearer will convey my wish to you to give me the opportunity of meeting you. The events have proceeded to such an extent that important material for a conversation is available. Many of the old friends are still here, but important new ones also joined up. The execution of our plans was hampered by difficulties which we visualised. The time appears to be opportune for the realisation of new plans. The day I could see you and talk to you again would be a very happy one for me. Regards and sincerest respect. 'Vater den Schlosskinder.' [251]

Naujocks claimed that 'the intellectual leaders' of the Austrian underground organisations were: Professor Heinrich, who was imprisoned for one year in a concentration camp; Professor Ottomar Spann, also held in a concentration camp with his sons; Professor Borodeikewitsch, who once taught history at Vienna University; and SS Obergruppenführer Werner Goettsch, Naujocks' old friend.

Naujocks was offering intelligence to the suspicious US military intelligence officers, telling them that if they sought to infiltrate agents behind enemy lines all they need was 'to make up a paper stamped *Geheime Reichssache* in red ink on the top and RSHA on the bottom with a signature of some SD leader.' Indeed 'all the agent will have to tell is the person he must report to.' The Germans would not be allowed to

---

[251] Translation of message, 23 October 1944, KV 2 /279 TNA.

question the bearer of such an identity paper for more information about his mission. Naujocks added more intelligence about Himmler, who was 'travelling constantly by a special armoured train (called *Sonderzug Heinrich*) through Germany.' He claimed that his friends in Austria had found out the exact timetable and location of the train so that the Allied air force could kill Himmler. His death would cause 'a great chaos' in Germany. 'No one man will be able to replace Himmler' and the feuds amongst Nazi leaders would 'cause a possible collapse of the home front.'[252]

He went on to explain that the SD transmitter in Vienna could be used for contacting the Allied secret services. He claimed that an officer named Wannelk responsible for the transmitter was 'mentally dominated by Goettsch.' The Americans were utterly bewildered and confused; Naujocks insisted that no SD high rank would notice the operation of the transmitter to contact Britain because everyone had their own codes. Naujocks was willing to find the SS Führerbuch for the Allies; all contact information of leading SS personnel was included there. Naujocks also said that all political leaders were held in concentration camps and would be executed before the end of the war. No one would be alive to lead Germans and Austrians post war. He proposed for an Allied propaganda campaign a warning that whoever executes prisoners of war or political prisoners would be sentenced to death.

Naujocks explained that in July 1944 he went to Vienna for a holiday. There he found his old friend, now Werner Goettsch, at 28 Colloredogasse. They talked about the war and the prospects of ousting Hitler. Both sounded willing to escape Europe and start a new life. Goettsch was thinking of joining the Freemasons and told Naujocks that he knew people in Vienna who would like to communicate with Allied Intelligence. Their aim was for a speedy Anglo-American victory and the establishment of an Austrian Republic to derail any Soviet plans for domination in central Europe. Naujocks replied that he would like to discuss this with these Austrians; he was willing to take risks to help them. He returned to Belgium and his duties there.

On 2 September 1944, the Allied advance in Belgium compelled the German occupation administration to withdraw. Naujocks and his service members reached Koblenz and then Berlin. On 6 October, he left by car for Vienna; he sought an opportunity to escape to the Allied lines carrying the message of the resistance group. During his journey he posed as an SS Sturmbannfuehrer.

---

[252] Interrogation report, Office of AC of S, G02, 20 October 1944, KV 2/ 279 TNA.

In Vienna, Naujocks spoke with his old friends Baron Georg Drash-Wartinberg and Goettsch, who arranged for Naujocks to see resistance leaders. In Wienzeile, Goettsch introduced him to Professor Heinrich, who claimed he was the leader of the Austrian Resistance Movement. Heinrich wanted an Austria free from Soviet occupation, and had drafted a message for his old friend, a certain Colonel Christie, who worked in the British Foreign Office. Naujocks keenly agreed to carry this message. The BBC should broadcast a code word when the message had reached the Foreign Office. Goettsch gave Naujocks 100 USD for his dangerous journey and a special SS pass, the Geheimdienstsache (Secret Service Business), which would enable him to pass without difficulty through the German lines.

Soon, Naujocks discovered that the Geheimdienstsache helped him 'to obtain every facility from the German military commanders with the advanced forces.' He made three attempts to escape to the US lines on 19 October. When asked by the Americans about Professor Heinrich, Naujocks told them that he knew almost nothing. London was informed about the letter to 'Colonel Christie of the Foreign Office.' MI5 found Christie and asked him about Heinrich. Christie, who had been an RAF group captain, remembered Professor Heinrich as a devoted Catholic at the University of Vienna. He had invited the Austrian to Arosa prior to the war. Heinrich was 'in a sense' National Socialist but 'he was not in agreement with the Nazis.' His ideology was Pan-Germanism. Christie had heard that Heinrich was at one time imprisoned by the regime.

Christie informed MI5 that Heinrich was just 'an armchair politician much too lacking in drive ever to have any real force'; he 'would be of no value to the Allies.'[253] S.H. Noakes, the MI5 officer who interviewed Christie, told him that the secret letter was brought by Naujocks. Christie replied that 'he knew the name well as that of a Nazi thug, though he had never met him.'[254] Subsequently Christie wrote to Noakes 'Heinrich, to the best of my knowledge, never joined up with Hauptmann Leopold and his Nazi roughnecks…we became good friends and he proved himself a very reliable source for information from behind the political scene in Austria, Czecho [Slovakia] and Germany.'[255] Heinrich, the armchair resistance leader, was a secret source of SIS, prior to the war. After the war Naujocks escaped prison waiting to be tried for war crimes. He was a true ghost. In any case it was evident to British Intelligence that resistance groups with potential did not exist in Austria.

In his turn Dulles disagreed with this premise and proved willing to

---

[253] S.H. Noakes memo, 18 January 1945, KV 2/280 TNA.
[254] Ibid.
[255] Letter by S.H. Noakes 19 January 1945, KV 2/280 TNA.

take risks with sources. Fritz Molden was a young man, born in 1924, who rose to become a key operative. He had deserted the Wehrmacht unit he served with and in summer 1944 joined the Italian partisans; he soon established contact with the OSS and offered to spy in Austria. His OSS code number was K-28 and he gained Dulles' trust. Primarily, Molden offered Dulles astonishing intelligence, even though it was fragmented in most cases and not verifiable.

In late 1944, he informed Dulles of the resistance organisation 'O5'. It was composed mainly of conservatives but gradually made contact and achieved some cooperation with Austrian socialists and communists. 'O5' was a cryptic abbreviation for Österreich with 5 standing for the fifth letter of the alphabet. It was a resistance organisation, not the whole of the resistance. In November 1944, Hans Becker, the military leader, and his associates established a seven man committee to direct the activities of the resistance. However, on 28 February 1945 the Gestapo raided a safe house, arresting him.

On 12 December 1944, the Provisional Austrian National Government (POEN, Provisorische Österreichisches Nationalakomitee) was formed; it was a descendant of the O5 committee of seven. Nonetheless, mass Gestapo arrests crippled the POEN. Molden was taking great personal risks by going in and out of Austria with forged papers to contact couriers and get the latest intelligence of the resistance and of the political-military situation in Austria as the Soviet forces advanced. Dulles was receiving reports which exaggerated the military potential of POEN. In the meantime, the SOE as well as the Soviet military intelligence discounted the value of the POEN, whose members cooperated with the military resistance group under Major Carl Szokoll. They planned for an uprising in Vienna under Operation *Radetzky* but the Gestapo received a prompt warning and averted their plans.

In January 1945, Dulles forwarded Molden's reports to OSS in Caserta for action. The OSS spymaster wanted 'intensified use of leaflets, particularly bearing factual news.' He passed on Molden's recommendation for propaganda as well as his information:

'Following places believed to be particular hideouts a. cellars and tunnels of old fortress Hohen Saltzburg, secret documents of OKW stored, b. cellars and tunnels of Jonnberg in Salzburg, c. cellars of Moenchberg in Salzburg...parts [of archives] of German Foreign Office formerly in Krummhuegel area Silesia moved to Schloss Hellbrunn near Salzburg...Head of Archiv-Kommission of German Foreign Office Professor Jagow recently instructed his staff to gather information for report on cruelties committed by Allied soldiers against German soldiers. Also on use of gas by Allied Armies.'[256]

The Austrian OSS operative suggested 'this looks like preparing alibis.' Molden claimed that Himmler had headquarters at Aigen-Glas near Salzburg and Goering maintained his own headquarters at a location between Reichenhall and Freilassing in upper Bavaria.

Molden's report was breathtaking: he claimed that the German field intelligence had captured Russian order of battle documents indicating that forces were moved to Poland. The Germans reached the conclusion that the Russian deployments in Hungary would be thus weakened. German generals planned to reach Budapest with reinforcements and defeat the Russians. [257] Molden claimed that the Wehrmacht generals had studied the tactics of the resistance in Stalingrad and Warsaw to employ the same for the defence of Vienna. [258]

Molden's intelligence on the Budapest front was deceptive. By late January 1945 the siege of Budapest, which had commenced on 26 December, escalated. Soviet forces put on strong pressure and by 13 February had conquered the city. Molden's reporting was inaccurate and dangerous if seen as credible and distributed to the upper echelons of US army and Allied forces.

On 25 February 1945, Dulles received Fritz Weston, an Austrian industrialist designated '503'. He had just arrived from Vienna. Weston told him that SD Sturmbahhfuehrer Dr Wilhelm Hoettl knew that Weston had contacts with the OSS and sought to start a secret channel of communication. In fact, as Weston told it:

'Hoettl informed him that Kaltenbrunner [the Austrian head of the RSHA] wanted to see him. Kaltenbrunner informed 503 that he and Himmler [were] most anxious to end war and as first step were contemplating liquidation of war mongers within Nazi Party especially [Martin] Bormann. [Himmler and Kaltenbrunner] were most anxious to establish contact with British and Americans [and asked 503] to make effort in this direction on his trip to Suisse and contemplated sending here high SS official to speak on their behalf

[256] Dulles to Caserta (OSS), 25 January 1945 in Petersen ed. *From Hitler's Doorstep* p. 435.
[257] Ibid.
[258] Ibid., p.436.

provided contact could be established.'[259]

Molden reported that the Free Austrian Committee set up by Russians at Debrecen in Hungary included only communists 'some disguised as Social Democrats or Christian Socialists.' Molden informed Dulles that he estimated that about 800 Austrian patriots were executed by the SS and Wehrmacht on a monthly basis. The operative's report was disorienting; he claimed that in Pocking in lower Bavaria was the 'Flieger Stafer Adolph Hitler' with specially made hangars which contained the newest Ju-290s transports with bulletproof glass and armour plates. Hitler might try to escape Germany by air to avoid arrest. Hitler was supposed to be 'greatly disturbed over delay'; the Ju-290s had to reach Berchtesgaden on 28 February. The planes would be not be ready until mid March.

Hoettl went to Bern and met with '502', an intermediary of Dulles. The American was 'convinced' Hoettl was the 'right hand man of Kaltenbrunner'. Hoettl offered his news from Vienna: he claimed that the SS in Vienna sought an end to the war and 'arrange [the] orderly transfer of administration to western powers.' The fear of the Soviet invasion paralysed all Austrians and they sought protection in an Anglo-American occupation. Hoettl presented a rough plan: the SS loyal to the 'war mongers', chiefly to Martin Bormann, the now all powerful leader of the NSDAP, should be eliminated.

Weston, the Austrian industrialist designated 503, met Kaltenbrunner between Hoettl's first and second trip to Bern. Hoettl claimed the RSHA chief tasked him with establishing contact with Austrian anti-communist resistance.

By that time, the battle of Vienna had ended. Dulles could not continue with the secret channel of communication with Kaltenbrunner. Stalin had started to blame the Allies for trying to cut a deal with Nazi leaders. Dulles had concluded that 'Wilhelm Hoettl's record is bad' and 'he desires to save his skin...'; the same applied to Kaltenbrunner. Hoettl had been offering Dulles frightening intelligence: the Nazi party 'is taking over power even from SS...Bormann becoming even more powerful than Himmler.' About 100,000 SS troops and reliable Wehrmacht units were headed by Hans-Adolf Prutzmann and Otto Skorzeny. Heinrich Himmler had named Prutzmann (who had committed war crimes in Russia and was directly involved in the Holocaust) Generalinspekteur für Spezialabwehr (General Inspector of Special Defence) and organiser of the Nazi resistance organisation called Werewolf.

---

[259] Dulles to Washington, 28 February 1945, ibid., p.459.

US Military Intelligence feared a Nazi last stand in the Alps, costing the lives of many Allied troops. Dulles keenly reported about the imaginary threat of German troops concentrating in the Alps. The US generals hesitated to speed up their advance into Germany and Austria. The immediate result was for the Red Army to get into Austria first.[260]

Hoettl insisted that the resistance group O5 was 'riddled' with Gestapo agents. The Austrian communists 'were [politically] unimportant but gaining greatly in prestige as result of Russians arriving first.' The Austrian population were 'entirely apathetic, want only peace and food and will support any regime assuring these.'[261]

The OSS was unaware that Major General Reinhard Gehlen, head of the Military Intelligence on the Foreign Armies East of the Wehrmacht, had urged Brigadefuehrer Walter Schellenberg (the head of RSHA Amt IV, foreign intelligence), the protégé of Himmler, to take over the organisation of the Nazi resistance. In March 1945, during a three-hour conference, Gehlen told Schellenberg that the Wehrmacht trusted him on this task. The general stated that the resistance would last for two more months before final defeat. Gehlen claimed that Himmler was 'the only man with the necessary imagination and energy' to lead the resistance, and thus to authorise Schellenberg to work with Gehlen and other generals. Gehlen revealed that he would ask for leave, while in reality he would work in secret to build up the resistance army; he had requested a full review of the Polish resistance army to take it as a model. At the end of the meeting, Gehlen asked Schellenberg to talk to Himmler and secure his approval.

Schellenberg told Himmler about Gehlen's plan. Himmler avoided telling him about the plan under Prutzmann and was furious. 'This is complete nonsense, if I should discuss this plan with [General Walther] Wenk [the chief of OKH) I am the first defeatist of the Third Reich. This fact would be served boiling hot to the Fueher. You need not tell this to your Gehlen. You need only explain to him that I strictly refuse to accept the plan. Besides - it is typical of the high class (sic) general staff officer to sit in Frankenstrupp nursing post war plans instead of fighting.' As he told his interrogators, Schellenberg 'quickly changed the subject, otherwise he thought Himmler would not have stopped talking and no-one could have predicted what orders Himmler might have given inspired by a momentary mood.' Schellenberg was not informed of any Nazi resistance

[260] Petersen, Neal H. 'From Hitler's Doorstep: Allen Dulles and the Penetration of Germany' in Chalou, George C. ed. *The Secrets War: The Office of Strategic Services in World War II* (Washington: National Archives and Records Administration, 2002), p.286.
[261] Ibid.

plan or action after this meeting. After the end of the war, Gehlen would offer his services to the Americans to establish a German intelligence organisation; they duly accepted the offer.

In the last months of the war, Dulles managed to secretly negotiate the surrender of SS troops in Northern Italy. Hoettl's reports gave Dulles hope that something similar could be achieved in Austria. Hoettl informed Dulles that he was in contact with a number of German generals, amongst them Albert Kesserling, ready to capitulate. He claimed that Hitler had ordered Kaltenbrunner to arrest Goering. Kaltenbrunner was ready to arrest even Himmler in case he proceeded to a Nazi resistance plan.

After the end of the war and the abolition of the OSS, Dulles returned to his private practice as a lawyer, until he was called to lead the CIA. Molden, the young risk-taking OSS operative, would become the son-in-law of Allen Dulles by marrying Joan, his daughter, in 1948; at that time he was serving as an Austrian diplomat in Washington. He would become an influential publisher in Vienna.

Dulles was a risk-taking spymaster in the sense that he keenly reported exciting but unverifiable information. Indeed, when assessing his secret sources, he relied mainly on instinct and first impressions.

9

Into Vienna

In February and March 1945, RAF and US bombers dropped 80,000 tons of explosive on Vienna; more than 12,000 buildings were destroyed. General Fyodor Tolbukhin, with the 3rd Ukrainian Front, advanced into Austria. Sepp Dietrich commanded the 6th SS Panzer Army, which had to be deployed around Vienna. By the end of March, the NKVD reached the front. Five regiments of the 3rd Ukrainian Army, almost 7,500 troops, had a mission to hunt spies, saboteurs and deserters in the rear. This NKVD would be the first intelligence organisation to be deployed in Vienna and start establishing their networks. By the first days of April the Soviet forces launched their overwhelming assault. The O5 resistance group, an Austrian organisation headed by Carl Szokoll, tried to sabotage Nazi resistance to ensure a quick Soviet victory. Back in 1943, he had met Colonel Claus von Stauffenberg, the officer who placed a bomb in the Führer's headquarters and took part in the July attempt by arresting Nazis in Vienna. Subsequently, Szokoll endured Gestapo interrogation and showed them that he was no conspirator. In late 1944, now Major, he established a group of officers to avert any resistance to a Red Army advance in Vienna, for the city to be spared further destruction. In April, during the chaotic days of Nazi defeat, his role was revealed and he was hunted by the Gestapo but survived - only to be arrested by the Soviet Army and accused of working for US Intelligence.

Stalin took a decision surprising everyone - Churchill, Roosevelt and his successor Truman, and the Austrian resistance. He sent a directive to the 3rd Ukrainian Army on 4 April. Hastily, Stalin had decided to support Karl Renner, a 75-year-old politician. The Russians would tell him that their mission was to destroy the Nazi occupiers and help him to restore democracy.[262]

Born in 1870, Renner was a Social Democrat who had served as Chancellor in 1918-1920 and President of the Parliament in 1931-33. He believed in the union of the German and Austrian republics. The Soviet forces started looking for Renner. He was found in Gloggnitz, a village an

---

[262] Stavka Directive on Karl Renner, 4 April 1945 in Bekes, Csaba et al. eds. *Soviet occupation of Romania, Hungary and Austria, 1944/45- 1948/49* (Budapest: Central European University Press, 2015), p.273.

hour south of Vienna. Renner did not hesitate to turn against the Soviet commander: 'You've come here as liberators...and we welcomed you as such. But if your troops continue to behave like Mongolian hordes, you'll find that the Austrians and, above all, the Viennese are not apt to accept you as friends but as enemies and beasts.'[263] The Soviet commander assured him that the discipline amongst Soviet troops would be preserved and civilians should fear no harm.

Meanwhile, as the Red Army and the SS and Wehrmacht forces clashed, the SOE launched new missions into Austria. An SOE wireless operator was parachuted into the Graz area but 'it was too hot [i.e. hostile] for him and he had to withdraw to the area held by Slovene Partisans where he is now.' In another operation in the Salzburg area, the SOE team did not signal back to their headquarters and thus it was assumed they were captured by the Gestapo. In parallel, secret couriers were dispatched from Switzerland to contact the resistance in Austria. The SOE rank and file was pessimistic that 'several long and detailed reports on the existence of a big coordinated resistance movement known as POEN are in all probability grossly exaggerated and bear the stamp of tendentious émigré wishful thinking.' Archduke Otto boasted of being the leader of a large resistance movement 'which is considered by us [SOE] to be non-existent.'[264]

On the night of 24 April, six Austrian SOE operatives were parachuted into Styria. On 3 May, they contacted the Wehrmacht command in Judenburg and demanded their surrender. The Wehrmacht officers sounded anxious for the British forces to arrive before the Russian advancing lines. 'Events have recently been moving so fast that operation orders have almost had to be changed from hour to hour' read an SOE report.[265] All SOE operatives were ordered that if they were approached by the Austrians they were not to accept their surrender but to contact headquarters for instructions.

Missions' tasks changed from sabotage to intelligence gathering only. The SOE groups were assigned to collect intelligence on the state of roads and railways, identify hostile forces and identify Nazis in hiding preparing a resistance movement against the Allied forces.

Leo Hillman, a courageous SOE veteran and Austrian Jewish refugee, carried out Mission *Electra* under the name Second Lieutenant Charles V. Kennedy. He was dropped on the night of 23-24 March, but lost his

---

[263] Bischof, Günter, *Austria in the First Cold War, 1945-55: The Leverage of the Weak* (London: Palgrave, 1999), p.35.
[264] A.D./X1 to X/A2, 5 April 1945, HS 6/20 TNA.
[265] Note on operational orders, HS 6/22 TNA.

wireless transmitter. He had no other choice but to walk to Vienna.

Once in the capital he reached the apartment of his contacts, a couple who informed him that the socialist underground was 'non-existent'; almost all had been arrested by the Gestapo. There was a growing suspicion between communists and socialists which resulted in non-cooperation against the Nazis. He was given a temporary address. Hillman could not contact the SOE and inform them of any news of the Russian advance toward Vienna. He tried to contact the Austrian resistance to contact the SOE in Italy. A socialist contact brought him to a meeting with resistance leaders in a safe house. There Hillman surprised everybody with a daring plan to raid the Gestapo headquarters at the Hotel *Metropole* at the Morzinplatz:

> 'I told them of my intention to stage a raid on Gestapo headquarters and I also called for open terror against all prominent members of the Nazi party. I was promised the cream of men and took charge of about 130 of them a day later. Most of my men were young deserters from the Wehrmacht who had no other choice but to follow me and obey my orders. They were a highly disciplined body of men who were well-suited for that type of work.' [266]

Nonetheless, by Easter, police and Wehrmacht patrols made it 'practically impossible to move in the streets without being challenged and asked for identity documents.' The resistance and deserters hid in ruins and cellars. Hillman had on him forged identity papers. He wrote:

> 'Two or three days before Easter I entered accompanied by one of my men Gestapo headquarters Hotel *Metropole* to reconnoitre the building in preparation for a hold-up which I intended to start on Easter Sunday. We spent about fifteen minutes inside the premises during which time I found out that the whole of Gestapo headquarters was to be evacuated on Sunday April 1. My intention was to shoot up the place, prevent the files from being destroyed and to capture hostages. It was arranged that a two-ton lorry and another car should take me and twenty-five men disguised as SS-men to the building's entrance and wait there with motors running. I was shocked to hear on Sunday morning that both vehicles

---

[266] Operational report on 'Electra', HS 7/146 TNA.

were requisitioned the previous night by the SS. On account of that I had to abandon the idea and call off the scheme.'[267]

He communicated with Wehrmacht soldiers stationed in the Rennweg barracks and persuaded them to sell their weaponry to the resistance. On 1 April, at a secret meeting with resistance leaders he discussed sabotage and propaganda with flyers. By 3 April, armoured vehicles patrolled the city roads and civilians were compelled to dig trenches. The resistance had commenced sniper attacks on SS units and command posts. Hillman remembered: 'The mass exodus of prominent Nazis which had started a day earlier reached its climax at about midnight when the principal roads were jammed with panicking Nazis pulling their baggage on handcarts, perambulators etc.; at some places they were sniped at by hidden foreign workers and various groups of resistance.'[268] At about 2200 the same day the first artillery shells exploded; the Russian attack had begun.

By Saturday 7 April, the Red Army and the Waffen SS clashed at Simmering; the resistance group headed by Hillman launched attacks against retreating SS troops. The Wehrmacht units were collapsing:

'Mass desertions of Austrian Wehrmacht soldiers had started a couple of days earlier and they enjoyed the help of the civilian population who supplied them with clothing and hid them in their homes and cellars…SS troops were given no assistance whatsoever and were met with open hostility at some places. It is stated that in Favoriten, a district chiefly inhabited by factory workers, wounded SS troops were thrown out of the houses in which they took shelter.'[269]

Resistance groups tried to put pressure on the Waffen SS caught between their fire and the Red Army. In the area between Schachthausgasse-Rennweg barracks and Baumgass 'the SS soon realised that they were caught between two fires and directed at least three furious attacks against them which were held by a handful of stout-hearted army deserters.' At 15 Schimmelgasse SS troops raided a house and killed a fifteen-year-old boy in front of his mother. The resistance groups pinned down the SS detachment, encircling them. The murderer of the boy was apprehended and executed in front of the house of his victim.

Hillman concluded that the resistance could not hold the Waffen SS

---

[267] Ibid; see also 'Report on Austria', 13 September 1945, FO 371/46603 TNA.
[268] Operational report on 'Electra', HS 7/146 TNA.
[269] Ibid.

retreat and decided to go to contact the Russian forces and ask for support:

> 'I left the building Paulusplatz 3 which was besieged by
> SS troops only accompanied by one of my men who spoke
> Russian. We slipped through a back-door into the open and
> by crossing two courtyards and jumping over a couple of
> walls we reached Schlachthausgasse where I shot an SS man
> who tried to stop us. Heavy fire was still being exchanged
> and as we approached the abattoir at St Marx we were met
> with a shower of bullets. I had taken a piece of white cloth
> with me and the fire stopped as soon as I waved it several
> times. Several heavily armed Russians appeared and my
> interpreter explained to them who we were and that we
> needed help at once.'[270]

The SOE officer was escorted to headquarters and interviewed by an NKVD officer who was fluent in English. The Russian agreed to help and immediately dispatched a company and a self-propelled gun. Together with Hillman they arrived in the key area, but the Waffen SS had further withdrawn. Hillman received an invitation to go to the Russian Corps headquarters. There he explained the overall tactical situation and told the Russian staff officers of a message from the members of the Social Democratic Party: they welcomed the Red Army. Hillman was not allowed to return to the field. On 13 April, the battle for Vienna was over.

For three weeks, he was kept under protective custody by the Russians. Resistance groups provided the Russians with lists of the addresses of Nazis. Hillman helped the Russians search flats to arrest Gestapo and Nazi officials. After three weeks he was released. Subsequently a certain General Blagedatov interviewed him and sent Hillman to Wiener Neustad to a transit-centre for former prisoners of war and foreign workers to be repatriated. Hillman did not possess genuine identity papers and had to return to Vienna where he stayed with the resistance.

On 21 May, the NKVD raided the house where he was staying and arrested him; 'In my absence my flat had been searched and I and my companion were taken to NKVD headquarters where we underwent a close interrogation in the course of which I was threatened with shooting if I did not confess to being a "fascist spy".' After an hour and a half, the NKVD received a phone call from Russian army headquarters to release

---

[270] Ibid.

Hillman.[271]

A few days later Hillman met a Belgian nurse in British uniform with the rank of lieutenant at the Klinik Denk. She told him that her name was Madelaine Boncopagnie. She invited Hillman to Linz and he agreed. She was to organise the transport of political prisoners from Dachau to the American zone of occupation. Eventually the Soviet military did not grant permission and she had to return to Vienna. She stayed at an apartment at 23 Operaring Strasse. Hillman stayed with her for the night to avoid being arrested again by the Soviets.

Nonetheless:

> 'on the same night a man whom I knew under the name of Doctor Sigrist and was the head of the British American Relief Association introduced himself to her and told her that she was not supposed to be seen in Vienna; as a British military person she might run into trouble. She believed him – apparently she had heard of him before – and accepted his invitation to stay at his home for a few days after which she would be taken to Linz by Allied officers. I also decided to wait for this opportunity but stayed for the night as it was raining heavily and I would have had a long way back home. I had given her a letter and a message to be sent to SO (M) [the SOE] from Linz in case I should run into trouble. With that she left accompanied by Dr Sigrist. At present he is being kept in police custody in Vienna and is alleged to be an imposter, possibly a member of the SS. He still claims to be an American citizen but it had been proved his real name is not Sigrist but Sieber...'[272]

Hillman never saw the mysterious nurse again. We could conclude that she was a communist or a Soviet agent in search of Nazis. Her stories to Hillman do not sound credible. Next morning, Hillman was arrested by three plain-clothes agents of the Staatspolizei. The janitor of the building at 23 Operaring had contacted the police telling them that a foreigner lived there unregistered. Hillman would have to be patient: 'Although I had mentioned the names of prominent people, amongst them Secretary of State for Social Affairs J. Roehm who would vouch for me, I stayed at the notorious police jail Elizabeth Promenade for six weeks during which

---

[271] Ibid.
[272] Ibid.

time I was kept at the level of starvation and had to share cell with nine Nazis. Six weeks later on 9 July I was released with apologies minus my wristwatch which apparently had been stolen from the file in which it had been kept.' After two weeks he left for Linz to return to Britain with the prisoners of war to be repatriated.[273]

---

[273] Ibid.

10

The Russian

A spymaster would employ all sources possible. NKVD Brigadier Ivan Pavlov, head of the administration of the troops of the 3rd Ukrainian army, responsible for 7,500 NKVD troops, was explicit:

> 'It is recommended to select those members of the local community to work as informants who have the possibility to help us search for people of interest and find them. Such persons would be for example:
> - less active members of National Socialist organisations and groups of bandits - under certain circumstances and if we can be sure that they will cooperate conscientiously
> - members of hostile counterintelligence bodies with good connections to local nationalists and the desire to do penance for their former connections to German National Socialists...'[274]

The Gestapo, SD and the Kriminalpolizei were the 'hostile counterintelligence bodies' whose members could be recruited by the NKVD. Pavlov's troops had to capture spies, 'small hostile groups', Soviet deserters and marauders. Top of the list of people to be arrested were Nazi police officials, commanders of concentration camps and officers of military courts, as well as leading public servants and publishers. The NKVD officers had to bear in mind: 'The principal methods of espionage on the territory of foreign states in which the Red Army operates are the same as those in our national territory. However, the methods for this kind of espionage depend directly on the operational situation and the specific features on the particular country.'[275] In 1946, the MGB (Ministry for State Security) succeeded the NKVD as a foreign intelligence and domestic security apparatus.

MGB Major Pyotr Deryabin, based in Vienna in the early 1950s, who

---

[274] Speech by NKVD Brigadier Ivan Pavlov regarding Espionage Activity, March 1945 in Bekes, et al. eds. *Soviet Occupation of Romania, Hungary and Austria*, p.264.

[275] Ibid., p.263.

defected to US Intelligence in February 1953, was nonetheless proudly stating that the Americans 'cannot really appreciate the diligence with which the Soviets pursued tiny tidbits of information against German Zeppelin agents' or secret agents of other missions. *Zeppelin* was an SS-sanctioned operation to send saboteurs behind the Red Army's lines. Post war the Soviet Intelligence had been looking for former Nazi operators to recruit them, before the Americans, as Deryabin had insisted.

A young diplomat working as personal secretary to the Austrian Foreign Minister, Karl Gruber, was a person of interest for the MGB and the Yugoslav secret service which maintained a presence in Vienna. HIs name was Kurt Josef Waldheim. He was born in 1918 and in 1936-37 completed his national service in the Austrian Army. Afterwards he studied at the Vienna Consular Academy and graduated in 1939, after the Anschluss. Waldheim applied to join the National Socialist German Students League. In early 1941 he was called up by the Wehrmacht and served on the Eastern Front, where he was wounded in the ankle by a grenade in December. His war service with the Army Group E in the Balkans included: interpreter and liaison officer with the 5th Alpine Division (Italy) in April/May 1942; 2nd Assistant Adjutant to the General Staff Quartermaster with Kampfgruppe West in Bosnia in June/August 1942; interpreter to the Italian 9th Army in Tirana, Albania in early summer 1942; 1st Assistant Adjutant to General Staff Chief of Operations in the German liaison staff with the Italian 11th Army and in the staff of the Army Group South in Greece in July/October 1943; 3rd Assistant Adjutant to General Staff Chief Intelligence Officer on the staff of Army Group E in Arksali, Kosovska Mitrovica and Sarajevo from October 1943 to January/February 1945. In 1945, Waldheim surrendered to British forces in Carinthia. He returned to Vienna and completed his studies at the university.

Colonel Anton Kolendic was the Yugoslav spymaster in Vienna under the title deputy chief of the Yugoslav military mission. He claimed that he had received a dossier from the Yugoslav prosecutor for war crimes implicating Waldheim. He, together with the MGB, would try to blackmail him to work for them, otherwise he would be prosecuted. Kolendic insisted that in 1947 the MGB 'realised the weakness of the Austrian communists':

> 'Their political positions were eroding rapidly although they were still in the government...the Russians figured that they could not count on this situation to continue for a long time and therefore began approaching people from the bourgeois parties. They could recruit people by, say,

facilitating the return of your son from a Soviet PoW camp; or by giving food or other favours; or by blackmail. [The Russians] were particularly angry with [Austrian Foreign Minister] Gruber, whom they considered a British agent - not merely a British sympathiser but an agent...I heard [Colonel] Gonda [of the MGB] and other Soviet officers, including generals, talk about an incident that could be staged to eliminate Gruber. Hence their interest in Waldheim, who was Gruber's secretary, working in Gruber's office...I am absolutely certain that Waldheim was recruited at that time. [Another former official who served as a personal aide to Tito said] we had to give him to the Russians.'[276]

Gruber had abandoned the neutrality approach of Renner and sided with London and Washington. In 1947-48 he had been handing in secret assessments of the growing Russian threat to Austria and the West. The Austrian minister was the one who introduced the concept of 'domino theory' in Europe, warning that the fall of Austria to communism would be followed by a general Soviet advance to Western Europe. Evidently, the NKVD had access to these confidential briefings (with or without the aid of Waldheim if he ever was recruited as an informer).

Eventually Colonel Gonda received the dossier on Waldheim. Kolendic was on friendly terms with the Russians. The Yugoslavs were directed not to approach Waldheim themselves.

Waldheim was recommended to Gruber by Fritz Molden, the trusted agent of Allen Dulles, the OSS spymaster in Bern (at that time Molden served as a private secretary to Gruber). He later became publisher of Viennese daily *Die Presse*. Molden was unaware of Waldheim's service in the Intelligence staff of the Wehrmacht high command. Waldheim insisted that in December 1941 a grenade wounded him in the ankle and he was medically discharged. By 1948, Waldheim's career took a meteoric course; he was appointed deputy in the Austrian Embassy in Paris. In 1951, he was named chief of the Ministry of Foreign Affairs personnel and in 1968 Minister for Foreign Affairs. Mirko Milutinovic Tito's long-time chief of staff said: 'I knew that Waldheim had been compromised...Tito did not regard Waldheim as a war criminal...'[277]

In 1971, Waldheim was elected Secretary-General of the United Nations. Washington, London and Beijing opposed his candidacy, but he

---

[276] Doder, Dusko ' '47 Soviet Bloc Bid to recruit Waldheim as Agent Described' *Washington Post*, 30 October 1986.
[277] Ibid.

was strongly supported by Moscow. Indeed, the KGB (the successor of the MGB) focused their activities on good publicity for Waldheim in the Soviet press. Waldheim always denied being approached by the Russians or knowing anything about war crimes.

In early post war Austria, the MGB would not venture into other Allied occupied areas: 'Espionage to be started and carried out only on areas secured by the troops' read the general orders. Intelligence officers should be very cautious: 'The selection of candidates to be recruited and the recruitment of informants itself is to be carried out exclusively by authorised reconnaissance officers, deputies of regiment commanders and their deputies...dossiers to be stored exclusively in the reconnaissance department of troops administration.' It was deemed 'absolutely essential that two reconnaissance officers are present at any meeting with an agent. For safety reasons it is recommended to secure the meeting point by taking appropriate measures.'[278]

The long negotiations with the Americans, British and French led to the demarcation of the occupation zones in Austria and in Vienna. All spymasters had to build up their espionage networks in ruined cities, with no electricity and water, a starving population, almost all families mourning a member fallen in the war and a rising black market which attracted the interest of some Allied soldiers. Soviet counter-intelligence (Smersh) officers held a low opinion of the tradecraft of their American and British counterparts in Vienna. The Americans were hastily trained in intelligence, the British were 'London policemen' while the French ranks were full of communists. A Smersh officer (writing under the pen name Romanov) remarked in hie memoirs that 'sometimes if we were lucky we even recruited Allied personnel themselves. Smersh took into account the strong pro-Soviet feelings which were then current among citizens of the western democracies.'[279] Servicemen felt lonely in the ruined city. The Smersh financed the 'procurers of girls'; a number of 'meeting houses' were under close surveillance.[280]

In any case, the Soviets deemed the British devious. In Styria, British authorities handed to the Russians General Krasnow, a former leader of the White Army in the civil war, and Shkuro wrote that 'the British lured them, about two thousand men in all, into a trap by inviting them supposedly to take part in a conference with Field Marshal Alexander. I

---

[278] Speech by NKVD Brigadier Ivan Pavlov regarding Espionage Activity, March 1945 in Bekes, et al. eds. *Soviet Occupation of Romania, Hungary and Austria*, p.263.
[279] Romanov, A.I. *Nights are Longest There: Smersh from the Inside* (London: Hutchinson, 1972, pp.158-161.
[280] Ibid., p.160.

found out these details later from our NKGB agents, who had been with Krasnow for a long time.' In 1945, in Linz, East Tyrol, British occupation authorities handed over to the Russians men, women and children, Soviet citizens now refugees in Austria; many women and their children were drowned in the Drava river, seeking to avoid capture by the Soviets.[281]

Romanov wrote of a mysterious woman who worked as an 'identifier' of potential agents. She was a Russian woman aged 28-30 and worked in Vienna; she was earlier an interpreter in the SD and mistress to a SS officer. Romanov wrote about her:

> 'I met her several times, always in the company of our plain-clothes officers. She was tall, with a boyish figure and her skin was the colour of white marble. Her eyes were always made up. A captain friend of mine told me that in bed she was capable of tricks that simply took one's breath away. He also said that she smoked either hashish or opium, I can't remember which. She often travelled without our officers to Vienna and to other towns, some in the western zones. The last time I saw her she was going into an open Admiral with Austrian number plates, which belonged to our operational branch. She was wearing a magnificent fur cape and had diamond rings on her fingers. Her escort, who was a Chekist officer, was dressed in a typical 'western bourgeois suit'…It must have been a month later that she shot herself with a pistol she had snatched from a driver-sergeant whose attention had wandered for a moment. The sergeant was subsequently tried by a Smersh tribunal.'[282]

Meanwhile, the OSS Colonel Charles Thayer was the best man available for US Intelligence in Vienna in 1945. Since 1937 he had served as a diplomat in Moscow and knew all about what it was like to be watched by the NKVD. He was fluent in Russian and during the war served with the OSS mission in Belgrade. He took an active part in the negotiations with the Russians on the demarcation of the occupied zones. He was one of the few who could understand Russian tactics, but did not have many spies at his disposal.

He was always trying to find out about Russian intentions and capabilities and his secret service opponents at the time, but the US

---

[281] Ibid., pp.151, 154.
[282] Ibid., p.175.

Intelligence machinery was weakening (the OSS would be abolished in October 1945). He wrote in his memoirs about how he uncovered the location of the NKVD headquarters in Vienna: 'I often tried to find out what the position of the GPU [NKVD] troops was in the chain of command.'[283] One day he asked Field Marshal Ivan

, the commander of Soviet forces, to allow him to go hunting in the Soviet occupation zone. The Russian agreed and soon Thayer was handed a special pass. He left with a 'prince', a von Hapsburg (though he does not name him in the memoirs, he could be either Felix or Carl Ludwig, the brothers of the last crown prince, Otto von Hapsburg) but once in the estate, early in the morning Thayer was asked to visit - under NKVD escort - the local unit's headquarters. Thayer protested but he had no choice. His pass did not deter the NKVD officer in charge from asking him questions and implying that he was spying on the positions of Russian units. The Russian officer told Thayer of the United States changing their policy towards Russia and wondered why. Thayer denied such a thing but remained angry. The Russian showed him a communist newspaper - 'See what you Americans are up to' - the British and the US were blamed for subverting the communist government in Prague. Eventually Thayer was released for a while only to be arrested again and led to the divisional headquarters for a new round of interrogation. He again showed his pass signed by Konev. The NKVD officer asked him: 'Of course you know how many divisions we have in the area, don't you, Colonel?' He continued: 'Well, you know the designation of the local division, of course, and now you have even learned where our headquarters are. Have you been able to make any estimate of our troop strength?'[284] By that time Thayer was frustrated, and replied that if he was accused of spying he would call US General Mark Clark, the commander of US forces in Austria, and file an official protest.

The interrogator replied, 'But we have to be careful with strangers.' Thayer and von Hapsburg were allowed to leave. They climbed on their US Army jeep and drove to Vienna. Soon, Thayer made a mistake. He stopped and asked for directions from a Soviet soldier. They were in the Soviet zone. The soldier lost no time: he pointed his bayonet at Thayer's stomach, and an officer soon appeared and led them to the town hall. Thayer was more than furious and demanded the soldier apologise in public. The Russian officers pleaded for a bargain; an apology in the town hall in front of them. They told Thayer that a public apology would

---

[283] Thayer, Charles, *Hands across the Caviar* (London: Michael Joseph, 1953), p.188.
[284] Ibid., p.193.

damage the Soviet prestige in the eyes of the Austrians. Thayer accepted this and the soldier was brought in front of him, shaking in fear. The American officer wanted to leave, and the Russians were more than happy. But Thayer was afraid of being arrested once more on the streets - it had turned into a very bad day for him, full of interrogation experiences. So he asked for an NKVD Soviet escort to take them to the US headquarters - his presence would deter other Russians from arresting them on their way. The Soviet officers keenly agreed. Thayer wrote:

> 'As we drove into Vienna I asked our young GPU [NKVD] man whether he wanted to be dropped at Marshal Koniev's (sic) headquarters at the Grand Hotel.
>
> "If you don't mind, I'd rather you dropped me at our headquarters," he replied.
>
> "'Our' headquarters? Where's that?"
>
> "You know, the Secret Police building over near the river."
>
> I had the answer to the question of what control a Russian field commander had over the political police. But it was certainly the hard way to find out.'[285]

In September 1945, an OSS X2 branch (counterintelligence) officer took a risky assignment. Dressed in civilian clothes, being fluent in German, he entered the Soviet zone in Vienna. When he returned, he claimed that he had made contacts and had revealing conversations with Russian officers, boasting 'with a good knowledge of Russian and two bottles of vodka you can get anything you want.'[286] The OSS headquarters in Salzburg assumed the mission a success, but this was not the case. Underestimating Russian counterintelligence would be a lethal mistake.

Camps for refugees and displaced persons were established. Usually single Ukrainians, Georgians, Armenians, Azerbaijans, Caucasians, Hungarians, Slovakians, former soldiers under the Wehrmacht or the Waffen SS would be found in these camps. They aimed first to persuade British and US Intelligence officers who interrogated them for war crimes that they could be of use in espionage against the Soviets as long as they were offered protection. By spring 1947, just before the formation of the

---

[285] Ibid., pp.193-195.
[286] Quoting 'Operational Status Report SICE, September 1945, 24 September 1945, RG 226 entry 215 box 8 in Alvarez, David & Eduard Mark, *Spying Through a Glass Darkly: American Espionage against* the Soviet Union (Lawrence KA: University Press of Kansas, 2016), p.153.

CIA, US senior military intelligence officers bitterly complained: 'intelligence derived from such Ukrainian groups is [not] worth the time and effort which would necessarily have to be expended on such a project. Experience has shown that information derived from such organizations has been both low-grade and ideologically biased.' Indeed, 'it has been impossible so far to elicit from our SB [Ukrainian] contacts the names of any of their subsources - this in spite of repeated attempts to get such data from them. Time and again mention has been made by our Ukrainian sources of the existence of "bunkers," supposedly small intelligence cells, in the American Zone of Germany as well as Czechoslovakia.'[287]

In Vienna, in October 1945, Project *Crown* was initiated: two arrested Russian Intelligence agents who had worked for the Abwehr claimed that they maintained a network of 300 agents and informed inside the Soviet Union. The Strategic Services Unit (SSU), the successor of the OSS, took up their handling, but in spring 1946 phone taps revealed the truth: they were heard celebrating 'how easy it was to fool the Americans.' Kauder, the chief Abwehr agent who initially recommended them, told the Americans that he believed that they were Russian double agents.[288]

Chancellor Renner feared Soviet espionage. In August 1945, he told an official whom he knew that was in contact with the OSS in Vienna that the Russians had placed many Austrian communists in the police - a sum of two battalions of communists hardened by partisan warfare with Tito and led by the current communist minister of the interior Franz Honner. The Chancellor insisted that his name not be put on paper as a source, fearing a Russian spy amongst the OSS staff. Indeed, from the Mitrokhin Archive, we know that at least three police officials were working for the NKVD: a secret agent codenamed 'Eduard' was recruited in 1945; 'Ventseyev' in 1946; and 'Peter' in 1952.[289] The 'kidnap campaign' of Austrians and other nationalities in Vienna was based on information supplied by communist police officials and public servants. A total of 400 people were estimated to have been kidnapped by Russians and Americans in 1945-1948. All Allied secret services had access to Austrian police records. Nonetheless, chaos ruled. The Americans complained:

---

[287] Quoting CE Operational Progress Report No. 5," 17 February 1947in CIA Draft Working Paper 'Long Experience in the Anti-Soviet Game; p. 25, available at:
<https://www.cia.gov/library/readingroom/docs/CIA%20AND%20NAZI%20WAR%20CRIM .%20AND%20COL.%20CHAP.%20%201-10,%20DRAFT%20WORKING%20PAPER_0006.pdf> accessed 23 July 2019.
[288] Report 12 September 1946 'Crown case' RG 226 entry 210 box 368 sited in Alvarez & Eduard, *Spying Through a Glass Darkly*, p.157.
[289] Andrew and Mitrokhin, *The Mitrokhin Archive*, p.363.

'It is in no way surprising that numerous reports obtained from Austrian police channels crop up now and then from two or three independent sources. An informant who has what he considers a choice bit of information, gossip or fabrication has little trouble in selling it (at a nominal price, of course) to one or more *Polizeidirektions* in Austria, and because each of the *Polizeidirektions* are penetrated by probably every US agency in Austria (and unfortunately not US agencies alone), the report gets wide dissemination. To further complicate the picture, the *Polizeidirektion* of, for instance, Salzburg, will immediately send the report to the *Stadtspolizei* in Vienna, from where it again gets into the extensive dissemination stream.'[290]

The Americans were interested in the services of Johann Sanitzer, the Gestapo spymaster. He would appear at a Vienna court in November 1948 to be tried not for war crimes but under the Denazification laws. The Americans were surprised though: 'the Russians made an attempt to get hold of him [Sanitzer] because they require him as a witness (for what I don't know)', wrote the American Intelligence officer who had taken up Sanitzer's case. He added: 'The Austrian court refused on the pretext that an accusation has already been made against him. Now he [Sanitzer] fears that the Russians will extradite him and put him to trial when the court no longer has a pretext or after he has served his time under the present sentence.' Sanitzer asked the Americans to arrange his trial to take place in Linz, claiming that the witnesses for his defence were afraid of the Russians and their 'expected reprisals'.[291]

Under Project *Caviar*, the SSU employed a German collaborator of Georgian descent, named Chalva Odicharia, an ardent nationalist with a 'too dark past'. Two NKVD informers spotted him in a refugee camp and brought him to NKVD headquarters. His choice was to work for them against US Intelligence. He agreed, but upon being released he approached the OSS and offered to work as a double agent. The OSS handlers developed a plan: the Georgian was to go back to the Russians

[290] CIA Chief of Station (Karlsruhe) to Chief (Foreign Division), 7 April 1951, available at: <https://ia801307.us.archive.org/27/items/BolschwingOttovon/BOLSCHWING,%20OTTO %20(VON)%20%20%20VOL.%201_0167.pdf > accessed 13 August 2019.

[291] Letter to Major James Milano, 10 November 1948, available at: <https://ia800206.us.archive.org/30/items/HoettlWilhelm/HOETTL,%20WILHELM%20%2 0%20VOL.%203_0020.pdf> accessed 25 July 2019.

and ask for their support to establish an anti-Russian émigré organisation in Vienna. Then, he would contact the Americans with Russian permission to gather intelligence; in parallel he would allow US Intelligence access to all his developing knowledge of his Russian handlers. The Russians were presented with the Georgian's proposal and asked for time to get authorisation from Moscow. The Americans described Major Valentin Rumiantsev, the one who handled Odicharia, as 'an ambitious officer, of keen intelligence, an open mind, and great resourcefulness.'[292]

Odicharia remained at large. But French military police arrived at the US occupation zone and asked for him to be handed over; he belonged to a Georgian 'Gestapo' that had operated in occupied Paris - he was a war criminal. The OSS remained excited by the prospects of their plan and decided to protect him, so they sent him to stay for a while in the Russian sector. The NKVD major accepted this. Almost a month later, a detachment of the Counter-Intelligence Corps (CIC, US Army) appeared wanting for Odicharia to be handed over to them as a war criminal. Again, the OSS officers in charge of the case risked everything and ordered him to remain in the Soviet sector for protection. Eventually, Rumiantsev ordered Odicharia's arrest and led him to a Soviet camp, where most probably he was executed as a war criminal against the Soviet Union in November 1945.

The top priority for US Intelligence was the Soviet order of battle. Fear grew that Stalin would threaten Austria and Western Europe. US Military Intelligence concentrated on the order of battle as the CIA was about to be formed. In early 1947 a Tass journalist was recruited as a spy under the codename 'Joy'; he recruited a Russian army major and together they would be the main two sources of Soviet military intelligence. The third, mass source would be Soviet army deserters. One CIA officer commented, 'at the time, first-hand information on the USSR was so hard to come by that the lowest dog-faced private deserting from the Red Army was considered a valuable source and immediately flown out of Austria to a defector center in Germany.'[293] Deserters carried with them genuine identity papers; most useful, in themselves for future secret missions into the Soviet occupied zones, as well as for creating near perfect copies.

---

[292] Caviar Project progress Reports, RG 226 entry, 216 Box 3, sited in Alvarez and Eduard, *Spying Through a Glass Darkly*, pp.162.

[293] Hood, *Mole: The True Story of the First Russian Intelligence Officer Recruited by the CIA*, (New York: W.W. Norton, 1982), pp. 30-31; Milano, James V. & Brogan, Patrick, *Soldiers, Spies and the Ratline: Americans Undeclared War against the Soviets* (London: Brassey's 2000).

Espionage involved the recruitment of poorly-paid cleaning ladies working in Russian headquarters in order to secure the contents of wastebaskets (Project *Paperchase*) in 1947. The Soviets had been employing clerks and cleaning ladies in the US and British and French military administration buildings. Whenever the Americans found a clerk or a cleaning lady already working for the Russians, they tried to recruit him or her as a double agent to spread false information. But they had to manage the protests of the spies that they had a family waiting them in the Soviet occupation zone and were really afraid for their lives. The Americans opted also for 'confusion agents': John Richardson, the CIA station chief, kept 'an eye open for "confusion agents," ordinary citizens tricked up to look like spies and waste investigation time. He became an expert on the bars and back alleys of the [Vienna] Innere Stadt' his son wrote later.[294]

Project *Claptrap* had an Austrian medical specialist directed by US Intelligence eliciting information from the Russian military personnel he treated. Under Project *Sybille*, US Army Intelligence handled a former Wehrmacht officer and his spy ring to identify NKVD informers in refugee camps. Project *Syracuse* concentrated on the recruitment of an Austrian financial adviser of the Renner government.

Moscow was shocked with the general elections of 25 November 1945. The Austrian Communist Party received only 5 per cent of the votes; a mere four seats in a 165-seat parliament. The Peoples Party under Leopold Figl won, with 49.8 per cent, ready to abandon the neutral policy of Renner. The communists were assigned only the Ministry of Electrification. Figl ordered large scale purges in the police services.

Nonetheless, the Ministry of State Security maintained trusted sources with access to police files and records. Russian spymasters opted for more aggressive tactics and strikes against US and British Intelligence. After all, Vienna and Austria were too small places for spies to hide.

The target was Richard Kauder, a former Abwehr officer who had developed a network during the war which channelled Soviet disinformation into the Wehrmacht. After some time, he had realised that he was passing his masters disinformation but continued in order not to lose his status - and possibly his life. At the end of the war, he offered his services to the OSS. They took him over as a key source, a spymaster directing all his sources (real and imaginary) against the Soviet occupation zone and Eastern European countries.

---

[294] Richardson, John H. *My Father The Spy: An Investigative Memoir* (New York: Harper Collins, 2005), p.83.

In 1946, Kauder worked for the SSU and was installed in an apartment in Salzburg. One early morning in January, an Austrian police officer in plain clothes, a middle-aged man, visited him. He introduced himself as Joseph Wiesinger. He asked him about his connection with US Intelligence and his wartime record with the Abwehr. Kauder declined to answer questions from a man who seemed to know many things about him. In reply, Wiesinger told him that he was about to propose a business deal, that he conducted no police investigation and was just looking into Kauder's past as a potential business partner. Wiesinger visited Kauder several times. He was followed by Kauder's driver, who found that he reported to the headquarters of the Soviet mission in the city. Ostensibly, he reported everything Kauder had told him.

Early in the morning in late January, two black sedans parked in front of the apartment block where Kauder was living. Three men climbed the stairs and the others remained watchful on the street. The man in charge wore a US Military Police uniform. Kauder's girlfriend answered the door. They were looking for him; she replied that she did not know where he was. They searched the apartment and found a radio transmitter and took it with them. They told her to tell him to stay in the apartment for his security and that they would come back.

She rushed downstairs after they had left and waited for Kauder to return. When he appeared at the street corner, she informed him about the visit. Kauder contacted his SSU handlers and inquiries to the US military confirmed that no police had been sent to Kauder's.

The Americans and Kauder decided to hit back. Later that day, Wiesinger called Kauder on the phone asking him to meet him at the Hotel Bristol. Kauder replied that they had better meet at his house. Already, a detachment of armed SSU officers and enlisted men were in the street and there were three in Kauder's bedroom. The unsuspicious Wiesinger agreed.

Two sedans with Soviet traffic plates appeared. A man in US Military Police uniform appeared with two others and reached Kauder's apartment. As soon as Kauder's girlfriend opened the door, the Americans pointed their pistols at the Russians. They did not offer any resistance. It was pointless. Major Mihail Yankowski was the 'US Military Police officer'. One 'civilian' wore a Red Army captain's uniform underneath his trench coat. The third man was an Austrian communist. Outside, their escort members were arrested; they wore Soviet army uniforms beneath their civilian attire. One Russian ran and escaped arrest.

The Russians were taken to SSU headquarters and photographed. A crisis meeting of US senior officers resulted in the resolution to hand them over to the Russians for the kidnap attempt. Major Yankowski maintained that he alone planned and executed this operation against a known Nazi war criminal. The Russians were transferred to Soviet custody on 25 January. A day earlier, someone tried to kidnap Kauder's girlfriend on the street by pushing her into a car; she ran away. Kauder was rushed to a US camp for protection, but he could no longer direct his network for intelligence collection in the Soviet Union, Bulgaria, Hungary and Yugoslavia.

CIC informants stated on several occasions in 1946-47 and 1948-1949 that attempts were made to kidnap Kauder. A CIC report, dated 22 March 1950, stated that Kauder was a homosexual and 'on this basis the Soviets once tried to kidnap him by trying to entice him by means of another person of similar tendencies to Enns where he was to be taken into custody and dragged across the demarcation line. This attempt, made in 1949, failed.' [295] The CIC reported on 21 March 1951 that Hans Kliemann, a former Abwehr officer, was suspected of working for the Soviets while Kauder was 'professionally associated with him'. In late summer 1951, Kauder was approached by Victor Altmann, an Austrian and naturalised British subject who considered working for SIS in Berlin. Kauder agreed to work for him to set up a spy ring in Austria. CIC reported in July 1952 that Altmann continued meeting Kauder in Saltzburg to discuss intelligence activities. A CIC report of 13 February 1953 stated that Kauder worked for SIS and US Intelligence until November 1951 'when he was dropped for submitting false information.' Altmann was now deemed to work for Israeli Intelligence in Austria. He continued meeting with Kauder. It was 'also rumoured that Kauder is or was working for the "National Liga", a Communist front group in Austria, however, this remains unverified' read an intelligence report. [296]

Meanwhile, the Russian forces were embarrassed by defections to the British and the Americans. In October 1948, two Soviet pilots, Anatoly Porfiryevich Borzov and Petr Afanasyevich Pirogov, flew a Soviet TU-2 bomber to the US occupation zone of Austria and asked for asylum. The Americans were surprised and did not know what to do with the bomber. The British insisted that in future similar episodes a team of experts would be ready to survey Soviet technology before returning the aircraft. Surprisingly, both pilots asked to be repatriated; they were executed by the MGB.

---

[295] Chief of Mission (Germany) to Chief of Ease (Salzburg) 12 March 1953, available at: <https://ia801309.us.archive.org/21/items/KAUDERRICHARDVOL2-0072/KAUDER%2C%20RICHARD%20%20%20VOL.%202_0072.pdf> accessed 26 July 2019.

[296] Ibid.

Boris Ivanovich Baklanov, an MGB investigator, defected in July 1947 in Vienna; he offered US Intelligence information about his assignments. In August 1947, two Soviet Intelligence translators, Mikhail Filipovich Denisov and Veronika Feodorovna Takacs, escaped to Czechoslovakia and asked for help from the British Embassy in Prague; the British mediated on the defectors' behalf in contact with the Americans. The following August, a young interpreter defected from an MGB counterintelligence unit to British forces in Germany. His debriefing was made available to the CIC. In 1949 in Vienna, Intelligence officer Vadim Ivanovich Shelaputin defected to the British and eventually emigrated to Britain and worked for the BBC.

MGB hit back; or one could say a US operation went wrong. On the night of October 30 1948, Soviet soldiers kidnapped and eventually beat to death Irving Ross, an American working for the Economic Cooperation Administration (the US agency to administer the US economic aid under the European recovery programme drafted by US Secretary of State George Marshall). His Russian girlfriend, Dana Superina, was also beaten but she escaped and was protected by the Americans. The *New York Times* (7 December 1948) claimed that the US Army in Austria feared escalation and another crisis like Berlin and that was why they did not retaliate immediately. As of today (2021) the files of the activities of Irving Ross remain classified.

The first post war SIS station chief in Vienna was George Young, an aggressive operator. He established a network of train watchers to keep track of the Soviet transfer of industrial machinery as well as of war materiel and troops. Decades later, he boasted in an interview, 'Keeping the Russians annoyed is rather an important part of intelligence work...We are trying to breed insecurity and uncertainly about their own people.'[297] Young was most proud of an operation he organised inside the Soviet zone, almost next to a checkpoint. A German had told him that the Wehrmacht had hidden a cache of aerial photographs of Soviet Union territories in this location. Young made a newsagent delivery of adult magazines at the checkpoint; the soldiers were preoccupied in reading these while his agents dug up and found the cache.

Young was wondering why some 'promising cases', one involving a Russian general in Vienna ostensibly willing to work for SIS, did not materialise. Anthony Cavendish (an SIS officer at that time) wrote in his memoirs:

---

[297] Quoted in Corera, *The Art of Betrayal*, p.28.

'It was only after Philby had been asked to resign [in 1951] that something clicked. Looking up the files, he [Young] found that either Philby or his friend David Footman, who resigned at the same time, had pooh-poohed all the suggestions [for commencing operations in Vienna].'[298]

Philby had returned to Vienna in late summer 1946 for his former wife and spy Litzi to sign the divorce papers. It was as strange as the end of a movie; the spy returned to the city that inspired him - witnessing the communist riots in 1934 and helping his comrades as a secret courier - to become a spy.

Young would write in an SIS circular in the late 1950s, when he was serving as vice chief of the SIS:

'It is the spy who has been called on to remedy the situation created by the deficiencies of ministers, diplomats, generals and priests. Men's minds are shaped of course by their environments and we spies, although we have our professional mystique, do perhaps live closer to the realities and hard facts of international relations than other practitioners of government.'[299]

In 1948, a new station chief, Peter Lunn, arrived in the city. He explored ways to access the intelligence of Russian military deployments. In Prague, the communists had taken over the government; in the streets of Vienna, rumours were rife that Stalin's next move would be a coup in Austria; in Berlin the Soviet blockade continued. In Vienna, the CIA station was examining plans for facilitating the escape of personnel dressed in traditional Tyrolean outfits. This was not a comic episode but proof of spymasters getting panicked with few resources of their own; until 1952 there was no Russian speaking CIA officer in Vienna.

Throughout 1947, a food crisis led Austrians into desperation. From March 1946 to June 1947, UNRRA supplied 65 per cent of food rations. However, a combination of factors such as adverse weather, a very poor potato crop (a major part of the Austrian diet), and the fact that UNRRA stopped shipments caused severe shortages. Inflation skyrocketed and

---

[298] Cavendish, Anthony, *Inside Intelligence: The Revelations of an MI6 Officer* (London: Harper Collins, 1997), p.196.
[299] Quoted in Macintyre, Ben, *A Spy Among Friends: Kim Philby and the Great Betrayal* (New York: Bloadway Books, 2015), p.185.

talks for an Austrian State Treaty (for the country to become once again a sovereign state) failed due to Soviet intransigence. By April, the government under Chancellor Figl was unable to distribute rations. The first food riots and strikes took place on 5 May. Communists escalated their attacks against the government. Figl, exaggerating, claimed an attempted communist coup. The British, Americans and French were not openly supporting the government. The Soviets too did not escalate tension. In September, the Central Intelligence Group (the predecessor of the CIA) distributed an alarming report that warned of general strikes in late September with the use of communist shock troops to claim to restore order but effectively to seize power and form a communist-dominated cabinet. Nonetheless an official of the CIA or a top-secret source whose name is not declassified added: 'it is recommended that the above unconfirmed information be treated with reserve.'[300]

The strikes did not bring the collapse of the Austrian government. Ominous secret reporting continued. A secret source of the CIA warned that for the last two weeks (early May 1948) the Central Committee of the Austrian Communist Party had 'begun to issue pistols - allegedly Walthers - to Party officials. Distribution is not determined by the rank of the individual in the Party but is based upon a Party evaluation of his reliability. At the present time (11 May 1948), it appears that all reliable Communist officials in Vienna down to the level of *Zelenleiter* (cell leaders) have been so armed.'[301] The same applied with the arming of right wing members. SIS officer Anthony Cavendish had been bringing small arms in his car to groups destined to become a government backup paramilitary force in case of emergency. The SIS planning entailed strategic demolition; technicians had been dispatched to arrange for the destruction of Austrian industrial and communication infrastructures in case of a Russian invasion.

British and US Intelligence operatives were surprised; in 1948, the communist English-language agency *Telepress* of Prague published a report revealing 'the USA had promised the Austrian "reactionary" circles through Mr Dulles to supply them with arms to fight against the communist danger and to equip an already existing anti-communist militia. [Austrian police officials assumed that] this announcement may be

---

[300] 'Plans for Communist Action in Austria', 18 September 1947, available at:
<https://www.cia.gov/library/readingroom/docs/CIA-RDP82-00457R000900440001-7.pdf> accessed 30 July 2019.
[301] 'Arming of Communist Party officials in Vienna' 11 May 1948, available at:
<https://www.cia.gov/library/readingroom/docs/CIA-RDP82-00457R001500420008-5.pdf> accessed 30 July 2019.

attributed to Peter Smollett, the *Times* correspondent in Vienna.'

French Intelligence operatives uncovered a secret forty-page plan for a takeover in Vienna by the Austrian Communist Party. The Communists assumed that the Western powers would not interfere in their coup.

Under Operation Squirrel Cage the CIA designated parachute drop zones for the supply of war materiel and backup networks. The CIA station received 'an elaborate report about a Soviet plan to invade Austria' from a case officer who had contacted a secret source at the Austrian Ministry of Foreign Affairs. John Erhardt, the US Minister in Vienna, was duly informed; the report was cabled to the CIA headquarters at Langley, prompting high level consultations. A senior CIA officer flew to Vienna in person to see the secret source and interrogate him. Eventually the Austrian confessed that he had made it up; the Soviet plan was a forgery.

Meanwhile, General Geoffrey Keys, the US forces' commander in Austria, demanded that the Austrian police be armed, to counter the Soviet threat. The available gendarmerie was 'more on paper than actual,' he assumed. In 1949 he urged for the secret stockpiling of arms for the gendarmerie. The recruitment was accelerated for the build up of a secret army. In their bid to find experienced Intelligence officers to man the newly-established Austrian police and paramilitary units, the authorities accepted the application of veteran soldiers. Karl Josef Silberbauer joined the Vienna police in 1954. In 1945-46 he had served a 14-month prison sentence for transporting Jews to concentration camps; he took part in the Holocaust. After his release he was a spy for US Intelligence on the Soviet occupation zones in Austria and Germany. Silberbauer did not only escort Jews to concentration camps; on 4 August 1944, Silberbauer, then an SS-Oberscharfuehrer in Amsterdam, led Dutch policemen into the old building on 263 Prinsengracht Street, arresting Anne Frank and her family, who perished in a concentration camp - her father, Otto, survived.

Meanwhile, an Austrian employee in telecommunications told a British Intelligence officer that the telephone cable serving Soviet headquarters ran under the British and French sectors of the city. Upon being informed of this, Lunn (the SIS station chief) asked for the blueprints and conceived the construction of tunnels to reach the cables and tap them. Vienna's streets were dangerous places to walk; the kidnapping campaign continued. Beneath the streets, British military engineers and Intelligence personnel had to dig as safely and as quietly as they could, and they had to calculate exactly where their tunnel would end, at the cables' main boxes.

Sir Harold Caccia, the former Chairman of the Joint Intelligence Committee, was appointed British minister in Vienna. Lunn informed him about his scheme, and he concurred that the results (information about the

171

possible Russian military threat) outweighed any risks. The operation took the code name *Classification/ Conflict* and was kept secret from the CIA; three tunnels were opened in total (operations *Conflict, Sugar* and *Lord*) and on three days a week recorded tapes were flown to London for analysis and incorporation of the information acquired into the threat estimates. In London a group of 100 White Russian and Polish émigrés took over the translation of the intercepted discussions, seeking to unearth more information. Nonetheless, amongst them, some had been recruited by the NKVD back in the 1930s.

The Americans had a source reporting Soviet telephone monitoring in Vienna in November 1948, but it is not known if they shared their reports with Lunn. One report told of the activities of the telecommunications building in Vienna:

> 'Soviet authorities had installed recording machines in Room 105 of the monitoring office. Conversations in French and English are monitored and Austrian interpreters are called upon from time to time to determine the relative importance of calls, since there are not sufficient recorders to cover all the lines tapped in Room 105... Rooms 105, 106, and 107 are used by the Soviets to tap Vienna city calls routed to them from their agents in the various city exchanges. This official [the secret source] had not heard that recording machines were being used.
>
> 'Room 105 is known to the Austrian employees as the room of the Soviet experts. All important proceed intercepts are brought there for transmittal to two Soviet officers. If both are absent, such intercepts are taken by an Austrian employee to the Soviet Censorship headquarters in Vienna IV, Technikerstrasse 5. Austrians are not allowed in the building, but they ask for the Zensurstelle and a Soviet official comes to the door and accepts the intercept.
>
> 'Telephone monitors were instructed during the week of 4-10 October 1948 to watch especially for calls concerning border crossing from Czechoslovakia, discussion of the Marshall Plan, and compensation transactions with [not declassified].'[302]

---

[302] 'Soviet Telephone Monitoring in Vienna' 16 November 1948, available at: <https://www.cia.gov/library/readingroom/docs/CIA-RDP82-00457R002000610003-3.pdf> accessed 30 July 2019.

Lunn, the spymaster who quietly and efficiently spied on the Russian military in crammed-with-spies Vienna had his nemesis: Kim Philby. In early 1963, he was serving as chief of the SIS station in Beirut where Philby had been working as a journalist since 1956. The previous chief and friend of Philby, Nicholas Elliot, failed to get a confession in return for immunity from prosecution. On 16 January 1963, Lunn asked Philby on the phone to report to the British Embassy; Philby feared arrest and an interrogation. He did not go to the Embassy. His house was not put under surveillance. Next day, Philby had his customary drinks at St George's bar. He did not look in a hurry. His wife, Eleanor, saw him: 'In the late afternoon, Kim grabbed his raincoat saying he had an appointment and would be back around six, in plenty of time to change for the Balfour-Pauls' party.' Glen Balfour-Paul was first secretary at the embassy. At about the time Philby left the house a rainstorm hit Beirut. About an hour later Philby called home. His son Harry picked up the phone and told Eleanor: 'Daddy's going to be late. He says he'll meet you at the Balfour-Pauls' at eight.' Eleanor assumed that Philby was about to meet a contact and that he was still working for SIS. At the party, she was alone; Philby had not come. She returned home and started worrying. Around midnight, she called the embassy asking for Lunn; she knew that he was working for SIS. She asked him if he knew where Philby was; she was worrying that something had happened to him with such bad weather. Lunn froze on hearing her question. He rushed to Eleanor's flat and asked her if Philby had taken something with him. In the early morning, Lunn reached Philby's house but during the storm of the previous night, Philby had boarded a Soviet cargo ship, the *Dolmatova*.

George Blake, a key KGB spy, was involved in the operation *Classification* and told his handlers about it; he gave a paper with technical details to a KGB contact in London in October 1953. SIS intelligence officer Anthony Cavendish wrote that the beginning of the end of the tunnels operation was an episode in central Vienna. A tram passing over the tunnel caused its collapse. British Intelligence managed to hush up this very public incident. No doubt it was nothing short of a miracle that in a small city like Vienna, occupied by four powers, with myriad spies and informers, the secret of the British tunnels (construction, maintenance and the tapping of Soviet lines) was kept from 1948 to October 1953.

The Russian spymasters had to deliberate on Blake's intelligence at a time when Moscow was in chaos and terror; on 5 March 1953 Stalin had died. The lethal race for his seat was on, with key contenders being Lavrentiy Beria (the notorious NKVD head) and Nikita Khrushchev, who eventually won. On 26 June, Beria was arrested at a Presidium meeting which Khrushchev orchestrated. In December, Beria was executed. Khrushchev started installing his own spymasters.

In 1951, the CIA station in Vienna began planning the same type of operation (tunnelling into the Soviet sector to intercept communications) and the British informed the Americans out of fear in case the latter exposed operation *Classification* by mistake. The same type of operation would be organised in Berlin; but again, Blake would inform the Russians about it.

The KGB did not inform the GRU about the tunnels in Vienna and in Berlin (constructed by a joint CIA-SIS operation) in order to avoid any leak about the name of the spy in the British ranks. No disinformation was spread by the Soviets; they did not have the time and resources to invent and implement disinformation on such a scale (hundreds of daily telephone and teleprinter communications). After all, the Korean War (1950-1953) was the immediate politico-military priority for London, Washington and Moscow. No doubt Moscow was worried with the formation of NATO in 1949, but Soviet self-confidence (and Western fear) was boosted with the successful test of atomic weapons the same year.

The Russian spymasters continued exerting pressure on the Austrian government and Anglo-American Intelligence. In 1948, Austrian Undersecretary Paul Katscher was kidnapped. Also, police detective Anton Marek, a leading anti-communist official at the Austrian Ministry of the Interior responsible for the police, was arrested by the MGB. The Americans assumed 'the Soviet aim' was 'to weaken the Austrian police and the Ministry of the Interior.'[303] Marek was accused of anti-communist activities and held until 1955. Together with Marek another detective was arrested, Franz Kiridus. They both were key officers of a police-paramilitary unit called Group 5; in cooperation with Anglo-American Intelligence they armed teams with weapons and explosives to take action in case of a communist coup or Soviet invasion.[304]

On 5 November 1948, at the Enns bridge, St. Valenin, Lower Austria, in the demarcation between American and Soviet zones, Peter Krauland, the Austrian Minister for Asset Protection and Economic Planning, and high-ranking official Margarethe Ottillinger (aged only 29 with a doctorate in commercial studies completed at the University of Vienna), were about to drive to the US occupation zone in a government

[303] 'Soviet Pressure on Ministry of Interior and Police' 25 June 1948, available at: <https://www.cia.gov/library/readingroom/docs/CIA-RDP82-00457R001600560006-1.pdf> accessed 30 July 2019.
[304] Riegler, 'The Spy Story behind the Third Man', pp.30-31.

sedan. Soviet border guards surprised them. Ottillinger was dragged out of the car. The shaken minister was ordered to continue with his journey. Ottillinger was charged with espionage on behalf of the United States and providing escape aid to a Soviet engineer. She had been working on the US Marshall Plan and had drafted a policy for lower allowances to Soviet steel companies. The charges of espionage did not lead her to execution; this was not what Moscow wanted. She spent seven years in gulags, falling seriously ill. She was released in 1955 at the end of the occupation and the signing of the State Treaty.

Meanwhile some kidnappings of Soviet deserters were outsourced to gangs. Benno Blum and his gang profited in the black market with Soviet support. Key contraband was American cigarettes brought from Hungary. The CIC followed their activities and they were further informed when one gang member deserted. Subsequently, the Americans arrested some members of his gang. The Soviets kept Blum for a while in protective custody. Once he was released, in April 1950, Blum visited his mistress in the French sector of the city. French and American military police rushed to the apartment. Blum made a bid to grab the pistol of one officer. He stayed firm, blocking the hammer with his thumb. Blum was shot dead by another officer.

Nonetheless, the MGB unmasked a CIC operation run by Johann Groissl, who had formed a spy-ring. Groissl was a battle-hardened Wehrmacht soldier; back in January 1944 he had been captured by the Americans and soon recruited as a spy on German prisoners of war. In 1946 he was released from prison. In April 1948 he was found in Vienna and recruited again by the CIC. He inducted Otto Schwab and their mission was to spy on the Austrian Communist party. Groissl joined the party and this enabled him to have access to party correspondence and files. However, three months after he had signed up, he was expelled; he was assumed to be a spy working in the 10th district of Vienna party offices. His name was made known to the MGB.

Groissl continued to work for the CIC and was looking to recruit more informers; he was known to offer money for espionage, and by early 1950 he had twenty-five informers. He met with and directed the majority of them himself. The informers under Schwab did not contact Groissl but he delivered the information to the CIC handlers. Schwab and Groissl had formed a railway observation network and kept track of Russian military deployments. They reported also on Russian military personnel. In February 1950 Groissl, Schwab and one of their associates, Kurt Zofka, broke into the offices of the Austrian Communist Party in the 10th district; the same office Groissl was expelled from as a spy in 1948. The Austrian police (where communist officers still remained, lying low) conducted a

175

rigorous investigation and few days later Zofka was arrested and handed over to the MGB. He confessed to the operation of the spy-ring; the information enabled the Soviets to identify Groissl as the leader of the ring.

The Russians were patient. Three months later Groissl was contacted by the Soviets. He could not hide any longer. He assumed that if he started working for them, his sentence would be lessened. He handed over some intelligence and in the following months some of his informants disappeared, arrested by the MGB.

In October 1950, one of Schwab's informers started working for the Soviets, blowing his cover. The Russian spymasters employed this informer and some others as double agents and soon uncovered Schwab. Groissl was captured in March 1951 and by January 1952 the whole spy-ring was destroyed; all twenty-five members were arrested by the Russians.

Meanwhile, former SS and Wehrmacht soldiers and Nazi functionaries (the large pool of Intelligence operatives for US and British Intelligence) were gradually gaining political support. In mid-October 1949, British Military Intelligence assessed the Nazi threat in Austria: 'there are about 433,000 "less-implicated" Nazis in Austria. In the elections on 9 October 1949, the new "Fourth Party", the League of Independents (V.d.U.), which openly appealed to ex-Nazi elements (who had recently been granted amnesty) surprisingly gained 12 per cent of the popular vote and 16 of the 165 seats. The party is extreme Right-Wing, and has been attacked by all sections of the Austrian press for being strongly influenced by its Nazi element.' British Intelligence warned: 'There have also been indications that leaders of the party have been in touch with the Russians.'[305]

Dr. Wilhelm Hoettl, the SD spymaster who was in contact with Allen Dulles in the last phase of the war, found himself employed once again as a spymaster, directing US Intelligence and former SS and Wehrmacht Intelligence officers into the Soviet occupation zone in Austria under Project *Mount Vernon* and in Hungary under Project *Montgomery*. His networks produced full intelligence about Soviet military deployments allowing strategic assessments during the Berlin crisis in autumn and summer of 1948.

The Berlin Blockade lasted from 24 June 1948 to 12 May 1949. Fear of an escalation of the crisis (involving an offensive in Austria as well as a coup against the government of Figl) directed the intelligence collection

---

[305] 'Germans Abroad' memorandum by MI4 (a), 19 October 1949 KV 3/418 TNA.

of the CIA, US Military Intelligence and the SIS. In August 1949, Hoettl wrote to Colonel James Milano of the CIC 'In the 10 months of our activity we rendered you 618 reports from line *Montgomery* and 1,600 reports from line *Mount Vernon*...As to the quality of reports you will admit, that I, as a former leading functionary of the German secret service, was able to form a somewhat correct judgment.'[306]

The issue with Hoettl (who was also interested in the 'Fourth Party') was that by mid 1949 it was discovered that he had provided US Intelligence with false information. And soon he was revealed to have contact with MGB spies, as we will explore in the next chapter.

---

[306]Hoettl to Major James Milano, 31 August 1949 available at: <https://ia800206.us.archive.org/30/items/HoettlWilhelm/HOETTL,%20WILHELM%20%20%20VOL.%203_0066.pdf> accessed 25 July 2019.

11

The Oblivious Spy

Allen Dulles concluded that 'Hoettl's record as a SD man and collaborator [of] Kaltenbrunner is, of course...bad and information provided by him [is] to be viewed with caution, but I believe he desires to save his skin and therefore may be useful.' The OSS in Washington feared a plot by Himmler using Hoettl and did not proceed to work with him. Hoettl was captured in Alt-Aussee, Austria. Almost immediately, he proposed an intelligence gathering scheme against the Red Army under the code name *Mount*. He boasted of maintaining 'a complex of agents in Romania, Hungary, Bulgaria, Yugoslavia, Montenegro and Albania, capable of reporting high-level political and military information.' He claimed that the 'central' radio transmitter was still operational in Vienna and could facilitate the communication with secret agents willing to work for the Americans against the Russians. The Hungarian cryptographers at his services would make sure the communications were secure. The X-2 of OSS tried to verify Hoettl's claims. Radio communication with Hoettl's agents in Budapest and Bucharest did occur; but these cities were by then under Soviet occupation and the Americans feared that the whole probing of Hoettl's claims would leak to the Russians. A certain OSS Captain Timm who led the investigations had four theories:

'a. The offer is genuine and his [spy] net may believe that they are still working for him.

b. Hoettl's offer may be an effort to entangle the Allies.

c. Hoettl's agents may actually be working for the Russians already.

d. The offer may be a distraction to divert the US from other networks or

operations.'[307]

William Donovan, the flamboyant and charismatic chief of the OSS,

---

[307] Ruffner, Kevin Conley, Eagle and Swastika: CIA and Nazi War Criminals and Collaborators (CIA: History Staff, 2003),p. 24 available at: <https://ia801301.us.archive.org/17/items/EagleAndSwastika/Eagle%20and%20Swastika.pdf> accessed 26 July 2019.

was informed of the scheme proposed by Hoettl. The war in Europe was over. Donovan ordered radio contact with Hoettl's agents. Eventually the spy ring dissolved or was discovered by the Russians. Hoettl remained in US custody, being a witness in the Nurnberg trials. In 1947, he was released and made a successful bid to offer his services as a spymaster. He drafted a number of papers on strategy and intelligence and found willing readers. A new war had started, the Cold War, and he could profit.

The SD spymaster, with a doctorate in modern history obtained at Vienna University in 1938, impressed the Americans, who gave him B (usually reliable); 3 (possibly true) marks: 'During the past twelve months that Hoettl has been in contact with this office [CIC] he has proven to be an excellent source for ideas, both concrete and theoretical, on the expansion of American Intelligence in Austria. His background as a former Deputy Chief of Amt VI RHSA for southeast Europe enables him to evaluate incoming reports on the Soviets with fairly complete accuracy.' [308]

In November 1948, John G. Erhardt, the US Minister in Vienna, was impressed by Hoettl's studies. C.L. Olson, the First Secretary, presented Erhardt a report on Hoettl's writings:

> 'The first report "The Necessity of a central American Intelligence Service": shows quite a good general knowledge of the factors involved. His somewhat detailed knowledge of competition between American intelligence agencies is a little surprising…As for the portion on the immediate activation of resistance groups in Eastern countries, the concept is not new. Such persons as General Donovan, Allen Dulles, Charles Thayer and Frank Lindsay, all ex-OSS men, have worked on it privately and have tried to sell the idea to the Army for some time without too much success at last reports.' [309]

Eventually Hoettl's papers reached Washington. [310]

Already, Hoettl was entrusted with two Military Intelligence projects by the CIC in Austria. Project *Mount Vernon* was activated on 1 October

---

[308] C.L.Olson to Minister (Erhardt) 1 November 1948, available at:
<https://ia800206.us.archive.org/30/items/HoettlWilhelm/HOETTL,%20WILHELM%20%2 0%20VOL.%203_0018.pdf> accessed 23 July 2019.
[309] Ibid.
[310] Ibid.

1948 and Hoettl reported to CIC Gmunden (Upper Austria) Field Office. He coordinated his spies from the house of Karl Kowarik, one of his close associates in Gmunden.

In January 1949 Hoettl was assessed as 'a very active, tenacious, and ruthless person, shrewd, versatile, and very ambitious…keeps a large correspondence with formerly prominent politicians, industrialists, financiers, and with persons involved in intelligence activities who could be of use to him in the future.'[311]

Hoettl employed Karl Kowarik, who had worked in the preparation of *Mount Vernon* since July 1948 and Kowarik 'has always shown a conservative attitude regarding all work done by sources and subsources.' Indeed 'Kowarik is not one to over-evaluate information received; on the contrary, he more often tends to under-evaluate' the Americans commented.[312]

Some of the sources of *Mount Vernon* sounded very promising. Source 10/6343 says:

> 'Makes a trip once weekly from Vienna over the Enns bridge to Attnag-Puchheim where a package containing reports is picked up, from the courier by a representative of the Gmunden Centre. When travelling through the Russian zone the courier wraps his reports in an old newspaper and places them on the baggage rack above the person opposite him in the train compartment, upon which bags, coats and other items are placed. Source also makes one monthly trip to the Gmunden Centre…he hides his package of reports inside the water tank of the men's toilet when passing through the Russian zone.'[313]

Briefly, some spies had a military and SS background. *Heinz* was working as a construction engineer in Vienna. He was a former Wehrmacht officer and he focused on Soviet military activities in the area. *Franz* was located in Baden. He had served as a sergeant in the Wehrmacht. Currently, he was working as an interpreter in the local

---

[311] 'Dr Wilhelm Hoettl' January 1949, p.13, available at:
<0002https://ia800206.us.archive.org/30/items/HoettlWilhelm/HOETTL,%20WILHELM%20%20VOL.%204_0002.pdf> accessed 25 July 2019.
[312] 'Net Project Mount Vernon' available at:
<https://www.cia.gov/library/readingroom/docs/ARMY%20CIC%20NETS%20IN%20EASTERN%20EUROPE_0002.pdf> accessed 23 July 2019.
[313] Ibid.

180

Soviet Army headquarters. He was fluent in Russian and gathered military information in his area. *Josef* worked initially in the offices of the Central Committee of the Austrian Communist Party in Vienna but was dropped by the CIC. Hoettl was proud of his sources: *Walther* was living in Leogen. He was a former SS lieutenant 'who worked under Skorzeny'; now he was a mechanic and was looking on general intelligence in the southern part of Burgenland and Styria. For the Americans the former SS lieutenant was 'a new addition and has to date submitted only a few reports, but according to Operations Chief [Hoettl] is a very good intelligence man, particularly in the industrial field.' Another SS/SD officer, *Erwin*, was living in Linz reporting on the Austrian Communist Party through subsources.

An indicative volume for a four-month period of reporting of *Mount Vernon* lists: 20 per cent of reports on Soviet military; 50 per cent of political/communist reporting; 15 per cent economic and industrial reporting; and 10 per cent general political reporting. Hoettl's spies were supposed to gather all intelligence they could encounter, including information on Austrian communist political and paramilitary activities, scientific intelligence, Soviet military, industrial and economic activities and Austrian politics.

The CIC was informed of the process of the Austrian spymasters: 'upon receipt of information by sources from subsources it [the information] is carefully checked. Once the source feels that the information is as complete and correct as possible, he forwards it by courier to the centre in Gmunden. When it arrives in Gmunden it is first processed by Kowarik who is a political and economic specialist, and also by [Werner] Moser a former SD officer who fought against the Russians during the past war. The information is then passed on to Koller who checks the new reports with reports previously forwarded and made references...once the information has gone through these three persons it is translated by...into English.' Twice a week these reports were dispatched to the CIC field station in Gmunden. Hoettl and the CIC officers wished to expand the operations: 'it is anticipated that in the near future radios will be established in four areas of the Russian occupied zone of Austria for expeditious reporting on Soviet military movement.'

The CIC concluded that there were some pitfalls; there was 'insufficient liaison with sources, which accounted for a great deal of time wasted by informants on reporting information of little or no intelligence value. More direct control of sources required by CIC Control Agent. Injudicious selection of sources and subsources by operations chief without consulting CIC Control Agent.'[314] Nonetheless, the operation under the promising Hoettl and his SD associates would continue.

Project *Montgomery* was activated on 10 July 1948 and controlled by the CIC Field Office in Gmunden. Hoettl was the spymaster who would have the operational control of the scheme to gather military, economic and political intelligence in Hungary. The spies were Austrians and their sources Hungarians. The spymasters under Hoettl were mainly Hungarians, former Military Intelligence officers who had worked with the Nazis and fought on the Eastern Front. One in the administrative personnel was Alojos Sike, a Hungarian officer taken prisoner by the Russians and released on 5 July 1948; he crossed the borders the same month and volunteered to work for Hoettl and his close associate Karoly Ney. Erich Kernmayr took over after the always undisciplined Ney. One could suspect that the Russians might have arranged something with Sike.

Key sources of military intelligence for Project *Montgomery* were: 10/5583 who lived in Salzburg and was an Intelligence non-commissioned officer in the Hungarian Army - he reported on military and political affairs in western Hungary. Source 10/6354, who travelled regularly to Budapest from Salzburg; he was an Intelligence non-commissioned officer in the Hungarian army, and he had access to intelligence in the Hungarian War Ministry too. It was reported: 'he contacts prominent persons' in the ministry and in the new communist army. Source 10/7114 was a former sergeant in the Hungarian gendarmerie; he lived in Salzburg and travelled to Hungary where he met another former sergeant who provided him with information on the border guards. Source 10/7874 was a police lieutenant in Budapest; he wrote reports on police activities and the general situation in the capital. Source 10/8474 was a Hungarian army 1st lieutenant writing reports on military activities in Budapest and the two military academies. Sixty per cent of the reports submitted to CIC were on military intelligence and twenty per cent on political/communist events and personalities.

Hoettl and the Americans arranged for the agents to have radio transmitters in case the border closed. All Project *Montgomery* secret couriers crossed the borders illegally at great personal risk of being caught as spies. After almost ten months of operations, the CIC review sounded positive; the listed mistakes were few: 'Issuance of Austrian identity cards to members of network who are non-Austrians and who are not good German (Austrian dialect) speakers. Injudicious selection of subsources. Placing a 'soldier' (Ney, Karoly) as a main operator in the net rather than

---

[314]Ibid.

182

an intelligence man.'[315] Karoly Ney 'is very difficult to handle, because of his unwillingness to take orders.' [316]

The CIC had been analysing Hoettl's reports and Intelligence officers sought to find cross references. Careful work over several months started revealing the truth:

> [report] of L/1063 of 14 Jun[e] [19]49: 'Romania-restricted are- This report is a slightly garbled version of newspaper reports, about 2 months old'
> L/11018 of 17 Jan[uary] [19]49: 'Members of a Hungarian Network in Vienna'- 'this report is substantially the same as that published in the Wiener Kurier of 31 Dec[ember] [19]48 with the addition of one name which is completely unknown to us'
> L/10318 of 1 Dec[ember] [19]48: 'Soviet Troops Concentration- the one point of real intelligence interest, that there really are Soviet troop concentrations on the Austro-Hungarian frontier, is never established; instead it is likely stated as a fact. The rest of the report is simply a set of theories that anyone could work out'
> l/1015 of 24 Nov[ember] [19]48: '[Heinrich] Guttman [Hungarian communist leader] and Soviet Policy- seems probably to be a complete fabrication'

The reporting of *Mount Vernon* did not reveal anything meaningful of Soviet Intelligence operations:

> 'Reports too few and too scanty in content to permit much evaluation. Inf[ormation] is of medium to low caliber in quality. Has about a 50 per cent batting average. Is good in naming Russian intelligence personnel, of which most mentioned are confirmed. So far as indigenous RIS [Russian Intelligence Service] informants and agents, little or none can be confirmed. General impression is that info[rmation] is bread-and-butter stuff...None of it is very important.[317]
> '[*Mount Vernon*] has produced the least confirmed information on the KP (Austrian Communist Party) of any network working on the problem. There has been little so

[315] Ibid., p.20.
[316] 'The Past of Dr Hoettl', p.18, ibid.
[317] Comments on Mount Vernon Miscellaneous Reports, ibid.

called documentary evidence which can be considered confirmed as authentic; most of it could easily be forged. Mount Vernon has a very low batting average on predictions of events to come, as evidenced by its report that Austrian elections would be held in May 1949...[Mount Vernon intelligence] is quite often sloppiest and contradictory.'[318]

Lieutenant Colonel Earl Tush, the head of USAR Air Intelligence branch, was angry with the reports of the CIC on the Yugoslav Air Force. The reports were based on Hoettl's sources of *Mount Vernon* and *Montgomery* projects:

'a. The information as reported in Report L-15442 has been discovered to be full of inaccuracies. To date there have been no confirmed indications of a 6th Air Div[ision] existing in the Yugoslav Air Force, and, if in existence, it is certainly not at Zemun [city near Belgrade]. Since the Tito-Cominform rift, the Yugoslav Air Force has fought desperately to keep to five divisions up to strength. Probably if the rift had not occurred, the 6th Air Div[ision] might have materialized.

b. Zemun is the location of the Yugoslav Air Force High Command, and the Air Transport Reg[iment] is located at Zemun Airfield. The Transport Reg[iment] is equipped with 25 to 30 aircraft (DC-3, and Ju-52 types). There have never been more than 12 fighter aircraft located at Zemun permanently, as confirmed by a recent survey of the Zemun Airfield by [US] Air Attaché in Belgrade (date of observation July 1949). There have been no confirmed reports of a paratroop unit being located at Zemun.

c. The 112 Air Regiment (not 112 Air Squadron as reported in L-15442), is subordinate to the 3rd Air Force Div[ision] which has its headquarters located at Mostar. The 112 Air Reg[iment] is located at Ljubljana equipped with approximately 30 Yak aircraft.

d. the following aircraft as reported in report are false: LA-7, Migg-11 (sic), and IL-18. None of these have ever been equipment of the Yugoslav Air Force. The tri-motored aircraft were undoubtly (sic) Ju-52 aircraft, but this office

---

[318] 'Comments on Mount Vernon RIS (Russia Intelligence Service] Efforts', ibid.

will not accept such aircraft, as part of the equipment of a tactical unit in Yugoslav Air Force, other than the Air Transport Reg[iment] located at Zemun.'319

CIC Major James Milano had to defend the decision to assign Hoettl the spymaster's position for *Montgomery* and *Mount Vernon*. Milano claimed: 'his reports recently (six months) have been extremely poor and have been on a steady decline. The reason is that he had not been paying any attention to his work as an intelligence operative for the United States Forces in Austria but has been engrossed in all sorts of political dealings.'320 Milano added 'due to the nature of his contacts and because of his background, we are in agreement that we do not believe that he will return and work for the Russians.' He might though try to work for British or French Intelligence. In any case, 'we will watch Hoettl very closely to ascertain his future movements from our CI (Counter Intelligence) point of view.'321

The Americans accused Hoettl of providing them with false intelligence from his journalist sources. He was seen in meetings with suspected (and eventually known) NKVD agents. The fear grew that he was trying to infiltrate Soviet spies into the newly established structures of West German Intelligence, namely the Gehlen Organisation. SIS too had grown suspicious. One of their Austrian agents (who had been an associate of Hoettl) was arrested in the Soviet occupation zone. The British came to the conclusion that it was Hoettl who 'signalled [betrayed] the agent to the Soviets because he refused to collaborate' with him in 'the fabrication of false intelligence'.322

On 7 July 1949, Washington cabled the CIC Station in Vienna: '...Hoettl has delivered a sufficient number of Nazi war criminals to the gallows, unbeknownst to his former associates, to afford us a strong hold

---

319'Suspected False Information' 10 August 1949, available at:
<https://ia800206.us.archive.org/30/items/HoettlWilhelm/HOETTL,%20WILHELM%20%2 0%20VOL.%203_0063.pdf> accessed 27 July 2019.

320 Undated Memorandum (possibly July/August 1949) 'Dropping of projects 'Montgomery' and 'Mount Vernon', available at:
<0002https://ia800206.us.archive.org/30/items/HoettlWilhelm/HOETTL,%20WILHELM%2 0%20%20VOL.%204_0002.pdf> accessed 25 July 2019.

321 Ibid.

322 Report ref. WIR-3385, 2952, CIA; Wilhelm Hoettl, Vol 5 document No 112, available at:
<https://ia800206.us.archive.org/30/items/HoettlWilhelm/HOETTL,%20WILHELM%20%2 0%20VOL.%205_0112.pdf> accessed 19 July 2019

over him. Should you decide that he had better be removed from the political scene, I am sure something could be done to hasten that process.'[323]

Meanwhile, the FBI ran a sting operation, uncovering two Austrians as spies, naturalised US citizens with war records with the US forces. Kurt Ponger and Otto Verber were arrested in Vienna on charges of espionage. Verber escaped to the Russian sector. But Yuri Novikov, the MGB officer-handler under diplomatic cover, was arrested. Ponger and Verber knew Hoettl since the Nuremberg trials where they served as interpreters; and in recent years they had been meeting him. The FBI maintained that in early 1949 Ponger was recruited by the MGB in Moscow and afterwards he recruited Verber. Together they approached an employee of the US forces in Austria (who turned them in to the FBI). He agreed to help them since he knew Verber from the Nuremberg trials, where he also had worked in an administrative post; Verber was provided with intelligence on agents of the US military and informants as well as on operations and policies.

Under the pen name Walther Hagen, Hoettl wrote a book about the secret intelligence during the Second World War entitled *Die Geheime Front* (The Secret Front). The publishing house was reportedly owned by his wife, but reports indicated it 'to be largely financed by Soviet funds though the journalist and allegedly French-Soviet double agent Alexander Vodopivec.' In his discussions with Austrian and American Intelligence officers, Hoettl claimed that he was the West German Military Intelligence representative in Austria. The Americans reviewed dozens of reports on Hoettl they had not paid much attention to earlier:

> 'There had been persistent reports for several years that Hoettl is a Sov[iet] agent. These are supported by a known connection between Hoettl and the *Nationale Liga* and by unclarified instances of direct association with Soviet agents...'[324]

In March 1953, after the arrest of Ponger, Hoettl was detained and rigorously interrogated, the main suspicion being that he was a Soviet agent. The long interrogation report read:

---

[323] Chief (Foreign Branch) to Chief of Station (Vienna) 7 July 1949, available at: <https://ia800206.us.archive.org/30/items/HoettlWilhelm/HOETTL,%20WILHELM%20%20%20VOL.%203_0060.pdf> accessed 25 July 2019.
[324] Report on Urban Josef Adolf, 6 April 1953, ibid.

'The interrogators have the impression that HOETTL is definitely concealing information on a number of points. He showed sensitivity in the polygraph examination to all questions pertaining to the concealment or destruction of evidence and, although he stated that he had not destroyed his files nor had he hidden other portions of his files outside of his house the interrogators are convinced that some destruction or concealment has taken place. Technically, HOETTL is not physiologically testable by polygraph. He has low blood pressure, almost meaningless. It was characteristic of his reactions on the polygraph machine that the strongest response was made to a question in which we absolutely knew that he was not lying. It is also characteristic that he reacted in some respect to every question and his breathing showed throughout a feeling of tension. From these observations, which will be reported technically by another interrogator, and from direct observation during the course of the interrogation, the interrogators are convinced that HOETTL is lying about or concealing some piece of information which to HOETTL is extremely important. This piece of information may be connected with his knowledge of the relations between Anton Boehm and Otto [von] Bolschwing.'

These were two close associates in the secret intelligence trade. Bolschwing was an SS-Hauptsturmführer of the SD and had worked under Eichmann; after the end of the war he worked for the CIC and the CIA. Hoettl understood that Bolschwing was a valuable intelligence operator for US Intelligence and that some of his past with Eichmann should be protected (see next chapter).

The report on Hoettl concluded:

'The interrogators have various theories about what Hoettl is concealing but the theories are all unsupported by concrete evidence. It is possible that he is a Soviet agent in contact with the Soviet-controlled *Tophole* complex [code-name for the Ponger spy-ring] either through Ponger or through somebody else. It is possible that he is a Soviet agent who nevertheless was unaware of Ponger's affiliation. It is possible that he is not a Soviet agent but is involved in some intrigue involving the future German Intelligence Service and present German Intelligence groups which he cannot afford to reveal to Americans. This last theory is partly supported by a number of curious circumstances surrounding the recent behaviour by members of the Gehlen group and by members of other US sponsored Intelligence operations which employ former German Intelligence officers.

'It is possible that Hoettl is sincere in his statements that he expects Mr Allen Welch Dulles to take personal cognizance of his case and that he is under the impression that his present interrogators are hostile to Mr Dulles. This fourth theory would explain his reactions to interrogation, but the theory cannot be accepted unless we assumed that Hoettl is naïve about the present organization of American intelligence. Such naivete is unlikely.

'At this writing [un-declassified name of one interrogator] is inclined to offer odds of ten to nine, or perhaps twenty to nineteen, that Hoettl is not under Soviet control and was unaware that Ponger and Verber were Soviet agents.'[325]

Correspondence from his intelligence activities was uncovered in Hoettl's house in Altanssee. A pistol was found, along with four blank Austrian identity cards, a sum of 1,265 British pounds and a forged passport from Lichtenstein with Hoettl's photo and a false name.

The Americans did not hide their frustration: 'the interrogation failed in its main aims…a. it was not possible for the interrogator to determine whether Hoettl is a witting Soviet agent. Hoettl claims that he is not a Soviet agent and points vehemently to what he affects to consider a consistent record of anti-Soviet and anti-Communist activity, b. it was not possible to determine whether Hoettl was a witting member of the *Tophole* complex or whether he was aware that Kurt Ponger was under control of Soviet Intelligence. He stated that he believed from the first Ponger's statement to him that Ponger had been a Captain in the OSS before becoming an interrogator at Nurnberg. He further stated that at no time in his association with Ponger, which began in Nurnberg and continued infrequently through October 1952, did Ponger indicate leftist inclinations or display curiosity about Hoettl's clandestine activities. Hoettl claims that he first thought Ponger to be a Vienna representative of Amt Gehlen and that later he concluded from Ponger's conversations and

[325] 'Preliminary report on Hoettl interrogation, 3 April 1953, p.5, available at:
<https://ia800206.us.archive.org/30/items/HoettlWilhelm/HOETTL,%20WILHELM%20%2
0%20VOL.%206_0040.pdf?> accessed 19 July 2019

interests that he had some loose connection with the Israeli Intelligence Service. He states, however, that he never considered at any time that Ponger was an active member of any intelligence service. According to Hoettl, Ponger appeared to be the least intelligent member of the group whom Hoettl met.' Ponger's wife Vera met Hoettl on one occasion for a period of 1½ hours. He told the Americans that he had the impression that she dominated her husband. Hoettl continued, telling his interrogators that 'upon learning through the newspapers that Ponger and Verber were alleged to be Soviet agents he assumed that Verber was the leader of the team but that Vera Ponger played an important and possibly dominant role.'[326]

The interrogators presented Hoettl with the two alternatives and he had to choose: he was either a member of the Ponger spy-ring or 'he was a complete dupe', fooled by the Soviets. Hoettl denied both:

> 'Being a proud man, he argued at length against the accusation that he must have been a fool to be taken in by Ponger and at the same time maintained that he never in any way tumbled to the true affiliations of the Verber-Ponger family although he was aware that the Pongers resided in a Soviet sector of Vienna.'[327]

Hoettl referred to former chief of the Secret Field Police (Geheim Feld Polizei) Wilhelm Krichraum, whom Ponger knew and with whom he discussed the Gehlen Organisation. Hoettl 'added that he did not believe Krichraum is a Soviet agent but made his statement in such a tone as to indicate that a good deal of suspicion does attach to Krichraum.' The interrogator commented 'this off-hand or indirect type of slander was characteristic of all Hoettl's remarks concerning previous colleagues...'[328]

Hoettl insisted that in his discussions with Ponger 'he did not blow to Soviet intelligence anybody who is engaged in sensitive activity against the Soviets who was not already known to Ponger.' About the Gehlen Organisation, Hoettl assumed that Ponger 'knew more than he himself did...Ponger urged him repeatedly to become a member of Amt (Service) Gehlen, saying that undoubtedly Amt Gehlen was the future German Intelligence Service.' Ponger argued (according to Hoettl) that 'the Americans had spent millions of dollars building up Amt Gehlen and would never permit another group to become important in German

---

[326] Ibid., p.3.
[327] Ibid.
[328] Ibid., p.4.

Intelligence.'[329]

Charts of spy networks were found in Hoettl's papers. These were to be offered to the Amt Gehlen. The Americans cross-referenced the lists of the dozens of names of principal agents and agents: '...these sources lists included only the name of notorious fabricators or of professional middlemen. There are no names on the list of persons who honestly collect intelligence, and all of the persons listed are, like Hoettl himself, primarily operations officers and arrangers.'[330]

Suspicion that Hoettl was acting as an unwitting informer of the MGB was regularly reported before Ponger's arrest. In early March 1953 it was reported to the chief of CIC in Vienna that Hoettl asked Ponger to talk to a US citizen who was in contact with the CIC and get them to persuade Hoettl to rejoin their intelligence apparatus.

A report dated 24 April 1950 read 'in a recent conversation with a confidential source of CIC, Hoettl stated that he is in contact with two American Jewish CIC agents, whom he knew from Nuremberg [trials], who keep him informed as to all that takes place regarding his person in Vienna.'[331] Hoettl must have been referring to Ponger and Verber, who presented themselves as CIC agents. No doubt, the SD spymaster had been taking advantage of the overall precarious situation to prove to the Americans that he should return to work with them. In the period August-October 1950 the communists instigated large scale strikes, demonstrations and riots. The economic crisis left no one unaffected: the US financial aid had been withdrawn and real wages dropped while inflation rose. The government accused the communists again of a coup, but the Austrian Communist Party did not intend this, nor had they received full Soviet support.

During this period of fear and chaos, on 18 October 1950 'a controlled American source reported that Ponger, presenting himself as an American literary agent, contacted Hoettl showing interest in his book and his future books from a business perspective.' Hoettl insisted that he was in 'constant' communication with Ponger, who worked as a photo-journalist and gave photos to Hoettl for his articles; in exchange Hoettl provided him with leads and contacts. In discussions with Hoettl and others Ponger claimed that he chose to live in the Russian sector 'so that

---

[329] Ibid.

[330] Ibid., p.5.

[331] G-2 to 430th CIC, Report, 12 February 1953, available at:
<https://ia600206.us.archive.org/30/items/HoettlWilhelm/HOETTL,%20WILHELM%20%2
0%20VOL.%206_0006.pdf> accessed 23 July 2019.

the Russians would let him alone, i.e. so that they would not observe him or place him under observation…as they learned that Ponger was not engaged in intelligence work, but rather occupied himself commercially with his pictorial service, they paid no more attention to him.'[332]

From 1 November 1952, Hoettl's name was placed on the special blacklist: 'long known in Austria as a fabricator of intelligence information. His reports normally consist of a fine cobweb of fact, heavily padded with lies, deceit, conjectures, and other false types of information.'[333]

Colonel Friedrich Wilhelm Heinz was assigned by the Americans the codename *Capote*. He worked for Amt Blank, the predecessor organisation of part of West Germany's Ministry of Defence. He had been receiving Hoettl's intelligence reports but assured the Americans that he had not paid him any money. *Capote* told Chief EE (Eastern Europe division, CIA):

> 'The only intelligence of value that Hoettl produced concerned the Austrian government, but all other, namely OB [Order of Battle of the Soviet Forces], Hungarian and Romanian political reports, reports on North Africa, Italy and Trieste were phoney. When I asked *Capote* why, if he knew Hoettl manufactured so much paper, he subsidized him, and maintained his close contact, *Capote* replied that he was trying to determine who Hoettl's excellent source on internal Austrian affairs was before completely severing the connection. *Capote* emphasized, however, that he was aware of Hoettl's [passing phony reports] and *Capote* was not making any disseminations of the questionably material. This was in May 1952.'[334]

The Americans had lost their patience: '*Capote* should be told that regardless of his associations with Hoettl, for the good of all IS (Intelligence Service) agencies working against satellites and Soviets, Hoettl must be removed to make way for more serious and positive

[332] Ibid.

[333] Chief of station (Frankfurt) to Chief EE, 29 September 1952 available at: < https://ia800206.us.archive.org/30/items/HoettlWilhelm/HOETTL,%20WILHELM%20%20%20VOL.%205_0123.pdf> accessed 23 July 2019.

[334] Chief of station (Frankfurt) to Chief EE, 12 September 1952 available at: < https://ia800206.us.archive.org/30/items/HoettlWilhelm/HOETTL,%20WILHELM%20%20%20VOL.%205_0113.pdf> accessed 23 July 2019.

intelligence gathering. I don't think he'll offer any argument and will play ball with us on this score.'[335] This was before Hoettl's connection with Ponger was established and the assessment that he might have been an informer of the MGB. There is no doubt that US Military Intelligence reporting on Soviet deployments in Austria and Hungary at a time of tensions in 1948-1949 was contaminated by Hoettl's forgeries and false intelligence.

Gehlen's Organisation was be penetrated by the MGB. A former SS Captain, Hans Clemens, was recruited by the Russians. A year later, he was admitted to the Gehlen Organisation and started to supply Moscow with 'valuable information' on the emerging West German Intelligence Services; his role was pivotal: 'This made it possible to prevent the exposure of valuable agents, and to disrupt operations directed against Soviet missions in the FRG [Federal Republic of Germany]'. Clemens recruited Heinz Felfe, a former SS comrade of his who also joined the Gehlen Organisation. According to a KGB report, once reviewed together, Felfe's, George Blake's and Kim Philby's intelligence led to 'the elimination of the adversary's agent network in the GDR' in 1953-1955.[336]

Capote admitted that Hoettl's reports of the Soviet order of battle were 'inflated' and had a mix of 'overt and semi-overt information' but he steadfastly maintained that Hoettl had 'the ability and does get bona-fide internal political information which, over a period of months, has proven to be true.' He was paying Hoettl 600 DMs per month for his political information, while allowing him to plan the expansion of a German-Austrian intelligence network to south eastern Europe. Hoettl boasted that he was Heinz's man in Austria.

By the end of May 1952, the CIC chief of station in Vienna was angry with both Hoettl and Heinz: '...support to Dr Wilhelm Hoettl is a Bad Thing [emphasis in the original], whether given by *Capote* or anybody else. Having for some time watched Hoettl from three different points of view, we each feel also that support to Hoettl is a waste of money and effort.' Besides 'the collection of internal Austrian political information was a low level (there is no other level for such information in Austria) does not require the talents of a very astute operator. Hoettl, like a couple of dozen other types in Austria, can turn out a sizeable volume of such information without interrupting his regular pattern of coffee house conversations. On the other hand, Dr Adenauer's

---

[335] Ibid.
[336] Andrew & Mitrokhin, *The Mitrokhin Archive*, pp.571-572.

handwritten commendation notwithstanding, we suspect that Dr Hoettl's analysis of the Austrian political scene is distinguished more by its rhetoric than by its profundity.' In addition, 'to assess Hoettl's OB [Order of Battle of Soviet forces] information it is only necessary to recall the case of Raimund Strangl, whose reports Hoettl rewrote and dizzied as his own to various customers, include *Capote*.'[337]

Heinz had shown German Chancellor Konrad Adenauer Hoettl's studies, enhancing the SD spymaster's standing. Strangl, a Viennese journalist, was arrested by the Soviets. In his appeal for clemency at the Soviet Supreme Court he stated: 'The earnings from espionage activity were the main source of income in my life.' He was executed in 1952.

Information about the past exploits of Hoettl was reaching the Americans. While an SD Sturmbannführer in Budapest by the end of the war, Hoettl (a father of three) was 'recognised by his superiors in the RSHA as one of the best qualified intelligence officials...Hoettl was so close-mouthed regarding his intelligence sources that his colleagues were unable to identity most of them.' One of Hoettl's best sources was Countess Franziska Palffy (born in 1897) 'with whom he carried on an intimate relationship.'[338] She had many contacts in Hungarian Intelligence 'and managed to obtain a continuous selection of Intelligence reports for Hoettl.' Hoettl 'reworked' the information, pretending to the RSHA that it was from his own spies. The spymaster was always demanding: 'on several occasions when Palffy's production dwindled, Hoettl let her know via subtleties that he had less time to spend with her socially because he had to meet his reports quota and that if he failed to do so he would be transferred to another post. Since Palffy didn't want to be separated from her paramour, she pressed her Hungarian contacts for more information and thus helped Hoettl enhance his position.' By the end of the war, she had escaped to Western Europe; in 1952 she was registered living in Kremsmünster in Upper Austria, close to the village where Hoettl had his villa. The Americans assumed that she was in contact with Hoettl, working with him again.

In October 1950 Hoettl was approached by Adolf Slavik with 'a proposal of collaboration with the Soviets. Slavik claimed he was acting

---

[337] Chief of Station (Vienne) to Chief EE, 21 May 1952 available at: <https://ia600206.us.archive.org/30/items/HoettlWilhelm/HOETTL,%20WILHELM%20%20VOL.%205_0086.pdf> accessed 27 July 2019.

[338] Chief of Station (Vienna) to Chief EE,15 April 1952, available at: <https://ia800206.us.archive.org/30/items/HoettlWilhelm/HOETTL,%20WILHELM%20%20VOL.%205_0074.pdf> accessed 25 July 2019.

on Soviet request.'[339] He was described as former chief of the Hitler Jugend and was used by the Russians.

The Austrian secret police kept Hoettl under surveillance. In January 1952 the Austrian police reported: 'it is confidentially reported that Dr Hoettl is currently negotiating with two representatives of General Swiridow on possibilities whereby the leadership of the former Waffen SS may be won over to work for Russian interests. The information stems from the circle of former SD personnel of the RSHA 6E, Budapest, who have no specific details.' The Americans discounted the report; 'the brevity and vagueness of the report suggest that it is a groundless denunciation by one of Hoettl's enemies.'[340]

Hoettl's enemies inside US Intelligence suspected him of working with Simon Wiesenthal, the Austrian Jew who became a legend in hunting war criminals. *Gruesome 201* was Karl Hass, a former SD officer; he had sent more that 1,000 Italian Jews to Auschwitz during the war and was responsible for killing 335 Italians in the Ardeatine massacre; he was finally tried in 1998. He worked for *Gruesome*, the 35th Detachment of CIC in Austria. The Americans suspected that Hoettl informed Wiesenthal that Hass was in Austria. On several occasions some CIC officers considered assassinating Hoettl: '[name not declassified] will attempt to find means of neutralising Hoettl. Tools at hand include [not declassified] who has indirect contact with Harry Mast (of the Gehlen Organisation), the *Gruesome* apparatus, which can deliver a poison-pen attack, and our contact with *Gragora* (codename for Counterintelligence Corps Detachment 430 of G-2 US Forces Austria), through which it may be possible to arrange indefinite detention of Hoettl...'[341] Eventually, Hoettl was not touched; probably because he worked for Colonel Heinz and the Americans did not want to jeopardise their relations with the Gehlen Organisation.

In October 1949, the Austrian police were informed that Hoettl and Karl Forner had been meeting; one of the interlocutors was Count Adam Rudmitsky, a former colonel of the Polish army who now was working for

[339]'Hoettl, Wilhelm', 17 October 1950, available at:
<https://ia800206.us.archive.org/30/items/HoettlWilhelm/HOETTL,%20WILHELM%20%20%20VOL.%204_0062.pdf> accessed 25 July 2019.

[340] 'Brandford/Alleged Hoettl/Soviet Connection', 30 January 1952, available at:
<https://ia800206.us.archive.org/30/items/HoettlWilhelm/HOETTL,%20WILHELM%20%20%20VOL.%205_0049.pdf> accessed 27 July 2019.

[341] Chief of Station (Vienna) to Chief (Foreign Division) 18 January 1952, available at:<https://ia800206.us.archive.org/30/items/HoettlWilhelm/HOETTL,%20WILHELM%20%20%20VOL.%205_0044.pdf> accessed 25 July 2019.

French Intelligence in Austria. They agreed for the Poles to send Hoettl intelligence reports for the Americans, but Forner stole these reports. Forner was involved in the kidnapping on 28 April 1948 of Colonel Diakov, a former career officer who had an official position in Austria before the war. Diakov was living in Vienna and was given a meeting place with Forner at a café at Judenplatz, Vienna. Forner was 'called to answer a phone call' when the Soviet agents appeared and arrested Diakov; 'they showed no interest for Forner' the CIC report commented.[342]

A confidential informant of CIC reported on 6 March 1950 that 'Hoettl had established contact with the French Intelligence through the former SS Sturmbannfuehrer of Amt VI, Werner Goetsch.' (Goetsch was a close friend of Naujocks, see chapter 8.) This officer 'openly worked for FIS' (French Intelligence Service). Hoettl 'receives Goetsch in his home very often, and both have been seen in Salzburg on numerous occasions.'[343] Erich Kernmayr claimed in February 1950 that Hoettl had 'indirect Intelligence connection with the Austrian Communist Party and the Soviets.'[344] Kernmayr was an SS officer, an assistant of Skorzeny in Budapest. Since 1947 he had worked for the CIC as an informer and had worked for Hoettl under project *Montgomery*.

In 1952, Hoettl showed that he had financial resources: he opened a boarding school in Bad Aussee in Styria and served as its director until 1980. Despite protests, the Austrian state authorities awarded him a cross of merit for his educational work. He died in 1999. All evidence cited in this chapter points to the direction that the ambitious Hoettl was the oblivious spy, ignoring the fact that his intriguing and his intelligence sharing with his former SD comrades-in-arms made him an unwitting source of Soviet intelligence. There is no evidence that the ever-suspicious Russian spymasters ever considered the kidnapping and interrogation of the SD spymaster.

American Intelligence officers frustrated by the lies and intrigues of Austrian former Nazi spymasters and their informers formed negative

---

[342] Chief of Mission (Vienna) to Chief (Foreign Division), 28 April 1950, available at: <https://ia800206.us.archive.org/30/items/HoettlWilhelm/HOETTL,%20WILHELM%20%20%20VOL.%204_0036.pdf> accessed 25 July 2019.
[343] 'Hoettl, Wilhelm, Dr.' 16 March 1950, available at: <https://ia600206.us.archive.org/30/items/HoettlWilhelm/HOETTL,%20WILHELM%20%20%20VOL.%204_0027.pdf> accessed 25 July 2019.
[344] Cable 'Hoettl, Wilhelm Dr.' 67 February 1950, available at: <https://archive.org/stream/HoettlWilhelm/HOETTL%2C%20WILHELM%20%20%20VOL.%204_0016#mode/1up> accessed 25 July 2019.

opinions of the Viennese in particular. CIA station chief Peer De Silva remarked they were 'generally a cynical, cold hearted lot...the Viennese are a breed apart from the rest of Austria: aloof, self-seeking, and often rude.'[345]

---

[345] De Silva, Peer, *The CIA and the Uses of Intelligence* (New York: Times Books, 1978), pp.125-126.

12

The Dark Nobleman

US Intelligence desperately needed reliable reports of the Soviet order of battle in Central Europe. The Berlin crisis had passed without escalation to war, but fear persisted of Stalin moving his thousands of armoured troops into Western Europe.

Otto von Bolschwing was born in 1909. He was descended from a noble Prussian family; his father, an officer, was killed on the Eastern Front in the Great War. The tall, suave, 'thin and athletic' Bolschwing had a pale complexion, short blond hair and blue eyes. As the Wehrmacht was collapsing, he proved himself a key tactical operator of US forces advancing into Austria. Lieutenant Colonel Ray F. Goggin of the 71st infantry regiment wrote on 7 June 1945: '…Bolschwing, a member of the "Tyrol Underground Movement", materially assisted the armed forces of the United States during our advance through Fern Pass and Western Austria prior to the surrender of the German Army. During our occupation, he personally captured over twenty high ranking Nazi officials and 55 officers and led patrols that resulted in the capture of many more.' On 16 August 1945, Lieutenant Colonel Howard F. Selk, the executive officer of the regiment, commended Bolschwing:

> '[He] has been closely affiliated with this organization for the past four months. During the regiment's stay in both Austria and Germany his able assistance in connection with Counter-Intelligence and Military Government matters has been virtually indispensable. In consideration of the many services he rendered our regiment, it is with pleasure that I commend him for his fine work and recommend him without hesitation to any Military organization with which he may come in contact in the future.'[346]

---

[346]Commendations of Otto von Bolschwing, available at: <https://ia801307.us.archive.org/27/items/BolschwingOttovon/BOLSCHWING,%20OTTO%20(VON)%20%20VOL.%201_0003.pdf> accessed 13 August 2019; see also Kevin C. Ruffner, Prussian Nobleman, SS Officer, and CIA Agent: The Case of Otto Albrecht Alfred von Bolschwing, Studies in Intelligence, 1998, available at: <https://numbers-stations.com/cia/Studies%20In%20Intelligence%20Nazi%20-

Bolschwing had told his American interrogators that he was compelled to join the Nazi party back in 1932 and had briefly served in the SD, as head of operations in Bucharest, Romania, but was imprisoned in 1942-43. The last years of the war he spent in Vienna being the manager of a pharmaceutical firm. The Gestapo arrested him in February 1945, but he was soon released with a bribe and joined the O5 resistance organisation. From 1947 he started working for the Gehlen Organisation, but he refused to share details of his secret sources.

By 1949 an extensive search of SS war records revealed 'General Heinz Jost (the head of SD Amt VI, prior to Schellenberg) considered Hauptsturmfuehrer von Bolschwing "extremely intelligent, supple and well-bred".' In Romania Bolschwing's contacts had opened access for him to secret reports on Moscow held by the Ministry of Foreign Affairs. It was noted that in June 1943 while in Vienna Naujocks had called on him to discuss matters of interest (see chapter 8).

US Intelligence took Bolschwing from the Gehlen Organisation and shielded him from inquiries from the Austrian authorities. The Americans had been changing the names of wanted Nazis they employed in intelligence operations, but this practice backfired:

> 'At the end of the war we tried to be very smart and changed the names of several members of the SD and Abwehr in order to protect them from the German authorities and the occupation authorities. In most cases these persons were so well known that the change in name compromised them more than if they were to face a denazification court and face the judgment which would have been meted out to them.'[347]

Initially, Bolschwing gathered intelligence regarding Austrian politics. In August 1950, the CIA handlers informed him, operating under the codename *Usage*, that they were no longer interested in reports on Austria but on Romania and Hungary and in particular on the Soviet order of battle. He boasted that his secret sources in Austria were indispensable

---

%20Related%20Articles/STUDIES%20IN%20INTELLIGENCE%20NAZI%20-%20RELATED%20ARTICLES_0014.pdf> accessed 15 August 2019.

[347] In April 1950 Chief (Pullah Operations Base) to Chief of Station (Karlsruhe) April 1950, available at:
<https://ia801307.us.archive.org/27/items/BolschwingOttovon/BOLSCHWING,%20OTTO%20(VON)%20%20%20VOL.%201_0042.pdf> accessed 13 August 2019.

to report on Central European and Balkan countries. Bolschwing 'showed himself enthusiastic' to activate spy-rings in Romania and Hungary since wartime. He had developed a network of Romanians with former members of the Iron Guard and was suspicious of British Intelligence. The Iron Guard was a Romanian fascist movement established in 1927. Their ideology was ultra-nationalist, anti-Semitic and anti-communist. In September 1940, Marshal Ion Antonescu incorporated the movement into his government but in January 1941 the members of the Iron Guard staged a mutiny. Antonescu purged them from the government and their leaders fled to Germany.

The American handlers reported Bolschwing as being:

> '...disturbed by the continuing British interest in Papanace [a close associate and former Iron Guard member for the Romanian spy rings]. He [Bolschwing] is now convinced that they want to assassinate him [Papanace]. He bases this belief on the fact that Papanace is one of the most eager proponents of Balkan unity, a plan which collides with the century old divide and rule tactics of Britain in Europe. *Usage* believes that the British want to get Papanace out of the way and install in his place a figurehead who could put the Papanace net at their disposal, but who would not insist on the Balkan federation plan which Papanace favors.'[348]

The Americans did not believe Bolschwing. They assumed that 'the British are worrying about a plan to unite the Balkans in the dim future when they are faced with the imminent possibility of a Europe forcibly united under the Soviets...the British interest in Papanace is, for the present at least, purely an intelligence matter.'[349]

Bolschwing presented a full plan for an intelligence operation against Hungary; he would call up a 'sleeping net already in existence which has between two and three hundred members.' He would give the Americans 'the true names of all these people who represent a tightly knit and well trained group.' The aim was to equip them with radio transmitters. He would also call up his contacts to establish a network in Romania.

The former SD spymaster submitted the first reports on Hungarian affairs by February 1951- his secret group under the cryptonym *XX* had

[348] Chief of Station (Karlsruhe) to Chief of Foreign Division,12 September 1950, available at:<https://ia801307.us.archive.org/27/items/BolschwingOttovon/BOLSCHWING,%20OTTO%20(VON)%20%20%20VOL.%201_0109.pdf> accessed 13 August 2019.
[349] Ibid.

produced intelligence; 'much to be desired…needs guidance' the general comment read. He had supplied the Americans with information on Hungarian production figures, labour unions, river navigation and railways. The CIC Salzburg station 'reacted strongly 'to the first reports on Hungary: '…the whole operation is based on fraud, and that the information which claims to originate from established sources within Hungary in reality consists of items from newspapers, old statistical works, and from current Hungarian publications with heavy but crude padding…'[350]

The information about Soviet troops was deemed 'the only factual report…the information may have been obtained from a refugee.' Indeed, 'the report was checked with the OB [Order of Battle] Section of G-2 USFA [Military Intelligence of United States Forces Austria], which considers the information possibly true; G-2 has had similar information from refugees. A check made directly to *XX 61* [an operative of Bolschwing] in Vienna might throw some light on whether or not a courier really exists and what his value is.'[351]

Bolschwing believed strongly that Jesuits in Hungary could be employed in intelligence operations; he had recruited a total of six priests. *XX 61* (Erno Karoly Heberstreit, a Hungarian Catholic living in West Austria), a chief operative of Bolschwing, 'was held in extremely high regard by all American case officers who had had dealings with him, but the reports produced by the operation were uniformly evaluated as of small value - vague, overt, outdated, rumours, padded newspaper articles, etc.' [352]

In July 1951, Bolschwing proposed an intelligence scheme to the Americans in Czechoslovakia:

> 'In order to convince us of the worth of this proposal, *Usage* [Bolschwing] sent *SLC-02* [one of his operatives] to Slovakia on 29 July…He returned on 9 August with a report, three samples of ammunition, a copy of the 1952 CSR production plan and three letterheads with the director's signature from the Zilina chemical factory…the report and

[350] Chief of Foreign Division to Chief of Station (Karlsruhe), 25 February 1951, available at: <https://ia601307.us.archive.org/27/items/BolschwingOttovon/BOLSCHWING,%20OTTO%20(VON)%20%20VOL.%201_0152.pdf> accessed 13 August 2019

[351] Ibid.

[352] Usage status as of 15 June 1951, available at: <https://ia801307.us.archive.org/27/items/BolschwingOttovon/BOLSCHWING,%20OTTO%20(VON)%20%20%20VOL.%201_0173.pdf> accessed 13 August 2019.

particularly the sample ammunition seem interesting, so we intend to explore this Slovakian proposal more vigorously. *SLC-02* expresses complete confidence, for instance, that upon completion of manufacture he can provide us with a plastic "RO-5" type anti-tank mine. We have almost completed operational data on the persons involved, both inside and outside Slovakia…'[353]

As Bolschwing submitted new reports he gained praise from US Military Intelligence and the CIA:

> '*Usage's* contribution to the overall USFA OB [Order of Battle] picture was discussed…all of his reports bear codename *Bismarck* whether they pertain to military, counter-intelligence, or political subjects…*Usage's* OB reports thus handled which are almost exclusively concerned with Air OB, while neither outstanding nor voluminous, are considered "good, useful and of value". In weighting this judgment, of course, *Usage's* comparatively late entry into this field should be given due consideration. It was pointed out by [name not declassified] that in *Usage's* case no time lag, processing or lengthy evaluation was involved since his reports were submitted in readable English and were promptly channeled through *Gruesome* (a CIC unit) to USGA G-2.'[354]

For security reasons, Bolschwing was assigned a new code name, *Grossbahn*. He was leading seven agents focusing on the Soviet order of battle in Austria. His American handlers were very satisfied: 'This is at present the most productive part of the *Grossbahn* complex of operations. Since May [1952] approximately eighty reports have been received here, all but a few of which have been disseminated. The evaluations received from Washington customer agencies have been varied, in general not too enthusiastic. In a number of cases, they have said that the info could best be evaluated by the Army in Austria. Customer agencies in the field, on

---

[353] Chief of Station (Karlsruhe) to Chief, Foreign Division, 22 August 1951 <https://ia601307.us.archive.org/27/items/BolschwingOttovon/BOLSCHWING,%20OTTO%20(VON)%20%20%20VOL.%201_0176.pdf> accessed 16 August 2019.
[354] Chief of Station (Karlruhe) to Chief Foreign Division, 7 December 1951, available at: <https://ia601307.us.archive.org/27/items/BolschwingOttovon/BOLSCHWING,%20OTTO%20(VON)%20%20%20VOL.%201_0190.pdf> accessed 16 August 2019.

the other hand, have shown extremely favorable reactions to the reports. For example, a memo from the Chief of the Intelligence Section of USAF characterized them as "extremely useful in helping this Headquarters maintain its Air Order of Battle of Soviet Air Forces units in Soviet zone Austria" and said that the information in them "is of great interest to this Headquarters as well as to USA, USAF, USFA. They were judged "quite reliable".'[355]

In addition, 'through a police official in Salzburg who has three or four subagents or informants, *Grossbahn* received police reports...most are of local interest...useful for counter-espionage. *Grossbahn* received also reports from an agent connected in Upper Austrian socialist circles but who maintains contacts in Austrian extreme rightist circles...valuable for counter-espionage.'[356]

The *Grossbahn* operations suffered a few setbacks. A spy-ring in Czechoslovakia was dismantled and the Americans assumed that it was 'a bad risk from the start.'[357] *Grossbahn* was an officially stateless person living in Austria so he could not buy a car because he had to show the source of his income to the Austrian authorities which would issue the required licence. His handlers repeatedly tried to help him in this respect but still by 1952 he did not own a car for his operations.

The overall report for intelligence provided by Bolschwing in 1952 was favourable. He had submitted 138 reports on the Soviet order of battle and only six were not disseminated. It was noted that the reports 'have been received with great favour by customer agencies in the field.' Bolschwing's reports 'constitute approximately 25% of the USAG OB take, exclusive of MIS [Military Intelligence Service] debriefings [of refugees and deserters].' His reporting 'has been extensive and competent, highly regarded by local customers...he successfully recruited the prospective agent he was asked to approach.' With reference to information on counter-espionage Bolschwing proved himself very efficient: 'a particular advantage has been his ability to do name checks on request speedily and in detail.'

To mitigate the damage of the collapse of the operations in Slovakia

---

[355] Summary prepared for [name not declassified] undated, 1952, available at: <https://ia801307.us.archive.org/27/items/BolschwingOttovon/BOLSCHWING,%20OTTO %20(VON)%20%20%20VOL.%202_0008.pdf> accessed 15 August 2019.

[356] Ibid.

[357] Extract from EASA-226 dated 24 October 1952, available at: <https://ia801307.us.archive.org/27/items/BolschwingOttovon/BOLSCHWING,%20OTTO %20(VON)%20%20%20VOL.%202_0043.pdf> accessed 15 August 2019.

'steps were taken to seal off *Grossbahn* from any efforts by CIS [Czechoslovakia Intelligence Service] to follow up leads obtained from the captured couriers.' Thus, 'there is no indication that *Grossbahn's* security has been endangered by the collapse of the Slovakian operation.'

The Americans worried that 'the serious threat' to Bolschwing's security was that one of his operatives, *CC-2*, had confessed that he was in contact with Wilhelm Hoettl, characterised as a 'well-known intelligence peddler suspected of connections with RIS [Russian Intelligence Service], inter alia' and 'has disclosed classified information to him.' It was Karl Hass, an operative for CIC, who first informed the Americans about the *CC-2* contact. *CC-2* 'has on his own initiative submitted his resignation, to be effective early 31 January 1953.' The interrogation of *CC-2* did not reveal that crucial information on Bolschwing was passed to Hoettl.

Bolschwing was to continue being a spymaster for US Intelligence until January 1954. His main motive was to become a US citizen; his sub-agents were loyal to him personally despite the risks.[358]

It is, indeed, surprising that one SD spymaster, Bolschwing, commanded the respect of his secret operatives who were recruited during the war and had witnessed the end of Nazi Germany.

Nonetheless, Bolschwing's health was deteriorating. In mid-January 1953 his handlers sounded alarmed: 'for several urgent reasons we are forcing *Grossbahn* to take a three to four week rest. He displayed evident signs of strain and in all fairness to him, as well as ourselves, we insisted that he "get away from it all" for a spell.'[359] 'Numerous gastrological symptoms as a result of considerable anxiety 'were noted. 'Therapy consisted of a rather rigid ulcer regimen combined with a sincere attempt to develop some insight on the part of the patient regarding the factors leading to his psychosomatic complaints.'[360]

At the end of March 1953, Bolsching noticed a man hidden in the bushes, watching his villa. He informed the Americans and the police who duly investigated, arresting a member of the Austrian Communist Party

[358] Project Grossbahn; Memorandum for the Chefi, Plans (CIA), 16 February 1953, available at:
<https://ia801307.us.archive.org/27/items/BolschwingOttovon/BOLSCHWING,%20OTTO%20(VON)%20%20%20VOL.%202_0068.pdf> accessed 15 August 2019.
[359] Chief of Base (Salzburg) to Chief Eastern Europe, 14 January 1953, available at:
<https://ia801307.us.archive.org/27/items/BolschwingOttovon/BOLSCHWING,%20OTTO%20(VON)%20%20%20VOL.%202_0061.pdf> accessed 15 August 2019.
[360] Medical report-Grossbahn, 1 May 1953, available at:
<https://ia801307.us.archive.org/27/items/BolschwingOttovon/BOLSCHWING,%20OTTO%20(VON)%20%20%20VOL.%202_0075.pdf> accessed 16 August 2019.

the first week of April. [361]

Bolschwing was about to move for a while to the United States; he would serve US Intelligence once he returned as a 'spotter, recruiter and developer of new operations.' For the time being, the CIA would try to 'dispose of - either by direct takeover, suspending or dropping - his recent operations prior to his departure.' [362]

Eventually, the CIA handlers concluded that Bolschwing's real identity as a US spy had been compromised: 'It was the consensus of opinion (Headquarters, VOB [Vienna Operations Base], and SOB [Salzburg Operations Base]) that agent's time in Austria had been used up; he was too badly compromised and too well identified as being a KUBARK [cryptonym of the CIA] agent in all circles.' A handler stated that 'GROSSBAHN was told that his days of usefulness in Austria were rapidly drawing to a close, and, if he were ever to realize his ambition of getting to the States and becoming a US citizen, now is the time to do it.' [363]

A review of the available files on Bolschwing indicated that he was once a member of Adolf Eichmann's staff. Worries led to a third interrogation with polygraph in September 1953; he was interrogated for 22 hours on three separate days during that month. The polygraph examiner noted that 'it appeared questions regarding subject's (Bolschwing) activities prior to 1945 cause more…tension and disturbance than questions regarding his activities subsequent to 1945.' [364]

He was asked if he had worked for Eichmann. He replied that he met him twice and that he refused to join his Sonderkommando. The examiner concluded that 'it does not appear that subject has been withholding any important information regarding Eichman[n], but, considering his initial reaction to the question, it is some minor fact related to the matter that subject is unwilling to mention.' [365] In 1959, Bolschwing, ostensibly a reputable businessman in pharmaceutics, applied successfully to become a US citizen.

After the trial of Eichmann in Israel, traces in files were discovered

---

[361] Report, 5 June 1953, available at:
<https://archive.org/stream/BolschwingOttovon/BOLSCHWING%2C%20OTTO%20%28VON%29%20%20%20VOL.%202_0080#mode/1up> accessed 15 August 2019.

[362] Grossbahn progress report, 10 August 1953, available at:
<https://archive.org/stream/BolschwingOttovon/BOLSCHWING%2C%20OTTO%20%28VON%29%20%20%20VOL.%202_0086#mode/2up> accessed 15 August 2019.

[363] Quoted in Ruffner, 'Prussian Nobleman, SS Officer, and CIA Agent', p.68.
[364] Ibid., pp.67-68
[365] Ibid., p. 68.

pointing to the direction that Bolschwing had indeed served in his staff in 1937-39. A CIA memo read:

> 'From 1937 (or earlier) until about 1939, he appears to have been principal agent of the Department II, Section 112 of the RSHA...At that time, Eichmann...was a member of this section. The examination conducted thus far has not made it possible to ascertain whether Eichmann was subject's case officer in the early years of their service...it does, however, appear that by 1938 Eichmann directed at least one or two specific phases of subject's work.'[366]

The real activities of Bolschwing prior to and during the war were revealed - to the dismay of the CIA (whose new generation of officers had to manage the crisis): '...the captured records contain evidence that, at least on one occasion,[Dr Franz Alfred Six the chief of Department II], Eichmann and subject [Bolschwing] conferred in detail about certain anti-Jewish activities of Section 112 and gave subject [Bolschwing] specific guidance. Other papers indicated that Dr. Six and Eichmann were well acquainted with subject and with his work.' Bolschwing was well-versed in plots:

> 'In 1937 or 1938, subject [Bolschwing] appears to have been directly involved in foreign currency manipulations specifically, at that time, the Nazis were exerting pressure upon persons of Jewish extraction in order to get them to leave Germany.'[367]

While SD spymaster in Bucharest, Bolschwing 'was closely associated with von Killinger, the German envoy in Romania. Von Killinger's activities have been linked with Eichmann's attempts to exterminate the Jews and he has been considered a war criminal.' CIA officers aware of the details of the voluminous files of Bolschwing sounded nervous: 'It is our assumption that subject may be named as Eichmann's collaborator and fellow conspirator and that the resulting

---

[366] 'Otto Albreach Alfred von Bolschwing', 2 February 1961, available at: < https://ia801307.us.archive.org/27/items/BolschwingOttovon/BOLSCHWING,%20OTTO% 20(VON)%20%20%20VOL.%202_0126.pdf>, accessed 16 August 2019.

[367] Ibid.

publicity may prove embarrassing to the US...'[368]

In 1978, the Special Litigation Unit (SLU) of the US Immigration and Naturalization Service (INS) investigated a former Iron Guard member named Valerian Trifa, who was a bishop in the United States. The role of Bolschwing in Romania in organising the persecution and execution of Jews emerged. A year later, in 1980, Nazi-hunter Simon Wiesenthal issued a report that Bolschwing was residing in the United States. The CIA was put under strong public pressure. A legal battle between the US government and Bolschwing ensued but the wealthy businessman died of progressive supranuclear palsy in March 1982.

---

[368] Ibid.

13

The Propagandist

'Take us to Smolka's,'[369] Major Calloway (Trevor Howard) orders his driver in the film *The Third Man*. Smolka was the name of a small tavern; Harry Lime (Orson Welles) waits there for the fateful phone call, before the manhunt commences leading him to the Vienna sewers.

The name Smolka was a secret joke between Graham Greene and Peter Smollett, the correspondent of *The Times* in Vienna. As a correspondent Smollett was described as 'the only newsman who could at any time get a personal statement from Tass (news agency).'[370]

The fear of a communist coup persisted in autumn 1948 as *The Third Man* was being shot. The Austrian police kept Smollett and his wife under surveillance. Smollett's wife was the Vienna director of the communist English language agency *Telepress* of Prague. The Austrian police insisted: 'It was from this agency that the report which caused much excitement reached the public in 1948 that the USA had promised the Austrian "reactionary" circles through Mr. [Allen] Dulles (the former OSS spymaster) to supply them with arms to fight against the communist danger and to equip an already existing anti-communist militia. This announcement may be attributed to Smollett.' In addition, 'it was Smollett who staged the thrust by the "eastern bloc" at the latest meeting of the Association of Foreign Correspondents in Vienna, at which Polish press correspondent was elected as the new president; he is considered to be a communist émigré.'[371]

Smollett had provided Greene with uncredited advice. Greene was accompanied by Elizabeth Montagu, a former operative of the OSS in Bern. Her assignment from the Hungarian-born film producer Alexander Korda was to search for pre-war contacts in Vienna.[372] Greene was quickly introduced to Vienna's dark secrets with black market stories, violence and kidnappings. As Montagu put it in her memoirs, 'Greene

---

[369] Smolka (as written in English lagunage documents); Schmolka (in German); Šmolka (in Czech).

[370] Confidential memorandum prepared by Mr W.R.Hutton, B.I.S., Chicago on the defection of John Peet, Reuters Berlin Chief of Bureau, 18 October 1950, KV 2/4169 TNA.

[371] 'Smollett/Smolka, Harry Peter', 30 October 1952, KV 2/4170 TNA.

[372] Riegler, 'The Spy Story behind The Third Man', p.7.

would talk to anyone he met, constantly searching for a theme on which to build his story.' The author met with Smollett once at the latter's villa at 27 Jagdschlossgasse (today's Seelosgasse). Montagu assumed that it was a 'very successful' meeting, ending with Smollet handing over a manuscript of a book he had written to Greene, to help him find a publisher. Smollet wrote about a blackmarketeer who diluted penicillin. Timothy Smolka, Peter Smollett-Smolka's son, assumed that his father told Greene only about the elaborate sewer system of Vienna ('He repeatedly spoke of it with great enthusiasm'). Eventually Smollet received from the film production company a total of £210 for 'giving advice on the film script' and 'providing assistance in Vienna in connection with the production'. His manuscript was not published.[373]

The story of Smolka is a labyrinth of machinations by a man despised by many of his peers while, surprisingly, maintaining access to and connections with many influential people of the elite. Peter Smolka was born on 17 September 1912 in Vienna. On 28 August 1930, he arrived in Marseilles aboard an Italian ship from Barcelona. He was arrested while taking photographs inside the fort of the port. The French assumed that he was a spy 'in the pay of Italy' and duly deported him the next day.

In September 1930, Smollett arrived in London to work as the correspondent of the Austrian daily *Der Tag* and enrolled at the London School of Economics. He attended political meetings in Britain and France. Casual informers of MI5 reported that he was known for his arrogance in the hotel where he was living and that he had 'communist tendencies'; 'it was alleged' that he took photos of poor people for propaganda. In March 1931, he left for Austria and returned in 1933 with his wife. Curiously, in November 1934 'with a certain H.R. Philby' he formed a small press agency called *London Continental News Limited*. Philby's full name was Harold Adrian Russell 'Kim' Philby and he was in Vienna at the same time as Smolka. In 1935 and in 1936, Smolka visited the Soviet Union for short periods. In 1936 Smolka went to Russia as a correspondent for *The Times,* where he participated in a Russian expedition to the Arctic.

Smolka finally made his reputation with a series of well-written articles for *The Times* describing his travels in the Russian Arctic, later turned into a best-selling book *Forty Thousand Against the Arctic: Russia's Polar Empire*, published in 1937. It received very positive reviews, but in effect it was subtle propaganda arranged by the NKVD.

In February 1937 he was assigned as the London representative of

---

[373] Ibid., p.10.

Praga Tagblatt and in November 1938 he became a naturalised British subject and changed his surname to Smollett. At about the same time he joined the staff of the *Exchange Telegraph* news agency. As Austrian Jews were fleeing their country after the annexation to Nazi Germany, an SIS operative under the code name *Victoria* 'conducted [Peter] Smollett (then a correspondent of the *News Chronicle* in Czechoslovakia) to the Czech-Austrian frontier in order to enable him to inspect and interrogate the refugees from Austria.'[374] This is one of the first traces that Smollett was known and perhaps provided information on a casual basis to the SIS, thus building up a 'legend' as loyal to the crown. His behaviour and attitude would have been reported by the SIS operative favourably.

Smollett was interested in working for the Ministry of Information (MoI), but on 31 August 1939 'he was informed that he was unsuitable.' Nonetheless: 'on the following day, however, we [MI5] waived our objection as he was well vouched for by Mr. Rex Leeper of the Foreign Office.' At that time Leeper was the head of the Political Intelligence Department of the Foreign Office.

In December 1939, the London representative of the French Committee of Information aired his suspicions that there was a leak of information from the News Department of the MoI to Switzerland. He feared that someone in the *Exchange Telegraph Ltd* had telephoned news bulletins to an associate in Zurich and the information quickly reached Nazi Germany. It was known that *Exchange Telegraph* had the monopoly news agency in Belgium, Holland and Switzerland. Most importantly 'it was alleged that Smollett had earlier threatened the head of [news agency] *Agencé Swiss* with reversion of his British visa if he refused to take the *Exchange Telegraph* news service.'[375] It was a clear hint that Smollett must have been behind this leak.

In 1939 Kim Philby, the 'certain H.R. Philby,' recruited Smollett for the NKVD. Smollett was given the code name ABO. Philby did not first get the authorisation from his NKVD handler and introduced Smollett to Guy Burgess. The new spy was now aware of two Cambridge spies and once Moscow was informed, they did not hide their anger at Philby's initiative to recruit Smollett.

At the MoI Smollett worked alongside Burgess before the latter joined MI5. Smollett showed his talent to claim more responsibilities and access to information. In January 1940, he was 'second in command' of the Foreign Publicity Division of the Ministry. He put forward his

---

[374] 'Harry Smollett aka Smolka', 28 May 1946, KV 2/4169 TNA.
[375] Memo on Smollett, 5 September 1942, KV 2/4169 TNA.

proposals that 'all reports from British press attachés should pass through his hands and be edited by him before being issued.'[376]

In June, as the British and French forces in France were defeated, the Foreign Office News Department informed the Home Office that the *Exchange Telegraph* had asked for permission for Mr. A.V. Smolka 'to continue his work of monitoring broadcasts from foreign countries.' A.V. Smolka was Smollett's father. His son personally intervened, calling the Home Office on the phone, telling them that he was working for the MoI and that the applicant was his father. The Home Office did not object to the man's employment.

In June 1941, it was reported to MI5 that Smollett's sister-in-law had told friends that she and Smollett were both communists and that he had applied for a Czech passport before becoming a British subject. 'Another source' in July claimed that Smollett was a communist with good connections to the Communist Party of Great Britain (CPGB).

Brendan Bracken, a press tycoon and friend of Winston Churchill, would become a key supporter of Smollett at the MoI. Bracken had been the proprietor of the *Financial Times* and *The Economist*. Upon the invasion of Russia in June 1941, he was appointed Minister of Information. He rushed to coordinate Anglo-Russian propaganda, effectively for Britain to support Stalin's war image. Smollett (ABO), to the surprise of all, was appointed the new head of the Russian section. Soon Smollett became the head of the Russian section of the MoI. He was a Whitehall insider with access to people and information critical to the war effort and to the evolving post war strategy of the British government. He was leading the effort for the dispatch of the British Publicity Mission to Russia. The mission was responsible for the publication of the Russian-language *Britanski Soyvznik*. Smollet's department sent some 300 to 500 British photographs to Russia every week and news items of some 2,000 words daily to the *Tass* news agency; he also arranged with the Russian Embassy in London for an exchange of films and radio recordings. Smollett had some contact with the Free German League of Culture, considered a pro-communist organisation.

W.T. Caulfield, an official of the MoI, was against the ever-expanding activities of Smollett:

'My interest in him [Smollett] arose chiefly from hearing that he had added Hungary to the list of countries which he looks after in the Foreign Division of the MoI. I believe he is

---

[376] Ibid.

nominally under Godfreay Lias…but actually he has a free hand…I, in general, feel misgivings that a Central European should have a position of influence and authority. He is of interest to me particularly by reason of his close relations with Andrew Revai the well-known Hungarian journalist who is the object of my strong but unsubstantiated suspicions. Revai is the brains behind the Zsilinsky/Almassy Group of Free Hungarians which is pro-Horthy, and is in bitter opposition to the Count Lonyai Group who are violently anti-Horthy and left wing democratic, apparently backed by the Czechs.'[377]

Miklós Horthy de Nagybánya was the Regent of Hungary, a staunch anti-communist. He had allowed the Wehrmacht to pass through Hungary to invade Yugoslavia and contributed 200,000 troops to the Eastern front.

Smollett supported Revai 'for a rather important job under aegis of the MoI in connection with Central European propaganda.' Caulfield was aware, since Smollett's phone line at the MoI was monitored, that he and Revai had agreed not to broadcast Lonyai's letter to the Hungarian people. Lonyai claimed to be the leader of the Free Hungarian Movement. Smollet and Revai antagonised him. Caulfield was wary of Hungarian intrigues. He knew that Lonyai's assertion was false. The British official had grown suspicious of Smollett: 'I am perhaps building on a rather slender foundation, and I do not know what special axe Smollett is trying to grind, but the episode [of not broadcasting Lonyai's letter] does leave me with the impression that his actions may not be governed solely by British interests coolly and calmly appraised.'[378]

It was also admitted that 'there is little in the file to confirm [that Smolka was a communist and had good connections with the CPGB]…from a rapid inspection' of his personal file the conclusion was that 'Smolka is very much too closely concerned with his own prosperity to commit himself to any side until he is sure that is the winning side.'[379]

Smollett expanded the policy for easing anti-Russian feeling amongst British public opinion. He showed his talent in manipulating resources; he promoted 'sympathetic British commentators' while he isolated 'Russian accented and openly partisan apologists.' Ivan Maisky, the Soviet ambassador, and his wife proved themselves always willing to support Smollett's carefully orchestrated propaganda schemes. Lady Violet

[377] Memo by W.T.Caulfeild, 5 August 1941, KV 2/4169 TNA.
[378] Ibid.
[379] Memo ADF2, 13 August 1941, KV 2/4169 TNA.

Bonham Carter, a BBC governor, and Maisky agreed to promote Soviet cultural achievements and avoid politics. The Soviet ambassador and his wife toured Britain making many public appearances in Pathé newsreels, reaching mass audiences in cinemas. In September 1941, it was announced that a full month's tank production would go to support the Soviet war effort. Surprisingly (for die-hard SIS and MI5 officers confronting Soviet espionage and propaganda throughout the interwar period) Maisky was allowed to make a speech to workers at a British tank factory standing by a tank named *Stalin*. British public opinion started viewing Stalin's Russia as an ally. To this end MoI promoted films arriving from Moscow, amongst them *A Day on the Soviet Front*, *Abundant Harvest*, *Odessa Besieged*, *Soviet Women*, *Salute to the Soviet*, *Daghestan*, and *A Day in Soviet Russia*. British films like *Merchant Seamen* and *Food Convoy* were connected to the overall pro-Soviet propaganda.

The BBC broadcast Shostakovich's *Leningrad* (Seventh) symphony on the first anniversary of the invasion of Russia in June 1942. More broadcasts followed about Stalingrad and the 25th anniversary of the October Revolution in 1942. In 1943 the 7th November was celebrated in Britain as the Soviet National Day and the next evening's BBC broadcasts were in honour of Russia. In 1944, on the occasion of the Red Army Day, Poet Laureate John Masefield read the *Ode to the Red Army*. In December 1944, the BBC broadcast the premiere of Prokofiev's *Toast to Stalin* on the occasion of the Soviet leader's birthday. Evidently, Churchill wanted this propaganda in order to gain some time, given Stalin's increasing pressure to open a second front in Europe.

The MoI and Smollett, as the Russian section head, coordinated efforts for cinema screens throughout Britain of the celebration of the 25th anniversary of the formation of the Red Army in 1943.

At the MoI, there was a research associate of Smollett who was a special case; she worked for the *Britansky Soyvznik* (the British propaganda weekly in Russian). Smollett was always interested in anything she said and, certainly, she would be one of the few people he had to treat perfectly for her to have a good opinion of him: she was Clarissa Churchill, the 22-year-old (in 1942) niece of the Prime Minister. She and her parents remained close to Churchill. A noted episode was that they lunched on 31 May 1940, one of the most dramatic days of the Dunkirk evacuation. She wrote in her memoirs: '...had lunch at my uncle's - which was a nightmare, with news of people's deaths coming in, and Winston's exhaustion, and the barbed-wire entanglements everywhere

212

- and then Johnnie my brother coming home, his clothes drenched by sea water having just escaped...'[380]

By January 1942 'the military advisers to the Ministry of Information were very perturbed about Smollett.' They distrusted him, seeing that he coordinated pro-Soviet propaganda. However, a review of his personal file and the monitoring of his phone calls did not substantiate any suspicions. The position of MI5 was:

> 'Whilst we had nothing against him from a security point of view, he seemed on the face of it a most unsuitable person to occupy his present position [head of the Russian section]. He is an Austrian Jew, 30 years of age, and does not appear to have any special knowledge of Russian though he seems to have paid short visits to that country. He has many associates in this country among Austrian refugees and it seems probably that he is, if not a Communist, at least strongly in sympathy with the movement...there is no evidence in our records which would justify us in having him removed, in fact he came up to us for vetting when he originally went to the Ministry. On the strong recommendation of Mr. Leeper of the Foreign Office we waived any objection.'[381]

'We know nothing to the personal detriment of this applicant' was the conclusion of MI5 on Smollett. In any case 'a reliable opinion expressed as recently as August this year [1941] was that Smolka is very much too closely connected with his own prosperity to commit himself to any side until he is sure that it is the winning one.'[382]

Sir Ivone Kirkpatrick, a seasoned diplomat (later to be a close associate of Prime Minister Antony Eden during his confrontation with Gamal Abdel Nasser which culminated in the Suez crisis in 1956), was appointed Director of the Foreign Division of the MoI. In July 1941, he was asked about Smollett and the broadcasts of the Hungarian section.

Kirkpatrick was 'very skeptical of Hungarians, whom he regards as incurable intriguers and unreliable. He has been told...that Hungarian broadcasts are rotten...he called Smollett up with Macartney [another MoI official] and told them to read the stuff [to be broadcast if they fall within BBC policy line].' For Kirkpatrick, Smollett was 'as bad as any of the

---

[380] Eden, Clarissa, *A Memoir* (London: Weidenfeld & Nicolson, 2007) e-book.
[381] Cross reference to extract from BIF minute re[garding] Smolka, 24 January 1942, KV 2/4169 TNA.
[382] Memo by Hogg, December 1941, KV 2/4169 TNA.

other Central European journalist intriguers.' Smollett had told Kirkpatrick that Revai 'was 100% all right, a most marvellous man, and they could dispense of him.' Nonetheless, the diplomat 'was not impressed' with this recommendation. Kirkpatrick remarked: 'there is little danger of information being passed out through the BBC - why should they bother when the complete Japanese embassy is just round the corner?' (Japan declared war on Britain on 8 December 1941). He sounded resigned; the BBC foreign services would 'always be a hotbed of intrigue, denunciation and allegation, though where there is smoke there is probably fire.'[383] Kirkpatrick was right, but he did not know it: Ernest Henri, an NKVD spy, was hired by Burgess at the BBC in January 1942 and he coordinated propaganda with Smollett.

In 1941 and 1942, 'information was received from two separate sources, both of a delicate nature,' that Smollett was 'a communist and had good connection with the CPGB' (Communist Party of Great Britain). New reports indicated that he was not a party member but a sympathiser. In May 1942, Brigadier O.A. Harker, the deputy director of MI5, received a note about Smollett: 'my friend has taken a strong instinctive dislike to this gentleman, who is said to be a Hungarian (sic) Jew whose name was originally "Schmolke" (sic). My friend has no evidence whatever against him, but I agreed to ascertain whether his instinctive feelings found any echo in the more prosaic records of your organisation. Don't, however, put your lads to too much labour over this, for, as I said, there is nothing that can be quoted as evidence against the man concerned.'[384] Harker's deputy was Guy Liddell. There is no mention in his diaries that Smollett was a person of interest for MI5 at that time.

In September 1942, during a lunch conversation between two intelligence officers (Fulford and Brooman-White) it came out that 'the certain H.R. Philby' 'is almost certainly our mutual friend in Section V [of SIS], Kim Philby.'[385] Fulford asked Brooman-White to contact Philby and have his opinion on Smollett.

Two days later Brooman-White replied:

'I spoke to Philby about Smollett. The press agency in question never actually functioned but Philby knew Smollett quite well at the time. He says he is an Austrian Jew who came to this country about 1920 [sic probably a typing mistake instead of 1930], did well in journalism and is

[383] Memo by W.T.Caulfeild, 19 July 1941, KV 2/4169 TNA.
[384] Brigadier O.A.Harker received on 12 May 1942, KV 2/4169 TNA.
[385] Fulford to Brooman-White, 10 September 1942, KV 2/4169 TNA.

extremely clever. Commercially he is rather a pusher but has nevertheless a rather timid character and a feeling of inferiority largely due to his somewhat repulsive appearance. He is a physical coward and was petrified when the air-raid began. Philby considered his politics to be mildly left wing but had no knowledge of the C[ommunist] P[arty] link-up. His personal opinion is that Smollett is clever and harmless. He adds that in any case the man would be far too scared to become involved in anything really sinister.'[386]

Philby, the spy who recruited Smollett, provided him with a sophisticated recommendation, reassuring MI5 that they had nothing to fear of him. Philby directed them to think of Smollett as 'harmless,' a 'coward' with a 'feeling of inferiority,' 'mildly left-wing.' In contrast, spies were considered courageous, ruthless and committed individuals.

In February 1944 Smollett had gone to Moscow on official MoI business. He remained with the MoI until June 1945. Afterwards he went to Prague as a correspondent for the *Daily Express*. In any case, despite the suspicions of Smollett being 'an ex-enemy alien,' 'no concrete evidence has been forthcoming that Smollett has acted against [the] security interests in this country (Britain).'[387] Smollett was awarded the Order of the British Empire for his copious efforts in propaganda. To a researcher of medals this award raises more questions about what Smollett had really done to deserve it.

In March 1946, the SIS station in Vienna filed a note on Smollett, then the correspondent of the *Daily Express* in the city:

'There are indications that he has been asking questions about Austrian Barracks Unit, and about our (SIS) Representative in Vienna. Also that he is cultivating Ernst Fischer, former Minister of Education and his wife, and is in contact with Tito Yugoslav circles in Vienna.'[388]

In London, the wartime role of Smollett as a spy could not be uncovered, because he had attracted suspicion as a selfish intriguer on Central European politics and propaganda while he was also a 'coward,' according to Philby. Smollett's critics were blinded into seeing him only as an intriguer, not a skilful spy.

---

[386] Broomn-White to Fulford, 12 September 1942, KV 2/4169 TNA.
[387] Letter to Kim Philby, 12 March 1946, KV 2/4169 TNA.
[388] SIS to Marriot (MI5), 29 March 1946, KV 2/4169 TNA.

An SIS operative under the code name *Victoria* reported that back in 1938, during and after the Anschluss crisis, she led Smollett (then a correspondent of the *News Chronicle* in Czechoslovakia) to the Czech-Austrian border in order for him to interview the refugees from Austria. *Victoria* added that Smollett's good relations with the Russians started during his participation in the Russian North Pole expedition in 1936. *Victoria* insisted also that Smollett's articles in post war Vienna were 'strongly biased in favour of Russia.'[389]

In November 1946, the SIS station in Vienna informed London that Smollett's articles were regarded by the Austrian government as 'Anti-Austrian.' Smollett organised 'tea soirees' in his villa in Hietzing, where 'leading Russian and Austrian communists' gathered.[390] In July 1947, SIS sent a message to MI5 for Smollett not to be allowed into confidential background talks by government officials to British correspondents.

In February 1948, Smollett took over as correspondent of *The Times* in Vienna. A Viennese SIS source considered him 'a communist'; 'certainly he is a very pro-Russian.' He had been writing also for the pro-communist weekly *Neues Osterreich*.

Surprisingly, in July, the SIS station reported that Smollett was 'working for American and other foreign intelligence sources.' No additional information was offered. In February 1949, SIS reported that Smollett's connection with the Austrian Communist Party was not 'over'; he was useful as a *Times* correspondent but 'regarded as Party member.' In May 1950, surveillance showed that Smollett was 'in close touch' with Soviet and Austrian communist circles in Vienna. In June, the SIS reported that he was given back his family metal factory in the Soviet occupation zone. It was a truly surprising Soviet decision. Smollett had resigned from *The Times* in May 1949 and started running his factory (of 200 workers). In October 1950, an American official submitted a confidential report that Smollett was 'a self-confessed communist, card-holder' of the Austrian Communist Party.

The SIS officers in Vienna did not hide their hatred: 'Subject [Smollett] still lives at Vienna XIII, Jagdschlossgasse 27, and suffers from severe diabetes. We wish Dr Banting had not discovered insulin.'[391] (Sir Frederick Grant Banting was the Nobel Laureate co-discoverer of insulin.)

George Orwell, the author of *1984* and *Animal Farm*, feared and despised Smollett. Historian Timothy Garton Ash insisted that Smollett was 'almost certainly' the 'civil servant' on whose advice in 1944 a

---

[389] Harry Smollett aka Smolka, 28 May1946, KV 2/4169 TNA.

[390] Extract from SIS source report, 16 November 1946, KV 2/4169 TNA.

[391] 'Peter Smollett- ex-Smolka', letter to Oughton (MI5), 20 June 1950, KV 2/4169 TNA.

London publisher rejected Orwell's *Animal Farm* 'as an unhealthily anti-Soviet text'. The disillusioned-with-communism Orwell (at that time seriously ill) feared an advance of Stalinism in Europe. He understood that the Soviet threat was not appreciated enough, so he decided to hit back. On 2 May 1949, he sent Celia Kirwan, a friend who worked for the Information Research Department (IRD) of the Foreign Office, a list of 38 names of journalists and writers deemed crypto-communists - amongst them Smollett. For Orwell, Smollett was 'almost certainly agent of some kind...a very slimy person.'[392]

Orwell's allegorical novella *Animal Farm,* deemed critical of Stalinism, was used in autumn 1951 by the CIA: they arranged for a total of 120,000 copies to be distributed with a CIA-subsidised newspaper in Austria.[393]

After the defection of Guy Burgess and Donald MacLean in May 1951, the SIS station in Vienna was notified to check on Smollett. Peter Lunn, SIS station chief in Vienna, reported back that 'he knows of nothing to connect the above [Smollett] with Burgess.'[394] The SIS station was instructed to report on Smollett in case he decided to defect. Lunn was reassuring: '[name not declassified] says that they do not now think that Smolka is likely to defect. [name not declassified] gave the impression that Smolka was a man who was much too intelligent to swallow the Soviet line.'[395]

Ironically, Smollett's name was found in a list of the MGB 'to be kidnapped' in Vienna in 1953. Smollett had to answer Russian suspicion that in the last years he was working for the SIS. After Stalin's death in March 1953, the operation was cancelled, but perhaps it was deemed difficult to remove the then wheelchair-bound Smollett, who was focusing his attention on his factory.

Godfrey Lyas, the *Times* correspondent in Vienna, met with Smollett and informed the SIS that Smollett had joined the Austrian Communist Party 'solely to enable him to acquire an interest in his late father's button factory, from which he derives a handsome living...Smollett is dying of

---

[392] Meeting with George Orwell, 1949, FO 1110/189 TNA; Ezard, John, 'Blair's Babe', *The Guardian*, 21 June 2003, available at: https://www.theguardian.com/uk/2003/jun/21/books.artsandhumanities accessed 22 July 2019.
[393] Quoting the diary entry of CIA Director Beddell Smith in Holzman, Michael, *Kim and Jim: Philby and Angleton, Friends and Enemies in the Cold War* (London: Weidenfeld & Nicolson, 2021), p.164.
[394] Letter from MI6 on Smollett, 28 June 1951, KV 2/4169 TNA.
[395] B1F Source report re Burgess and MacLean, KV 2/4170 TNA.

an obscure disease, and he is only kept alive by liberal use of American drugs.'[396]

In London, the frantic investigations of MI5 to discover what was leaked to Moscow by Burgess and Maclean led to an astonishing discovery: documents were found in Burgess's flat connecting him with Smollett. The examination of typewritten documents confirmed that they derived from Smollett's typewriter. The date range of the documents was October 1941-May 1942. The documents included:

> 1. Loose sheets of typewritten notes describing conversations with government officials (amongst them one summary of a telegram received by the Admiralty from Admiral Myers in Moscow)
>
> 2. A handwritten note containing some details of a bombing raid
>
> 3. An extract from a letter from Sir Stafford Cripps to Eden dated 20 September 1941
>
> 4. A typewritten copy of an Admiralty telegram to the British military mission in Washington dated 30 January 1942
>
> 5. A long handwritten note describing conversations of Smollett with officials, dated April 1939
>
> 6. Handwritten notes taken from official dispatches from Moscow, the date of which was probably 1936

After close examination, MI5 experts concluded that documents one to four were written by Smollett. Of course, Smollett would have written dozens of reports for Moscow in the key period 1939-1945 and afterwards. It was Burgess's sloppiness that allowed the documents to be found by MI5.

J.B. Woodburn of the Central Office of Information was asked by MI5 about the documents and replied that 'it was unlikely that Smollett would have made such notes...for any Ministry of Information purposes...it would not have been part of Smollett's duties to interview members of the Service Departments, though he would have had close official connections with the Foreign Office.' Woodburn remembered that Smollett's 'intimacy' with Sir Stafford Cripps's family 'might have come through Sir Stafford Cripps's daughter' who worked in the MoI during the

---

[396] Memo by M.R.Wade, 'Harry Peter Smollett aka Smolka' 6 November 1952, KV 2/4170 TNA.

war.

Cripps was a noted left-wing wealthy barrister. Churchill appointed him ambassador to Moscow assuming that he could develop a rapport with Stalin. In 1942, he returned to London and boosted pro-Soviet propaganda in Britain; Churchill appointed him Member of the War Cabinet, Lord Privy Seal and Leader of the House of Commons; in late 1942 he headed the Ministry of Aircraft Production, and in 1945 he joined the Labour Party.

MI5 officers studied, yet again, Smollett's record of service. On 2 September 1939, he was hired by the MoI to do press relations work among foreign journalists. In 1940, he was exempt from military service; in November 1940, he was appointed head of the section on propaganda in Switzerland; in June 1941, he was named head of the Russian section; in March 1943 was appointed director of the Soviet relations division. From April to July 1944, he visited Moscow on behalf of the Ministry and helped the US information agencies there. He was awarded the Order of the British Empire for his service to the MoI in 1944 and in May 1945 he submitted his resignation; he left on 1 July 1945.

The voluminous service correspondence revealed that Smollett was denounced by an anonymous employee of the MoI in December 1939 as a German secret agent responsible for the disappearance of some documents. However, 'the letter was dismissed as a nonsense after it had been established that no papers had disappeared.'[397]

In November 1961, Smollett travelled with his wife to London to attend a reception in his honour. The MI5 lost no time; they sent an officer to interview him. To avoid suspicion, Smollett agreed. During the interview, he admitted 'lifelong acquaintanship (sic) with Lissie Philby.' He also claimed 'that Philby was a sleeping [business] partner and that friendship with Kim was never strong because he disapproved of his right-wing political affiliations.'[398] It was a lie that he assumed that Philby was a rightist; this was what Philby pretended throughout the 1930s and 1940s as a cover.

The MI5 officer asked him about the documents found at Burgess's. 'After some hesitation,' Smollett 'admitted that he was their author.' He claimed that Burgess, then serving in MI5, was interested in any official government discussion, putting emphasis: 'MI5 liked to know what people were thinking.' Smollett told his interrogator that he did not object to helping Burgess in this. Nonetheless, Smollett admitted himself to

---

[397] Note by A.S.Martin, 12 February 1952, KV 2/4170 TNA.
[398] Memo by A.S.Martin, 2 November 1961, ibid.

being a 'fellow-traveller' until 1951, when he was disillusioned with communism. He informed his MI5 interviewer that 'his doctors give him only a year or so more to live.'[399] The attorney general, back in 1957, had concluded that no evidence to be presented in a court of law was found to support the charge that Smollett had acted as an agent of a foreign power.

The conclusion of the MI5 officer read:

> 'Smollett, even in his present paralysed condition, is a forceful personality with a quick, shrewd mind. He said nothing which was demonstrably false but, in the interrogator's opinion, he was probably lying when he described the circumstances which led him to write the "Burgess documents"; and that he could have been lying when he described his relationship with Philby. His claim to have lost his Communist faith should therefore be taken with reserve.'[400]

Smollett left London on 4 October 1961 and returned to Vienna. He died in 1980. Until his death he may have been in some kind of contact with the KGB. After all, he was a wealthy businessman with many connections in Austria and in Britain. And Soviet spymasters never had the reputation of leaving behind trusted sources - despite occasional suspicions.

Throughout his espionage career, Smollett was disliked by his peers as a cowardly intriguer. One could argue that this dislike shielded him from suspicions and accusations that he could be a spy for Moscow. John le Carré explores the concept of misdirecting counterintelligence with personal animosity in *Tinker, Taylor, Soldier, Spy*. Bill Haydon tells George Smiley who uncovered him as a spy: 'He [Karla, the Soviet spymaster] reckoned that if I were known to be Ann's lover [Smiley's wife] around the place you wouldn't see me very straight when it came to other things.'[401]

[399] Extact from MI5 (D Branch) Summary of Soviet Satellite and Chinese Intelligence Services in the UK, 'Harry Peter Smolka', 10 November 1961 KV 2/4170 TNA.
[400] Memo by A.S.Martin, 2 November 1961, KV 2/4170 TNA.
[401] Le Carre, John, *Tinker, Taylor, Soldier, Spy* (New York: Pocket Books, 2002), p.373.

14

Panic

In May 1951, the defection of Burgess and MacLean panicked British Intelligence. In February 1954 Pyotr Deryabin, a seasoned officer of NKVD, responsible for counterintelligence in Vienna, defected; a series of defections of Russian officers occurred in the first half of 1954. A year earlier, the Soviet Intelligence apparatus experienced the aftershock and chaos of the death of Stalin and the power struggle between their head Beria (notorious for repeated terror campaigns) and Nikita Khrushchev. Russian spymasters were in a state of panic.

Major Deryabin, born in 1921, was a member of the Communist Party and a war hero, having been wounded four times before being transferred to Smersh and later to the Ministry of Internal Affairs (MVD) (it was merged with MGB and the KGB was established in March 1954).

While in Vienna Deryabin ordered a Greek operative under the surname Khadhiveronius (probably Hatziveronis) to kidnap a former *Zeppelin* operative (the SS-sanctioned operation to send sabotage agents behind the lines of the Red Army), a woman called Avdey. Trusted informers suggested she worked for British Intelligence. By October 1953, the operation of her kidnap had not begun. A new order sent from Moscow ordered Deryabin to proceed with her abduction. But on 13 February 1954 Deryabin defected to US Intelligence.

Deryabin was afraid of being purged and executed as a Beria loyalist. A day before his defection, a junior official of the trade mission had defected; Deryabin would be held responsible. He felt that he had no other choice; he reached a CIC officer (who he had located from surveillance) and offered to defect. The CIA station was duly notified. Deryabin offered intelligence: he told the CIA he had been running a spy under the codename *Stroitel* (constructor in Russian). He was a Russian émigré from Czechoslovakia working as the chief engineer for military construction projects in Austria. The Americans realised that he was their agent too under the codename *Greatcoat*. After a most informative debriefing, Deryabin was informed that the only way to escape Vienna was to travel through the Soviet-occupied zone of Austria in a military crate. He was put inside and tried to feel as comfortable as possible. Four armed CIC officers accompanied the crate and loaded it onto the train's baggage car for the American zone. Two other armed CIA officers were seated in the next car. The journey was uneventful and they all reached

Linz.

In Baden in February 1954, a Soviet general (unnamed in the CIA reports) summoned his officers and warned them about the penetration efforts of US Intelligence. Amongst other things, in order to scare them, he said that the Americans had 'performed acts of sabotage, terror, and even murder.' He mentioned two suspected episodes: a woman soldier was pushed off a train and killed, and a Soviet lieutenant was found dead on a railway track - cause of death, his fall.

The general stated that 'there were plenty of indications that US agents were responsible for the death.' He spoke about leaflets calling to defect found close to Soviet barracks in Austria 'and even inside the military compounds.' He did mention 'several cases of US agents kidnapping Soviet officers' children in Vienna.'[402]

SIS and CIA officers reported on Soviet secret services' reactions to Deryabin's defection. An SIS report read:

> '[name or technical source of information not declassified] have enabled us to watch the effect on Soviet officials there [in Vienna] of recent defections and desertions to the West. We have been able to observe the extreme anxiety of the Soviet authorities to win back the allegiance of Soviet defectors, and to take all possible steps to prevent others from taking the same course. A deputation of senior officers, including two colonels, thought it worth their while to make two visits to Klagenfurt to try to persuade a private (Batanov) to repent of his defection to the British in March 1954. They were unsuccessful.'[403]

In February 1954, a soldier named Khodosov from an MVD escort section defected. A manhunt was launched involving all MVD officers in Austria, and Red Army search teams. British Intelligence concluded that severe punishments awaited these officers. So SIS top rank and file argued that the strategy of neutralising Soviet spymasters was to urge their soldiers to defect by any means possible. Since severe punishment awaited the officers and spymasters after a defection, the defectors turned into 'executioners'; the authority of the spymasters would be weakened. Moscow would be 'wasting' spymasters, punishing them, and the

[402]Morale of Soviet Armed Forces, 13 October 1954, available at:
<https://www.cia.gov/library/readingroom/docs/CIA-RDP80-00810A005000420008-5.pdf> accessed 3 September 2019.
[403] Effects of Recent Soviet Defections and Desertions, 25 May 1954, KV 5/107 TNA.

relations between army, intelligence services and communist party would be damaged.

In April 1954, Vladimir Petrov, the third secretary of the Russian Embassy in Austria, defected. He was not a mere diplomat. He was a Lieutenant-Colonel of the MVD engaged in espionage. His wife, Evdokia, was not only an accountant at the Embassy but an MVD captain engaged in coding secret messages to Moscow. It seemed that Petrov feared the post-Stalin purges and for some time had collected secret documents to offer Austrian Intelligence.

The nervous reaction of Moscow was noted everywhere. SIS reported:

'In Paris, following on Petrov's defection [one and a half lines not declassified; probably technical secret source] an extraordinary meeting was called of all Soviet officials serving in Paris and their families, at which they were warned that the British and Americans had redoubled their efforts to bribe Soviet citizens into defecting or failing that to kidnap them. Special counter-measures announced included forbidding officials to go out alone in the evenings, or to frequent cafés and other public places. Children of Soviet officials were not to be taken for walks in parks. A particular watch was to be kept on any members of the staff known to be addicted to drink. No one was to travel by train, and by air only on aircraft flying straight to East Berlin. Soviet officials were described as disgusted with the tightening of the regulations and inclined to take the line that they were well able to look after themselves. Their morale was reported as outwardly good, but everyone was afraid of showing signs to the contrary.'[404]

Rumours spread that the Soviet ambassador in Paris had been checking personnel files to find anyone deemed 'weak' ideologically. The case of Sergei Ivanovich Volokitin, an MVD officer in Paris, was noted. He flew with his family to Geneva on 29 April and there he changed planes for a direct flight to Moscow. They disappeared without trace behind the Iron Curtain.

Retired Major General Hugh Alexander Sinclair, the Chief of SIS, ordered for the (above) SIS memorandum to be shared with MI5. Philby

---

[404] Effects of Recent Soviet Defections and Desertions, 25 May 1954, KV 5/107 TNA.

wrote about Sinclair in his memoirs:

> 'Sinclair, though not overloaded with mental gifts (he never claimed them) was humane, energetic and so obviously upright that it was impossible to withhold admiration.'[405]

In reply, MI5 elaborated on the security context:

> 'The Doctors dilemma of January 1953 [the 'Doctors' plot' to kill Soviet leaders, staged by Stalin], the MVD/KGB merger of April 1953 and the arrest and execution of Beria and his colleagues in July/December 1953 must all have had an extremely unsettling effect on MVD personnel throughout the service. There is some evidence to support this contention. It is understandable therefore that during and for some time after such events responsible MVD officials could be most anxious to avoid leaving themselves open to the popular charge of "lack of vigilance". This I feel probably accounts for the zeal showed by the deputation of senior officers in Austria who have called twice in person on the private soldier who defected in March 1954 in Austria, and for the mobilisation of the entire MVD in Austria to hunt for the second soldier defector. It is also true that under the Soviet system failure of subordinates is often attributed to their superiors in all walks of state and party activity. I think it is therefore credible that the feeling in the MVD in Austria…was that officers more senior than his C[ommanding] O[fficer] would be severely punished. This type of retribution is all the more likely in times of stress as was shown in the 1938 purges which culminated in the removal of many senior NKVD officials who were blamed for the misdemeanours of their subordinates.'[406]

MI5 urged some caution:

> 'While MI6 (SIS) are entirely right in taking the view expressed that no defector, even a "scruffy malcontent", is insignificant, I feel that a more balanced view on the

[405] Philby, Kim, *My Silent War* (London: Grove Press, 1968), p.141.
[406] Memo, 4 June 1954, KV 5/107 TNA.

remainder of the paragraph [of the SIS memo] is called for. The value of procuring the defection of scruffy malcontents who have little if any useful information to offer about the MVD and whose resettlement in the West can be fraught with major problems (sometimes for us) must be set against what is always their hypothetical value as "executioners" of their senior officers in the MVD. This consideration of course applies only to the type of uniformed MVD troops found in occupied countries. These are rarely concerned in intelligence operations of any significance against the West, their function being largely in the nature of security guards on vulnerable points, communications, etc.'[407]

Indeed, 'the removal of senior MVD officers as a result of procuring the defection of MVD privates may admittedly cause upheaval but this effect can neither be relied upon nor calculated and as often as not remains concealed from us. The events...describe "a degree of MVD panic" however in view of the series of MVD defections (Rastvorov, Khokhlov and Petrov) all within a few months they are hardly to be wondered at.'[408]

Panic caused paranoia and mental illness. In early 1953 a four-man KGB team went to Vienna to review the performance of the separate stations of military counter-intelligence, counterintelligence and foreign intelligence. At a breakfast, General Andrey G. Graur (one of the four-man team) told the other KGB officers that 'he was recruited by the British Intelligence last night.' He spoke calmly. All the rest were surprised. He continued, claiming that he was drugged by British secret agents in doctors' coats in his hotel room. They injected him with a special liquid and he had revealed top secret information; he also agreed to be their secret agent. The rest of the KGB officers concluded that the general had had a mental breakdown. A Soviet Air Force military flight took him back to Moscow and he was admitted to a hospital.[409]

John Le Carré elaborated in *Tinker, Taylor, Soldier, Spy* on the workload of SIS officers reaching out to defectors. George Smiley, the hero of the book, talked of mass defections of all Soviet embassies' ranks (from intelligence officers and clerks to drivers) from Singapore and Nairobi to Washington; he had to interrogate them. [410] In his turn,

---

[407] Memo, 4 June 1954, KV 5/107 TNA.
[408] ibid.
[409] Bagley, *Spymaster*, p.132.
[410] Le Carré, *Tinker, Taylor, Soldier, Spy*, p.200.

Deryabin offered the British more intelligence on current security of Russian installations in Vienna. He pointed out that it was an 'exaggerated conception', the 'good' security of Soviet establishments. Indeed 'whereas there is only one officer charged with this responsibility in Moscow, the Vienna group consists of seven. These seven, however, are never operating at maximum efficiency, because they are either overloaded with other types of assignment or one of them is ill...the effective strength is two or three officers.'[411]

Nikita Khrushchev, the new all-powerful Soviet ruler, would surprise his own KGB as well as Anglo-American Intelligence by isolating Molotov (Stalin's foreign secretary) and drafting a strategy for concluding a treaty for the end of the occupation of Austria. The Austrian State Treaty, re-establishing full sovereignty of the country, was signed on 15 May 1955 by the representatives of the occupying powers and the government of Austria. The occupying powers had to withdraw from Austrian soil by October 25.

Peer de Silva, the CIA station chief in Vienna, had to confront the panic of moving out. He wrote in his memoirs:

'Our intelligence apparatus in Vienna and the American Zone would have to be dismantled and cut back from several hundred staff people to a few score, who would then be housed in the American Embassy on the Boltzmanngasse...Our own station went through a weeding out, as we cut down. We also relocated station officers who were to stay, under suitable cover in an independent Austria, without the benefit of military cover. It was some comfort to realize that my Soviet counterparts, in their headquarters at the embassy, were undergoing the same traumatic compression.'[412]

Meanwhile, in summer 1955, the CIA station:

'...had long maintained several American surveillance teams, replenished with new blood from time to time to keep down the risk of being penetrated or identified by the

---

[411] Extract from MI6 report re[garding] Organisation of MVD, URRS, given by Major Deryabin, former Russian intelligence officer, 30 November 1955, KV 5/107 TNA.
[412] De Silva, Peer, *The CIA and the Uses of Intelligence* (New York: Times Books, 1978), p.87.

Soviets. The members of these teams included Hungarians and Czechs, who had been in refugee centers and were long residents of Austria. From July to October [1955] we kept them almost fully employed in pinning down the movements of known Soviet intelligence officers, when the newly established Soviet Embassy was rearranging its personnel organizations and finding ways of accommodating a large KGB and GRU rezidentura. In terms of percentage, the Soviet intelligence organs would be about four times larger in manpower than our station.'[413]

Meanwhile, for eight months until the battery of the transmitter ran low, the CIA station eavesdropped on KGB consultations in a private residence rented by the head of the rezidentura, named Colonel Sokolnikov. De Silva remarked: 'we felt that Sokolnikov had never been aware of the plant. We had been careful at all times to turn off the transmitter, with a signal from the listening post, when Soviet sweepers were at work in the house, as was routine from time to time.'[414] The results were claimed to be impressive. De Silva wrote in his memoirs:

> '...we had a stream of remarkable intelligence as Colonel Sokolnikov held frequent operational meetings with his staff in that room. We learned the identities of a number of local Soviet agents and were able to double several of them. We also acquired a great amount of positive intelligence. Sokolnikov and other members of his *rezidentura* and sometimes embassy staff officers would meet to review world affairs and current Soviet policy. On our side, the Political Section of the embassy and the Department of State in Washington were impressed with the substance and volume of the reports.'[415]

De Silva and Sokolnikov kept in contact with each other and decided on the unthinkable: to have dinner, accompanied by some of their staff. The enemy spymasters would share food and drinks. On 23 October 1956, during the dinner, a radio broadcast surprised everyone: 'We interrupt for an important announcement. In Budapest at this moment, extensive demonstrations are underway involving Hungarian students and young

---

[413] Ibid., pp.88-89.
[414] Ibid., p.114.
[415] Ibid., p.117.

people, who are attacking Hungarian government buildings, in particular, the radio station and the AVH Headquarters.' De Silva wrote in his memoirs 'conversation in the living room died out at once, and everyone listened to the news, as it continued…some student demonstrators have been killed by gunfire…There are some reports, not yet confirmed, that Soviet troops and tanks have been engaged in actively opposing the demonstrators with small arms and machine guns.'

The CIA spymaster turned off the radio. Sokolnikov stood up and said 'I think it better that my comrades and I return to our embassy. I hope you all understand.'[416]

---

[416] Ibid., p.102.

15

Chaos and the Spy

October 1956: crisis and revolution in Hungary. The CIA, without the permission of the US ambassador in Vienna, managed to dispatch two contract agents. 'The first had no operational mission and little intelligence briefing, except of the most general sort...His experience showed how easy it was for someone, who had partial use of the language and sufficient courage and imagination, to get around even in chaotic times, and to make contacts without difficulty.' The other agent reached the town where his mother was living and stayed until after the Russian invasion of November 4, 1956.

Neither the CIA, the SIS nor the KGB warned that student demonstrations in Budapest would escalate into a full armed revolt, bringing down the communist government. It seemed that Hungarian émigrés, broadcasting with the CIA-funded Radio Free Europe, urged their compatriots to revolt. This was not authorised by either the CIA or the SIS. Nonetheless, Radio Free Europe opted to re-broadcast local radio programs calling for a revolution. Of course, Moscow blamed London and Washington for instigating the crisis.[417] R.A. Butler, the Lord Privy Seal, rushed to reassure the House of Commons that the Her Majesty's Government had no 'intention of exploiting events in Eastern Europe to undermine the security' of the Soviet Union.[418] The SIS under Sir Dick White maintained some groups of Hungarians for sabotage and stay-behind operations in case of a full-scale Soviet invasion in Western Europe. There were hidden arms caches in woods close to Budapest but the order was explicit for them not to commit any act of sabotage.[419] Both the British Legation in Budapest and the Foreign Office in London did not foresee that the intra-communist political crisis would turn into an armed revolt against the Soviet presence.[420]

On 23 October, in a matter of hours, thousands of ordinary

---

[417] Cormac, Rory, *Disrupt and Deny: Spies, Special Forces, and the Secret Pursuit of British Foreign Policy* (Oxford: Oxford University Press, 2018), p.84.

[418] Ibid.

[419] Ibid.

[420] Cable, James, Sir, 'Britain and the Hungarian Revolt of 1956' *International Relations*, Vol 9, Issue 4 (1988), p.322.

Hungarians took up arms, and confronted and lynched members of the Hungarian Communist Party and the AVH (State Protection Authority). Budapest and other cities turned into places of chaos and killings; civilian casualties, dead and wounded multiplied by the hour. The streets were not safe for anyone. The AVH apparatus was collapsing. Initially, in Moscow, Kruschchev and Field Marshal Zukov assumed that the best policy was to withdraw the Soviet forces from all of Hungary. During these dramatic days, the Suez crisis had captured the full attention of London, Paris, Washington and Moscow. A secret alliance of Britain and France with Israel led to the invasion of Egypt to topple Egyptian leader Gamal Abdel Nasser. Eisenhower strongly opposed British Prime Minister Anthony Eden's bid.

In Budapest, the CIA maintained only one officer, Geza Katona, a second-generation Hungarian-American, a medium-built man 'with a Hungarian-style handlebar mustache.' [421] He stayed in the country from 1950 and focused on general overt intelligence gathering, 'cover duties...he mailed letters, purchased stamps and stationery,' all 'support tasks,' and was not involved in espionage.

In Vienna, the CIA station under Peer de Silva had at that time no Hungarian operations section: 'On the agent-roster there was one Hungarian...his activities were not directed against Hungarian targets.'[422] For spymasters, the Hungarian troubles period was 'too short to effect' any 're-organization to meet a crisis, whose exact nature, duration and final significance could not be rightly judged at any time.' The CIA station in Vienna 'reacted to the suddenly fluid and frenetic circumstances of the situation the only way it could, which was by throwing everyone into the job of covering the crisis on a hit-or-miss basis, somewhat the way a newspaper office does, when suddenly confronted with a catastrophic event.'

The US ambassador in Vienna was clear: CIA agents should not enter Hungary. De Silva dispatched informers close to the Austrian-Hungarian border, not as teams but individually. A large number of informers were fluent in Hungarian: 'This [their dispatch close to the borders] was done with relative alacrity considering that no plan for the use of such personnel previously existed and that the magnitude and outcome of the crisis was uncertain during the earliest days.'[423]

Meanwhile, in Hungary, General Ivan Serov, the chairman of the

[421] Marton, Kati, *Enemies of the People: My Family's Journey to America* (New York: Simon & Shuster, 2009), p.157.
[422] The Hungarian Revolution and Planning for the Future, Vol.I, p.76.
[423] Ibid.

KGB, was in an agony of indecision. His spies had not warned of the coming of the revolution. He desperately sent agents to report on what was going on. Key members of the Politburo, the influential Mikhail Suslov and Anastas Mikoyan, had arrived in the city to consult with the Hungarian government (assuming that the Hungarians needed Soviet military support to defeat the insurgents). It was Andropov who called on the Politburo members to be in Hungary in order to share the blame in case of an escalation of the crisis.[424]

The Politburo members met the government and communist party officials on 24 October. They reported back:

> 'We said [to the Hungarian Central Committee members] the purpose of our arrival was to lend assistance to the Hungarian leadership in such a way as to be without friction and for the public benefit, referring especially to the participation of Soviet troops in liquidating the riots. The Hungarian citizens, especially Imre Nagy, related to this with approval.'[425]

On 26 October, the British Legation informed the Foreign Office: 'The Hungarian people almost to a man are in revolt...' Next day it was reported: 'rapid spread of fighting in Buda - increasing reports of indiscriminate Russian firing everywhere.' On 31 October, outside Budapest, a reconnaissance team of Lieutenant Colonel James Noel Cowley, the British military attache - most possibly an SIS officer was with them - reported that they could not be certain if the Russians would withdraw their forces further; they continued guarding the international airport.[426] Cowley, a decorated tank officer wounded in Normandy, managed to inspect thoroughly a T55A Soviet tank captured by the rebels.[427]

---

[424] Bagley, Tennent H. *Spymasters: Startling Revelations Cold War Revelations of a Soviet KGB Chief* (New York: Skyhorse Publishing, 2013), p.118.

[425] Mikoyan-Suslov Report, October 24, 1956 in Granville, Johanna trans., 'Soviet Documents on the Hungarian Revolution, 24 October - 4 November 1956,' *Cold War International History Project Bulletin*, No. 5 (Woodrow Wilson Center for International Scholars, Washington, DC), Spring 1995, p.30.

[426] Cable, ''Britain and the Hungarian Revolt of 1956', p.322.

[427] Obituary: Colonel Noel Cowley, The Telegraph, 26 April 2010, availabe at:<https://www.telegraph.co.uk/news/obituaries/7636192/Colonel-Noel-Cowley.html > accessed 28 October 2020; Smith, Nicholas, 'The Beast of Budapest' September 2018,available at: < https://www.historynet.com/the-beast-of-budapest.htm> accessed 28 October 2020.

Meanwhile, KGB officers discovered that Red Cross trucks with humanitarian supplies also carried crates of hand grenades for the rebels. The KGB had been struggling to find evidence of Anglo-American direct support to the rebels.[428]

Already the SIS and the Foreign Office were informed of events by the publications of British correspondents. Noel Barber of the *Daily Mail* reached Hungary on 25 October, and stayed in Budapest. Next day, he returned to Austria to file his first report on events as well as photographs.

At the Foreign Office, Tom Brimelow, the Head of the Northern Department (Hungary and Soviet Union), voiced his pessimism: the rebels did not stand a chance. He assumed that Moscow was confronting a dilemma: either crush the rebellion, or concede and weaken their position vis a vis the other communist states in Eastern Europe. At Whitehall (suffering from the Suez crisis), no Cabinet or Chiefs of Staff meeting discussed the crisis in Hungary between 23 October and 30 November 1956.[429] London was, though, willing to provide medical and food supplies. Between 29 and 31 October, the RAF transported 95 tons of food and 16 tons of medical supplies to Vienna to arrange for distribution to the thousands of refugees from Hungary.

Meanwhile, at the British Legation, diplomats and SIS officers arranged to transport diplomats' families (eleven wives and six children) and nineteen stranded British subjects out of Hungary. A lorry and six cars were to be used, manned by skilful Hungarian drivers and three Legation staff members. They reached the borders before the Russians sealed them. A similar US convoy was denied exit from the country by the Soviet border commander. They were compelled to return to Budapest. James Cable, the then first secretary at the British Legation in Budapest, remarked:

> 'Waiting impatiently to hear from Vienna of the safe arrival of our families, we took little notice of the view expressed from Moscow by Sir William Hayter: "I find it hard to believe that the Soviet Government intend to go into reverse in Hungary." He thought additional Russian forces were entering Hungary only to cover the withdrawal of those already there...We knew, only too well, how ignorant diplomats in a Communist country could be - until revolution

---

[428] Bagley, *Spymaster*, p.123.
[429] Cable, 'Britain and the Hungarian Revolt of 1956', p.323.

removed the pads the police had fastened over their eyes and ears.'[430]

The days of the crisis in the Legation building were described laconically by Cable:

'While the battle raged, we had little normal work to do. We kept away from windows (neglect of this precaution had been the death of a Yugoslav Second Secretary); we burned some of our files; we ransacked our dwindling stores to feed our guests [British and other subjects taking refuge in the Legation building]. (Minister Sir Leslie Alfred Charles) Fry, whose intentions were always kindly, hurried down many flights of stairs to assure the correspondent of the *Daily Worker*, hyper-sensitive after the loss of his faith, that he was welcome in the Legation and need not risk a Russian bullet outside. We were heartlessly amused (fighting was then in progress at Port Said) to hear that the Egyptian Legation had been looted by a Russian officer and five of his men.'[431]

Meanwhile, General Serov informed Mikoyan by cable:

'From the network of agents, which has contact with the insurgents, doubt is arising about whether to continue the struggle. The more active part of the opposition wants to continue fighting, but says, however; if we do not stop for a while, we must still keep our weapons in order to attack again at an auspicious moment...An organised observation of the American embassy confirms that the employees at the embassy are leaving the city with their things. The American [diplomats] Olivart and West in a conversation with one of the agents of our friends [Hungarian secret services] said that if the uprising is not liquidated in the shortest possible time, the UN troops will move in at the proposal of the USA and a second Korea will take place.'[432]

The hard line communist First Secretary Ernő Gerő and former Prime Minister András Hegedüs fled to the Soviet Union. Imre Nagy, a

---

[430] Ibid., p.325.
[431] Ibid., p.327.
[432] Serov to Mikoyan, 28 October 1956, ibid., pp. 31-32.

communist functionary who had served as Minister of the Interior just after the war, took over. The Russians assumed Nagy loyal to Moscow. Indeed, back in the 1930s while in Moscow (during the Great Terror) he had worked for the NKVD. For them, the young Nagy was 'a qualified agent, who shows great initiative and an ability to approach people.'[433]

Katona realised that the US Legation under an acting chargé d' affairs 'was not ready for anything of a more serious nature.' Indeed, 'we were in the strange position that, strictly speaking, we did not even have a minister! Unfortunately, even these quite discernible portents had sounded no alarm bells in America. Nothing was stirring in Washington.' [434]

The lone CIA officer had to cope with poor instructions:

> 'I have to say that Washington's instructions were not entirely explicit, not exactly precise. The usual response that was given to any question we raised was "What do you think?" We would then attempt to steer by this and kept on writing our reports, which wouldn't always reach Washington on time...One thing is for sure: no direct contact was made between the Legation and the Nagy government. I can state that with complete certainty.'[435]

Imre Nagy replaced the hard-line communist leader Ernő Gerő, who had fled to Russia. Katona had to deal with anyone wishing to talk to the Legation. Indeed:

> '...there were more than a few Hungarians who dropped in on us, not just with information, but with the aim of giving us advice of a political nature, pleading for us to take action, to intervene somehow; however, these were all private individuals and not one of them represented the Nagy government in any official capacity.'[436]

On 30 October, Suslov and Mikoyan reported to Moscow:

---

[433] Granville, Johanna, *The First Domino: International Decision Making During the Hungarian Crisis of 1956* (College Station Texas: Texas A&M University Press, 2004), p.23.

[434] Kovacs, Peter, Jordan Thomas Rogers, Jordan Thomas, Nagy, Ernest A. 'Forgotten or Remembered? - The US Legation of Budapest and the Hungarian Revolution of 1956' *Miskolc Journal of International Law*, Vol. 4. (2007) No. 1. p.18, note 37.

[435] Ibid., p.26.

[436] Kovacs, Jordan, Nagy, 'Forgotten or Remembered?', p.27.

'The political situation in the country is not improving; it is getting worse. This is exemplified in the following: in the leading party organs there is a feeling of helplessness. The party organisations are in the process of collapse. Hooligan elements have become more insolent, seizing regional party committees, killing communists.'

Nagy's role was now suspicious:

'Last night according to the instructions of Imre Nagy, Andropov (the Soviet ambassador in Budapest) was summoned. Nagy asked him: is it true that new Soviet military units are continuing to enter Hungary from the USSR? If yes, then what is their purpose? We did not negotiate this. Our opinion on this issue: we suspect that this could be a turning point in the change in the Hungarian policy in the [UN] Security Council. We intend to declare today to Imre Nagy that the troop-movements were in accordance with our agreement, that for now we do not intend to bring in any more troops on account of the fact that the Nagy government is dealing with the situation in Hungary. We do not yet have a final opinion of the situation - how sharply it has deteriorated...We think it essential that Comrade [General] Konev come to Hungary immediately.'[437]

It was a clear hint that a Soviet invasion was the only option for Moscow, as Foreign Office officials had foreseen.

In the interval, the always careful Katona looked to follow the instructions of non-US-intervention. He was informed that the eight US marines in the Legation had put on civilian clothes and left the building. Katona was angry:

'There was no holding them back! They went off to the Kilián Barracks, even had themselves photographed with the freedom fighters, and they practically begged to be allowed to go off in uniform to help the Hungarians. "The Russians only need to give us Marines one look, and they'll be taking to their heels!" This spontaneous fervour obviously did not

---

[437] Mikoyan-Suslov Report, 30 October 1956, Granville, trans., 'Soviet Documents on the Hungarian Revolution, p.32.

have much grounding in reality, but it was characteristic of the spirit of our military personnel.'[438]

In his turn, De Silva admitted that as spymaster he could not do much:

'As far as can be ascertained, there was and could have been no plan for the specific operation deployment of this (intelligence) personnel, for the same reason that a general crisis-plan or reorganisation within [not declassified] was impossible - no one knew enough of what was happening to place personnel or assign tasks. The sole operating principle was to find out as much as possible and for this reason personnel were sent to the border areas and were spread out so that there was some coverage on an on-and-off basis of all points which had been reported open.'[439]

At the Austrian-Hungarian borders, only CIA informers operated, not as teams, but individually. Indeed 'the fact that staff members [not declassified] were prohibited from going to the border areas was not so great a loss from the information collection point of view (since they lacked the necessary language) but it complicated the management of the personnel who were dispatched to the border, most of whom stood in need of daily guidance.'[440]

Rebels came to the borders to be in contact with CIA informers and ask for help. In the same areas, as well as in Budapest, Western journalists operated freely as well as 'agents of intelligence services.' De Silva was clear 'there was competition for news.' The Hungarian rebels spoke to anyone willing to hear them. Thus, 'none of what we [the Vienna CIA station] picked up was any better or any worse than what any good newsman could or did pick up, except that we had a central office [not declassified] with a large staff who could try to put the pieces together, compare incoming information with radio, State Department and liaison material.'[441]

Very soon, it became apparent that the rebels near the borders did not know what was going on in Budapest. De Silva was frustrated: 'the fact that we were not getting news from the storm center of the revolution at Budapest or on a country-wide basis meant not only that our intelligence

---

[438] Kovács, Jordan, Nagy, 'Forgotten or Remembered?', p.27.
[439] The Hungarian Revolution and Planning for the Future, p. 78.
[440] Ibid., p.80.
[441] Ibid., p.82.

was one-sided but also that much of our planning, which was based on this intelligence, was one sided.'[442]

He concluded that the capital was isolated because 'everyone else [except journalists and truck drivers] in Budapest was much too busy or too keen on watching developments to bother about the outside world or even to bother to any extent about what was going on in other parts of Hungary.'[443]

The CIA headquarters at Langley was compelled to react on 27 October when it was informed that some cities in Hungary were in rebel hands. The CIA station in Vienna asked for instructions on US policy in case the rebels asked for arms and ammunition. Next day, Langley replied that only CIA officers would gather intelligence. 'Agents sent to the border must not get involved in anything that would reveal US interest or give cause to claim intervention.'[444]

On 29 October, headquarters gave further instructions to the Vienna station for them to find out the names of the rebel leaders. It was repeated that no arms should be supplied. In any case, 'At this date [29 October] no one [in the CIA] had checked precisely on the exact location and nature of US or other weapons available to the CIA. This was done finally in early December [1956].'[445] Even if President Eisenhower had wanted to arm the rebels, there were no arms available, and the motors of Soviet tanks were just about to start.

Meanwhile, office frenzy spread as described by De Silva. CIA officers were:

> '...reviewing the rosters of dropped agents from old [not declassified] operations who had had w/t (wireless transmitter) training who were located both in Europe and in the USA. (Among others, headquarters attempted to find the exact address of a former [not declassified] agent who had been resettled, it was thought, [not declassified]. This was a little like the scene in an old comedy where in the frantic search for a missing person, people begin to ransack the bureau drawers).'[446]

The watchful Yuri Andropov, the Soviet ambassador, a 42-year-old

---

[442] Ibid., p.83.

[443] Ibid., p.84.

[444] Ibid., p.91.

[445] Ibid., p.92.

[446] Ibid.

promising party functionary, was invited to the inner council of Nagy's government on 1 November. He reported back:

'Nagy proposed that, since the Soviet Government had not stopped the advance of the Soviet troops, nor had it given a satisfactory explanation of its actions, they confirm the motion passed that morning regarding Hungary's giving notice of cessation of Warsaw Pact membership, a declaration of neutrality, and an appeal to the United Nations for the guarantee of Hungary's neutrality by the Four Great Powers. In the event that the Soviet Government stopped the advance of the Soviet troops and withdrew them beyond its own borders with immediate effect, [the Government of the Hungarian Peoples' Republic will form a judgment on compliance on the basis of the reports of its own armed forces] the Hungarian Government would withdraw its request to the United Nations, but Hungary would still remain neutral...One hour later the Embassy received the note from the Ministry of Foreign Affairs, stating that since a strong Soviet Army force had crossed the border that day and had entered Hungarian territory against the firm protest of the Hungarian Government, the Government was leaving the Warsaw Pact with immediate effect.' [447]

It seemed that Nagy sought to humiliate Moscow, compelling them to withdraw their forces. The Russians agreed to negotiate on this. The CIA report read: 'this [the announcement of Hungarian-Soviet negotiations for the withdrawal of Soviet forces] breath-taking and undreamed-of state of affairs not only caught many Hungarians off guard, it also caught us off-guard, for which we can hardly be blamed since we had no inside information, little outside information, and could not read the Russians' minds.' [448]

Katona and the rest of the Legation in Budapest, isolated, reported on the formation of the coalition government under Nagy. During the interval, Hungarian rail workers, employing their stations' teletypes, reported to the rebels and the Americans of Russian military movements in the Northeast corridor of Hungary (Zahony-Nyregyhaze); in their messages they provided 'exact numbers and exact directions' of the

[447] Andropov Report, 1 November 1956, Granville, trans., 'Soviet Documents on the Hungarian Revolution', p.34.
[448] The Hungarian Revolution and Planning for the Future, p.95.

movements of Russian troops. Nonetheless, in the mass traffic of messages received by US Intelligence, the Hungarian rail men's reports did not ring any alarm bells. De Silva was explicit:

'In the days following these reports we were, however, dickering in rather long cables [not declassified] on the proposed make-up of a coalition government and were revising our program for the satellites [Eastern European countries]. In summary our reporting was good in local events in West Hungary and on the atmosphere and make-up of the local Revolutionary councils in that area. We knew little of what was happening in Budapest or of the encircling movements of Soviet troops and we had no composite picture of the status of the Revolution in the period between its first victory [with the coming to power of Nagy] and its suppression by the Russians. We did not have the kind of information on which quick deft moves of our own could have been based, either in the nature of support to the Revolution or of improved intelligence coverage.'[449]

The events in Budapest left a mark on KGB officers. Young KGB officer Vladimir Kryuchkov served as third secretary in the Russian Embassy in Budapest and witnessed the collapse of communist rule, the killings of AVH personnel and - he concluded - Nagy having betrayed Moscow. Decades later, it was Kryuchkov who in 1989 gave Gorbachev the dossier on Nagy revealing that he was an NKVD agent, ostensibly to discredit him; two years later Kryuchov staged the failed coup in Moscow. In 1967, Andropov became KGB chairman; he never forgot his Budapest experience. In 1968, he urged for the military response to the Prague uprising. He served as Secretary General of the Soviet Communist Party in 1982-1984, as the Russian intervention in Afghanistan dragged on.

Budapest was encircled by Soviet armoured and mechanised divisions under Marshal Ivan Konev at about 2130 hours, 3 November 1956. The KGB under General Serov took action against the Hungarian government. They invited the Hungarian Minister of Defence, Pál Maléter, to discuss the Soviet withdrawal. The meeting place was the Soviet Military Command at Tököl, near Budapest, on 3 November. During the conference, Serov, according to some accounts, entered the room armed with a pistol and personally arrested the Hungarian

---

[449] Ibid., p.106.

delegation.

Next day, under operation *Whirlwind,* seventeen Soviet divisions crushed Hungarian resistance. Street battles raged in Budapest and a curfew was imposed. Katona 'was unable to report on the site and types of Soviet troop units moving at night in the Budapest area.' He was handling public contacts, people reaching the US Legation asking desperately for any help to save themselves. Katona was doing whatever he could to help them. Indeed, after his return to Langley, he was secretly decorated for his humanitarian (not espionage) activity.

Meanwhile British students entered Hungary to help the rebels. Cable hinted of SIS help when writing:

> 'More adventurously, various British students made their way (before the border was properly closed) to Hungary, where the British Legation went to some trouble to get them out of the country - occasionally out of gaol as well.'[450]

By 10 November, all resistance was suppressed. The revolt cost the lives of 2,500 Hungarians and 700 Soviet troops. Nagy fled to the Yugoslav Embassy but once he tried to go to Yugoslavia he was arrested by the Soviets. He was tried in secret and executed by hanging in 1958. According to the UN High Commissioner for Refugees, by May 1957, 199,000 Hungarians had fled their country. [451]

No doubt Austria, and in particular Vienna, yet again became the centre of émigré communities; some of them immersed in intrigues. Soon the press reported many Soviet defections. De Silva was amazed at the fake news:

> 'We were besieged by cables, asking about those non-existent troop units and these hordes of Soviet defectors; where they were, why hadn't this been reported, and did I need extra help in screening them? The simple fact was there were no hordes of defectors during the revolution, not in the weeks and months following the crushing of the revolt.'[452]

Intelligence gathering on Hungary intensified in the closing months of 1956 and the beginning of 1957: 'There was no lack of Hungarians who were willing to go back across the border, which was not a tight Iron

---

[450] Cable, 'Britain and the Hungarian Revolt of 1956', p.328.

[451] Ibid.

[452] De Silva, *Sub Rosa*, p. 127.

Curtain, as it had been.'[453] Meanwhile, secret agents of the AVH infiltrated the refugee waves. De Silva wrote: 'it is doubtful that we were completely successful in this endeavour [in finding the agents], but we were able, especially with the help of Austrian security authorities, to identify and neutralize a large number of hostile agents.'[454]

De Silva would be transferred to the CIA station in Saigon. While serving there he would be informed about an incident in Vienna. The KGB spymasters and their counterparts in Czechoslovakia and Hungary proved themselves astute. Since about 1951, the CIA station in Vienna had been in liaison with a high-ranking Austrian police official in their inter-service co-ordination. He was polygraphed without any suspicion. The Austrian had access to CIA personnel, case files and tradecraft. In 1962, a Hungarian Intelligence officer defected to the CIA in Vienna. He pleaded for protection; he feared for his life. He was kept under guard in an Austrian police station. A couple of days before he was flown to the United States, he complained and screamed that he had been poisoned. A few of hours later, he died. De Silva recorded:

> 'An examination of the circumstances leading up to the death led inescapably to one Austrian official. He was the number-three man and the person, during all of my years in Vienna, who had been the daily liaison with my staff. Investigation proved him to be an agent of the Czech intelligence service. It was he who killed the Hungarian, with the poison supplied by the Soviets.'[455]

---

[453] Ibid.,p.136.
[454] Ibid., p.139.
[455] Ibid., p.145.

Epilogue

Austria, and Vienna in particular, unquestionably the commercial and economic hub of Central Europe throughout the twentieth century, shaped the operational mindset of spymasters, as this book has shown. In this study, we have elaborated on the spy game of secret sources and tradecraft. The secret intelligence reporting influenced foreign policy and strategic decision making in dramatic events, the riots of 1934, the Second World War in Austria, the annexation to Nazi Germany in 1938 and crises of the late 1940s during the Berlin blockade.

Much effort has been made to provide a detailed and precise account of archival material and narrative. The historical record shows that the NKVD and its successors, the MGB and the KGB, always employed a phenomenal number of strategically-placed spies; one could claim almost nothing was kept secret from them in Austria and in Vienna. The Russian spymaster was interested in secret intelligence, not recruiting communists. Philby himself admitted, 'it may seem strange that, having rejected party discipline, I should have submitted willingly to the discipline of the OGPU, but the explanation is simple. None of the OGPU officials with whom I had dealings ever attempted to win my total acceptance of the party line. All they required was rigid adherence to instructions on the technical level [of espionage].'[456]

The SIS carefully watched both the communist and the Nazi threat with the help of a few Czech secret agents. Nazi Intelligence patiently plotted the uncovering of British spy rings, which were indeed few due to interwar spending cuts. As the war progressed, the Gestapo directed parachute missions and deceived the NKVD. The post-war success of SIS was the tunnels project, kept secret in a Vienna crowded with spies, producing ample military intelligence of Russian deployments and procedures.

US Intelligence (the OSS and its successors, the SSU, CIG, the CIA and their military counterparts the CIC and the MIS) had to confront the moral and operational dilemmas in trusting Nazi spymasters to get military intelligence about the Red Army and the Soviet occupation zone in Austria. Nazi spymasters proved themselves astute in maintaining post-war networks of informers in Austria, Hungary, Romania and Czechoslovakia. Collaborators of Eichmann and other war criminals

---

[456]Extract from notes handed by Philby, 12 June 1964, KV 2/4428 TNA.

escaped justice while they acted as spymasters. There was an American tolerance towards Gehlen and the BND. The German spymaster employed Himmler's daughter as a secretary with access to top secret material. Gudrun Burwitz-Himmler was a devoted Nazi who helped Nazis escape and Neo-Nazis facing charges in courts of law; she supported the *Stille Hilfe* (Silent Assistance).

The American demand for information influenced the supply economics of the intelligence market in Austria: the supply of real and fake intelligence and the high demand drew prices up. Given the punitive and unforgiving reputation of Russian spymasters, we could assume that few may have tried to sell them false information.

Vienna, the capital of the now independent Austria, was the epicentre of collecting intelligence on Eastern European countries, the safe base for the CIA and SIS. As we have shown, the chaos of the Hungarian Revolution inhibited the spies from collecting intelligence. Spies are after secret information usually kept safe in locked documents or coded transmitted correspondence. This simply means the opponent keeps his house in order, so gradually the spy arranges to have access to the organised environment of the opponent. But once a coup or a revolution breaks out, the house of the opponent, his organisational environment, is shaken and might collapse. During the crisis, information spreads - people talk about their aspirations, fears, plans and views; well-kept secret documents either are destroyed or are no longer relevant to the developing political, military and security situation. Opposition leaders might yet decide their response, which is why the related intelligence is not available even to their own spymasters. The spy becomes a newsman, with many informers (none of them loyal and confidential to him/her only), just reporting what is going on - which is no more secret.

Drawing lessons-learned from the experience of the spymasters is not always safe and sound; all of them encountered unique situations that forged their understanding of secret intelligence and the cost to be paid to acquire information or actionable intelligence.

BIBLIOGRAPHY

Archives

a.Unpublished

FO, HS, KV series The National Archives, UK.

CIA Records/database, Freedom of Information Act (FOIA).

b. Published

Foreign Relations of the United States Series.

Granville, Johanna trans., 'Soviet Documents on the Hungarian Revolution, 24 October - 4 November 1956,' *Cold War International History Project Bulletin*, No. 5 (Woodrow Wilson Center for International Scholars, Washington, DC), Spring 1995.

West, Nigel, ed. *The Guy Liddell Diaries: MI5's Director of Counter Espionage in World War II, Vol.1: 1939-1942* (New York:Routledge, 2005).

Memoirs

Blake, George, *No Other Choice* (London: Jonathan Cape, 1990)

Brinson Charmian & Dove, Richard, *A matter of intelligence: MI5 and the surveillance of anti–Nazi refugees, 1933–50* (Manchester: Manchester University Press 2014).

Cavendish, Anthony, *Inside Intelligence: The Revelations of an MI6 Officer* (London: Harper Collins, 1997).

Churchill, Winston S. *The Second World War: The Gathering Storm* (Boston: Houghton Mifflin, 1948).

De Silva, Peer, *The CIA and the Uses of Intelligence* (New York: Times Books, 1978).

Eden, Clarissa, *A Memoir* (London: Weidenfeld & Nicolson, 2007).

Gedye, G.E.R. *Betrayal in Central Europe: Austria and Czechoslovakia- the Fallen Bastions* (London: Harper, 1939).

Gisevius, Hans Bernd, *To the Bitter End* (Boston: Houghton Mifflin, 1947).

Jansa, Alfred, *Erinnerungen Aus Meimen Leben* [Memoirs of My Life] (Vienna: 1954).

Hechelhammer, Bodo, *Spion ohne Grenzen: Heinz Felfe - Agent in sieben Geheimdiensten* (Munchen: Piper, 2019).

Hood, William, *Mole*: *The True Story of the First Russian Intelligence Officer Recruited by the CIA*, (New York: W.W. Norton, 1982).

Milano, James V. & Brogan, Patrick, *Soldiers, Spies and the Ratline: Americans Undeclared War against the Soviets* (London: Brassey's, 2000).

Milne, Tim, *Kim Philby: A story of Friendship and Betrayal* (London: Biteback, 2014).

Modin, Yuri, *My Five Cambridge Friends: Burgess, Maclean, Philby, Blunt, and Cairncross by Their KGB Controller* (New York: Farrar and Giroux, 1994).

Nicholson, Leslie (writing as John Whitwell), *British Agent* (New York: William Kimber & Co, 1967).

Panetta, Leon, *Worthy Fights: A Memoir of Leadership in War and Peace* (New York: Penguin, 2014).

Philby, Kim, *My Silent War: The Autobiography of a Spy* (London: Macgibbon & Kee, 1968).

Philby, Eleonor, *Kim Philby: The Spy I Loved* (London: Hamish Hamilton, 1968).

Romanov, A.I. *Nights are Longest There: Smersh from the Inside*

(London: Hutchinson, 1972).

Richardson, John H. *My Father The Spy: An Investigative Memoir* (New York: Harper Collins, 2005).

Schellenberg, Walter, *The Labyrinth: Memoirs Of Walter Schellenberg, Hitler's Chief of Counterintelligence* (New York: Da Capo Press, 2000).

Schuschnigg, Kurt, *Austrian Requiem* (London: Victor Gollancz, 1947).

Suduplatov, Pavel & Suduplatov, Anatoli, with Jerrold L. Schecter and Leona P. Schectre, *Special Tasks: The Memoirs of an Unwanted Witness—A Soviet Spymaster* (New York: Little, Brown & Co, 1994).

Taylor, J.H. 'DUPONT Mission' (October 13, 1944-May 5, 1945) Available at:<https://www.scrapbookpages.com/DachauScrapbook/DachauTrialsJackTaylorDebriefing.html> accessed 1 July 2019.

Thayer, Charles, *Hands across the Caviar* (London: Michael Joseph, 1953).

Wilkinson, Peter, *Foreign Fields: The Story of an SOE Operative* (London: I.B.Tauris, 2002).

Winterbotham, Frederick, W. *The Nazi Connection* (New York: Dell Books, 1978).

Novels

Greene, Graham, *The Third Man & The Fallen Idol* (London: Heinemann, 1950).

Le Carré, John, *Tinker, Tailor, Soldier, Spy* (London: Hodder & Stoughton, 1989).

_____, *Smiley's People* (London: Hodder & Stoughton, 1992).

_____, *The Secret Pilgrim* (London: Hodder & Stoughton,

1991).

Interviews

'MI6's 'C': We warned Putin what would happen if he invaded Ukraine' *The Sunday Times*, 23 April 2021.

'Alex Younger: "The Russians did not create the things that divide us — we did that" Interview to Roula Khalaf, *Financial Times*, 30 September 2020.

Books & Articles

Aderet, Ofer, 'SS Man who arrested Anne Frank became Intel officer in Postwar West Germany' available at: <https://www.haaretz.com/1.5149888> accessed 16 July 2019.

Alvarez, David & Eduard Mark, *Spying Through a Glass Darkly: American Espionage against* the Soviet Union (Lawrence KA: University Press of Kansas, 2016).

Aldrich, Richard & Cormac, Rory, *The Black Door: Spies, Secret Intelligence and British Prime Ministers* (London: William Collins, 2017).

Aldrich, Richard, *The Hidden Hand: Britain, America and Cold War Secret Intelligence* (New York: Overlook Press, 2002).

Andrew, Christopher & Mitrokhin, Vasili, *The Sword and the Shield: The Mitrokhin Archive and the Secret History of the KGB* (London: Basic Books, 1999).

Andrew, Christopher, 'Intelligence, international relations and "under theorisation",' *Intelligence and National Security*, Vol.19, No.2 (Summer 2004).

Anonymous, 'Obituary: Colonel Noel Cowley', *The Telegraph*, 26 April 2010,

Ashley, George, *CIA Spymaster: George Kisevalter- The Agency's Top Case Office who handler Penkovsky and Popov* (Gretna: Pelican

Publishing, 2004).

Bagley, TennentL H. *Spymaster: Startling Cold War Revelations of a Soviet KGB Chief* (New York: Skyhorse Publishing, 2013).

Bard, Mitchell G., *Forgotten Victims: The Abandonment of Americans in Hitler's Camps*. (Boulder CO: Westview Press, 1994).

Barker, Thomas, M. 'Partisan Warfare in the Bilingual Region of Carinthia' *Slovene Studies* Vol.11 Issue 1-2 (1989).

Bassett, Richard, *Hitler's Spy Chief: The Wilhelm Canaris Mystery* (London: Phoenix, 2011).

Beer, Siegfried, 'Rund um den "Dritten Mann" Amerikanische Geheimdienste in Österreich 1945–1955' in Erwin A. Schmidl ed. *Österreich im Frühen Kalten Krieg 1945–1958. Spione, Partisanen, Kriegspläne* (Wien: Böhlau, 2000).

_____ "The Third Man" and British Intelligence, *History Today*, Vol. 51, Issue 5 (2001).

Bekes, Csaba et al. eds. *Soviet occupation of Romania, Hungary and Austria, 1944/45- 1948/49* (Budapest: Central European University Press, 2015).

Bischof, Günter, *Austria in the First Cold War, 1945-55: The Leverage of the Weak* (London: Palgrave, 1999).

_____ et al eds. *The Marshall Plan in Austria* (London: Transaction Publishers, 2000).

Bobi, Emil, *Die Schattenstadt: Was 7.000 Agenten über Wien aussagen* (Wien: Ecovin, 2014).

Borovik, Genrikh, *The Philby Files: The Secret Life of Master Spy Kim Philby* (New York: Little Brown & Co, 1994).

Brown III, Ralph W, 'Making *the Third Man* look pale: American Soviet conflict in Vienna during the early cold war in Austria, 1945 1950', *Journal of Slavic Military Studies*, Vol.14, Issue 4 (Autumn 2001).

Bułhak, Władysław & Friis, Thomas Wegener, eds. *Need to Know: Eastern and Western Perspectives* (University Press of South Denmark, 2014).

Burr Bukey, Evan, *Hitler's Austria, Popular Sentiment in the Nazi Era, 1938-1945* (Chapel Hill: The University of North Carolina Press, 2000).

Cable, James, Sir, 'Britain and the Hungarian Revolt of 1956' *International Relations*, Vol 9, Issue 4 (1988),

Carver, Tom, 'Philby in Beirut' *London Review of Books*, Vol.34, No.19 (October 2012).

Chalou, George C. ed. *The Secrets War: The Office of Strategic Services in World War II* (Washington: National Archives and Records Administration, 2002).

Corera, Gordon, *The Art of Betrayal: Life and Death in the British Intelligence* (London: Weidenfeld & Nicolson, 2011).

Cormac, Rory, *Disrupt and Deny: Spies, Special Forces, and the Secret Pursuit of British Foreign Policy* (Oxford: Oxford University Press, 2018).

Danks, Catherine, 'The Anglo-Soviet Alliance: What Manchester Thinks?' Available at: <http://espace.mmu.ac.uk/618804/1/UdSUArticle7thJune.%20%28 29.pdf> accessed 1 September 2019.

Doder, Dusko ''47 Soviet Bloc Bid to recruit Waldheim as Agent Described', *Washington Post*, 30 October 1986.

Dorril, Stephen, *MI6: Fifty Years of Special Operations* (London: Fourth Estate, 2000).

Dulles, Allen W. *The Craft of Intelligence* (Guilford CT: Lyons Press, 2006).

Ezard, John, 'Blair's Babe', the *Guardian*, 21 June 2003.

Finch, Charles, 'Murderous Husbands, Flapper-Era Gun Molls and Korean Assassins: The Best Winter Thrillers' *New York Times*, 28 January 2019.

Foges, Peter, 'The story of H.P. Smolka, Soviet spy and inspiration for The Third Man' *Lapham's Quarterly*, 14 January 2016.

Fry, Helen, *Spymaster: The Secret Life of Kendrick* (London: Marranos Press, 2018).

Doerries, Reinhard R. *Hitler's Intelligence Chief: Walter Schellenberg* (New York: Enigma Books, 2009).

Hamann, Brigitte, *Hitler's Vienna: A Portrait of the Tyrant as a Young Man* (London: Tauris Parke Paperbacks, 2009).

Hastings, Stephen, 'Obituary: Nicholas Elliot' The *Independent*, 18 April 1994.

Haidinger, Martin, *Wilhelm Höttl - Spion für Hitler und die USA* (Nurnberg: Carl Verlag, 2019).

Holzman, Michael, *Kim and Jim: Philby and Angleton, Friends and Enemies in the Cold War* (London: Weidenfeld & Nicolson, 2021).

Granville, Johanna, *The First Domino: International Decision Making During the Hungarian Crisis of 1956* (College Station: Texas A&M University Press, 2004).

Grose, Peter, *Gentleman Spy: The Life of Allen Dulles* (Boston: Houghton Mifflin, 1994).

Jeffery, Keith, *MI6: The History of the Secret Intelligence Service, 1909-1949* (London: Bloomsbury, 2010).

Stefan Karner, Stefan & Stelzl-Marx, Barbara eds. *The Red Army in Austria: The Soviet Occupation, 1945-1955* (Lanham, MD: Lexington Books, 2020).

Khalaf, Roula, 'Alex Younger: "The Russians did not create the things that divide us — we did that" *Financial Times*, 30 September 2020.

Knightley, Philip, *Philby: KGB Masterspy* (London: Andre Deutsch, 1988).

Klussman, Uwe, 'Spionage im ZweitenWeltkrieg: Stalin's Mann in der Gestapo' *Der Spiegel*, 29 September 2009.

Karner. Stefan Stelzl-Marx, Barbara et al eds., *The Red Army in Austria: The Soviet Occupation, 1945-1955* (Lanham, MD: Lexington Books, 2020).

Kolpakidi, A.I., D.P. Prokhorov, *VneshnayarazvedkaRossii* ['The Foreign Intelligence Service of Russia'] (Saint Petersburg, Moscow, 2001).

Kotkin, Stephen, *Stalin: Paradoxes of Power, 1878-1928* (London: Penguin Books, 2015).

Kovacs, Peter, Jordan Thomas Rogers, Jordan Thomas, Nagy, Ernest 'Forgotten or Remembered? - The US Legation of Budapest and the Hungarian Revolution of 1956' *Miskolc Journal of International Law*, Vol. 4, No. 1 (2007).

Kurt Bauer, 'Hitler und der Juliputsch 1934' in Österreich' *Vierteljahrshefte für Zeitgeschichte*, Heft 2 (April 2011).

Lathrop, Charles, E. ed. *The Literary Spy* (New Haven: Yale University Press, 2004).

Leidinger, Hannes & Moritz, Verena, *Russisches Wien: Begegnungen aus vier Jahrhunderten.* (Wien: Böhlau, Wien 2004).

Longerich, Peter, *Heinrich Himmler (*Oxford: Oxford University Press, 2012).

Lownie, Andrew, *Stalin's Englishman: The Lives of Guy Burgess* (London: Hodder Paperbacks, 2016).

MacDonogh, Giles, *1938: Hitler's Gamble* (New York: Basic Books, 2009).

Macintyre, Ben, *A Spy Among Friends: Kim Philby and the Great Betrayal* (London: Broadway Books, 2014).

Madeira, Victor, *Britannia and the Bear: The Anglo-Russian Intelligence Wars, 1917-1929* (Woolbridge: Boydell Press, 2014).

Mallet, Robert, 'The Anschluss Question in Italian Defence Policy, 1933-37', *Intelligence & National Security*, Vol.19, No.4 (Winter 2004).

Marton, Kati, *Enemies of the People: My Family's Journey to America* (New York: Simon & Shuster, 2009).

Mueller, Michael, *Canaris: The Life and Death of Hitler's Spymaster* (Annapolis: Naval Institute Press, 2007).

Moritz, Verena et al. eds. *Gegenwelten: Aspektke der osterreichoschsowjetischen Beziehungen* (Salzburg: Residenz Verlag, 2014)

Morley, Jefferson, *The Ghost: The Secret Life of CIA Spymaster James Jesus Angleton* (New York: St. Martin's Press, 2017).

Neugebauer, Wolfgang, *The Austrian Resistance, 1938-1945* (Vienna: Steinbauer, 2014).

O'Sullivan, Donal, *Dealing with the Devil; Anglo-Soviet Intelligence Cooperation during the Second World War* (New York: Peter Lang, 2010).

Pelinka, Anton, *The Dollfuss/Schuschnigg Era in Austria* (Routledge, 2003).

Persico, Joseph E. *Piercing the Reich- The Penetration of Nazi Germany by American Secret Agents during World War II* (New York: Viking, 1979).

Petersen, Neal H. ed. *From Hitler's Doorstep: the Wartime Intelligence Reports of Allen Dulles, 1942-1945* (University Park: Pennsylvania State University Press, 1996).

Pirker, Peter, 'British Subversive Politics towards Austria and Partisan Resistance in the Austrian-Slovene Borderland, 1938-1945' *Journal of Contemporary History*, Vo. 52 No.2 (April 2016).

Plasser, Fritz et al eds. *New Perspetives on Austrian and World War II* (New York: Routledge, 2017).

Pringle, Robert, W., *Historical Dictionary of Russian & Soviet intelligence* (Lanham, Maryland: Scarecrow Press, 2006).

Riegler, Thomas, 'The Spy Story Behind the Third Man' *Journal of Austrian-American History*, Vol.4 (2020).

Riehle, Kevin, P. 'Early Cold War evolution of British and US defector policy and practice', *Cold War History*, Vol. 19 No.3 (2018).

Rubin, Barry, *Istanbul Intrigues: a True-Life Casablanca* (New York: McGraw-Hill, 1989).

Schafranek, Hans, *Sommerfest mit Preisschießen. Die unbekannte Geschichte des NS-Putsches im Juli 1934* (Wien: Czernin, 2006).

_____, *Söldner für den Anschluss: die österreichische Legion 1933-1938* (Wien: Czernin, 2011).

Sherry, Norman, *The Life of Graham Greene*, Vol.2, 1939-1955 (London: Vintage, 1996).

Smith, Michal, *New Cloak, Old Dagger: How Britain's Spies Came In From the Cold* (London: Victor Gollancz, 1996).

Smith, Nicholas, 'The Beast of Budapest' *History-net*, September 2018, available at: < https://www.historynet.com/the-beast-of-budapest.htm> accessed 28 October 2020.

Suppan, Arnold, *The Imperialist Peace Order in Central Europe: Saint-Germain and Trianon, 1919-1920* (Vienna: Austrian Academy of Sciences Press, 2019).

Swarz, Martin Ben, 'A new look at the 1956 Hungarian Revolution: Soviet opportunism, American acquiescence' (PhD thesis, Tufts University, Boston, 1988).

Traussnig, Florian, *Militarischer Widerstand Von Aussen: Osterreicher in Us-Armee Und Kriegsgeheimdienst Im Zweiten Weltkrieg* (Wien: Bohlau Verlag, 2016).

Turner, C. *The CASSIA Spy Ring in World II Austria* (Jefferson: McFarland, 2017).

Weber, Thomas, *Becoming Hitler: The Making of a Nazi* (Oxford: Oxford University Press).

Wenninger, Florian, et al eds. *Das Dollfuss/Schuschnigg-Regime 1933-1938:Vermessung Eines Forschungsfeldes* (Wien: Bohlau, 2013).

West, Nigel, *Spy Swap: The Humiliation of Putin's Intelligence Services* (Barnsley: Frontline, 2021).

West, Nigel &Tsarev, Oleg, *The Crown Jewels: The British Secrets exposed by the KGB Archives* (London: Harper Collins, 1999).

West, W.L. The Quest for Graham Greene (London: Weidenfeld & Nicolson, 1997).

Westerfield. H. Bradford ed. *Inside CIA's Private World: Declassified Articles from the Agency`s Internal Journal, 1955-1992* (New Haven: Yale University Press, 1995).

Williams, Warren Wellde, 'British Policy and the Occupation of Austria, 1945-1955' (PhD Thesis, University of Wales, Swansea, 2004).

INDEX

Abwehr, 21, 41-2, 53, 55,60, 63-9, 73, 79, 82, 95-101, 107, 111-12, 119, 141, 157, 160, 162, 191
Adenauer, Konrad, 186
Alberovaya, Sonia, 31
Altmann, Victor, 162
Amt Gehlen, 141-2, 179, 181-3, 185, 187-8, 191, 234
Andropov, Yuri, 223, 226, 229, 231
Angleton, James, 13, 19
Animal Farm, 209
Antonescu, Ion, 192
Anschluss, 53, 61-3, 71, 74, 82, 114-15, 151, 208
Armia Krajowa, 79
Armistice (1918), 28, 79,
Auschwitz (concentration camp), 67, 187
Austrian-Hungarian empire, 9, 24-5, 38, 222, 228
Austrian Legion, 48, 50, 57, 76, 89
AVH (State Protection Authority), 220, 222, 231-2

Bailey, W.S. 118
Balfour, Arthur James, 24, 167
Banting, Frederick Grant, 209
Barber, Noel, 224
Bazna, Elyesa, 119
Beck, Ludwig, 95, 97
Becker, Hans, 138
Beigl, Kurt, 121
Belgium, 98, 134, 137, 202
Benton, Kenneth, 67
Benes, Edvard, 41
Beria, Lavrentiy, 168, 214, 217
Bern, 116, 121, 132, 134, 140-1, 152, 200
Best, Sigismund Payne, 135
Blake, George, 168
Blum, Benno, 169
Boehme, Franz, 53
Bonham Carter, Violet, 204
Bormann, Martin, 103. 140-1
Britain, 22, 32, 38, 55, 62, 87, 137, 149, 162, 192, 201, 203-8m 211-12, 221
Brandenburg (regiment), 95

255

Denisov, Mikhail, 171
Doctors' plot, 227
Dollfuss, Engelbert, 16, 20, 43-55, 61, 67, 80, 82, 105, 125-6
Donovan, William, 181-2
Drau/Drava (river), 131-3, 136
Dulles, Allen, 128, 139-41, 145-150, 160, 173, 179, 181-2, 191, 210
Dzerzhinsky, Felix, 22

Earle, George, 43, 46, 48, 50
Economist (weekly), 213
Eden, Antony, 124, 216, 221, 233
Edward IV, 28
Eichmann, Adolf, 66-7, 190, 207-8, 245
Einstein, Alfred, 49
Eisenhower, Dwight, 140, 233, 240
Elliot, Nicholas, 12, 176
Elser, Georg, 104
émigrés, 23, 40, 67, 80, 85, 90, 152, 167, 171, 175, 209-10, 224, 232, 243
Erhardt, John, 174, 182
Esterhase, Tobby, 23
Evidenzbureau, 43, 49, 57
Exchange Telegraph Ltd, 212-13

Federal Republic of Germany, 195
Fey, Emil, 50, 52
Figl, Leopold, 168, 173, 180
Financial Times, 213
Fleckner, Hans, 136
Foley, Frank, 66
Forbes-Dennis, Ernan, 27-9
Foreign Office, 72, 121, 124, 142, 145, 212-3, 216, 220-1, 232, 235, 238
Free Austrian Movement, 124
Free German League of Culture, 213
Free Hungarian Movement, 214
Friedman, Litzi, 16

Gaitskell, Hugh, 16
Gallagher, Rory, 12
Galicia, 26
Gedye, George Eric Rove, 125-130
Gehlen, Reinhardt, 149-150, 188, 191-3, 195, 197, 201
Geheim Feld Polizei, 192, 204
Germany, 10, 20, 23, 26, 39-40, 45-6, 49, 53-4, 57-8, 60-1, 67, 69-70, 77, 79, 84,
89-91, 96, 102, 104, 106, 109, 120, 124-5, 127, 129, 139, 144-5, 148-9, 165-167,
171, 174, 194-5, 202, 206, 212
German Students League, 159